DATE DUE

AMERICAN GOVERNMENT
The U.S.A. and West Virginia

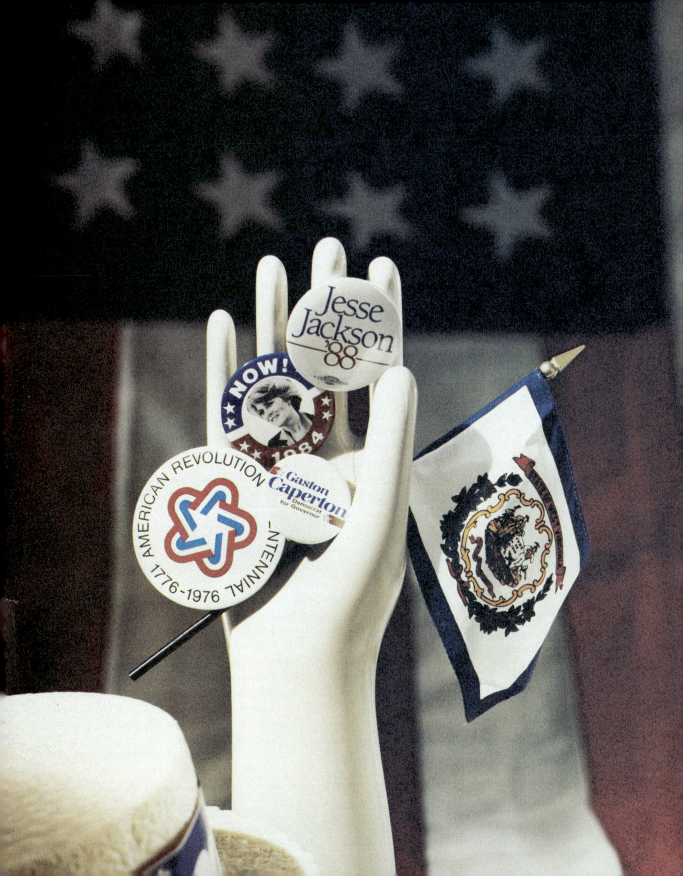

AMERICAN GOVERNMENT

The USA and West Virginia

DISCARD

William E. Coffey

Associate Dean for Faculty Relations
Office of the Chancellor
California State University System
Long Beach, California

Frank S. Riddel

Professor of Social Studies
Marshall University
Huntington, West Virginia

Published by
The West Virginia
Historical Education Foundation, Inc.
Marshall Buckalew, *Editor*
Charleston, West Virginia
1990

For Dr. Ed Welch:
May your influence in
West Virginia be reflected
in the lives of its people and
its government.
Marshall Buckalew

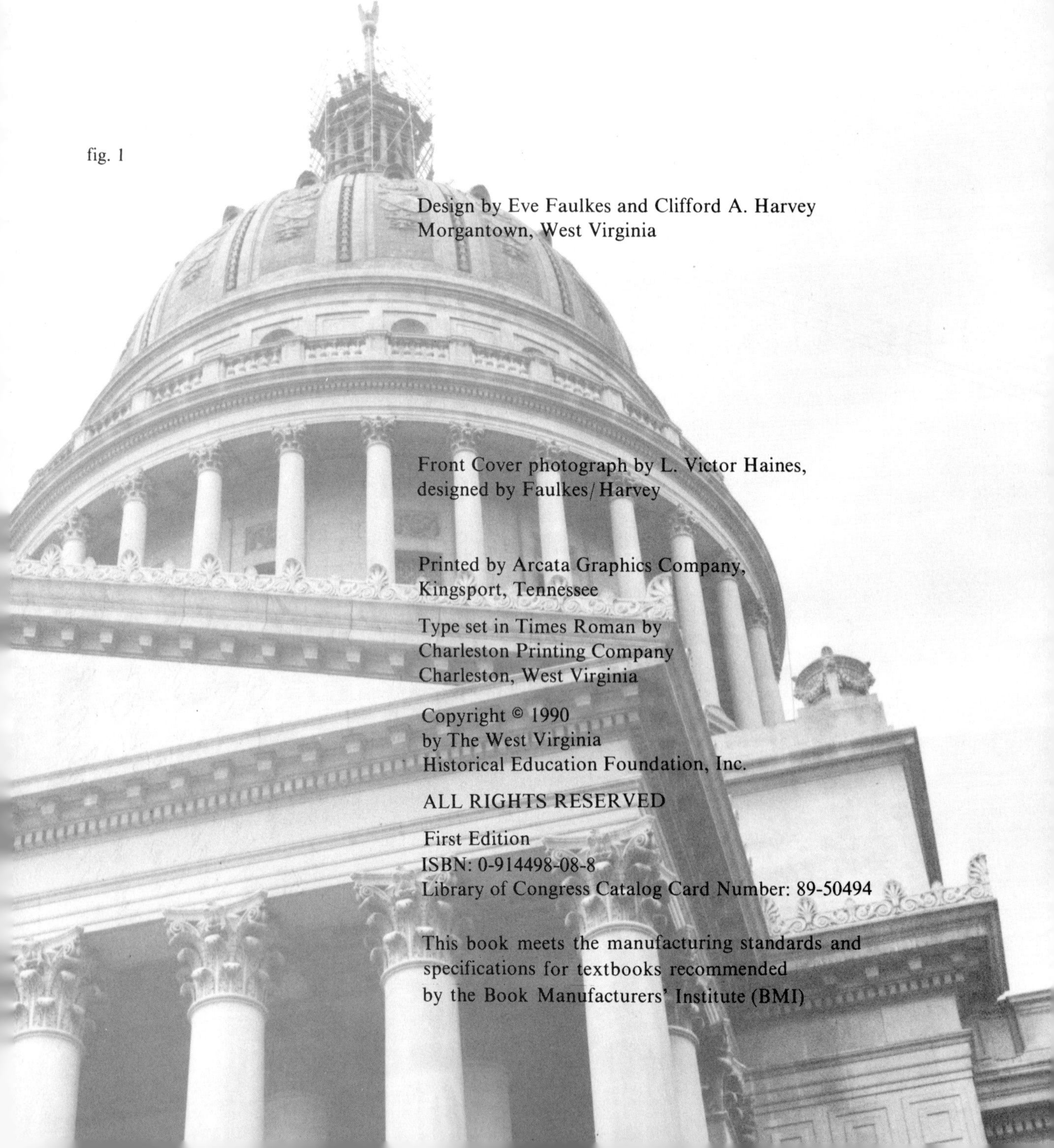

fig. 1

Design by Eve Faulkes and Clifford A. Harvey
Morgantown, West Virginia

Front Cover photograph by L. Victor Haines,
designed by Faulkes/Harvey

Printed by Arcata Graphics Company,
Kingsport, Tennessee

Type set in Times Roman by
Charleston Printing Company
Charleston, West Virginia

First Edition
ISBN: 0-914498-08-8
Library of Congress Catalog Card Number: 89-50494

This book meets the manufacturing standards and
specifications for textbooks recommended
by the Book Manufacturers' Institute (BMI)

Preface

One of the major points made in this text is that the well-being of our democracy depends upon the participation of citizens in the political system. However, intelligent political decisions and actions by citizens require an understanding of how our government is organized and how it works. That is why you are taking a course in American government. The knowledge you gain from it should help you become a useful citizen.

You and your teacher are facing an interesting but difficult task. In only one semester you must cover the complex subject of American government at the national, state, and local levels. *American Government: The U.S.A. and West Virginia* has been especially designed to make that task somewhat easier.

The first part of the text describes the development of the federal government, the principles upon which it is based, its structure, and its most important functions. Even though these complex topics are dealt with in only eight chapters, all the material that is absolutely necessary to understand our national government has been included.

The last eight chapters of the text are concerned with state and local governments. Most texts devote only two or three chapters to this topic and do not concentrate on West Virginia. Yet, our state and local governments are closer to us and influence our lives even more than the federal government. A major strength of this text is the extensive coverage of West Virginia's state and local governments.

Not only is the text designed to enable you to cover the three levels of American government in a single semester, it contains several features that should assist both students and teachers. Every effort has been made to make the text easy to read and understand. Difficult vocabulary has been avoided when possible. Words that may not be understood have been listed at the beginning of each chapter. Important terms are underlined, and short definitions of familiar synonyms follow many of the underlined words. Many charts, maps, and pictures have been included to illustrate points made in the text. Review questions appear at the end of each section of the chapters.

fig. 2
To "govern" means to steer

Supplementing the text is a *Teacher's Manual,* which contains a great deal of useful material on each chapter. For example, the manual contains a list of suggested activities prepared by the authors of the text that can be used to expand your knowledge of the topic being studied. We strongly urge teachers to make extensive use of the manual in order to strengthen students' understanding of the material contained in the text.

William E. Coffey
Frank S. Riddel

Editor's Note:

In order to meet the textbook adoption schedule for West Virginia Studies established by the West Virginia Board of Education, this textbook had to be printed before the United States Census Report for 1990 was completed. The most reliable estimates for 1990 have been used. The teacher who requires exact statistical information for 1990 should use a library or write to the United States Department of Commerce, Bureau of the Census, Washington, D.C. 20230.

fig. 3
This Uncle Sam whirligig was created by Bill Muehling, an exhibitor at the Stonewall Jackson Jubilee

fig. 4, right page
This preamble to the Constitution was commissioned by the Commission on the Bicentennial of the U.S. Constitution in 1987 to represent all 50 states.

We the people of the United States, in Order to form a more perfect Union, establish Justice, insure domestic Tranquility, provide for the common defense, promote the general Welfare, and secure the Blessings of Liberty to ourselves and our Posterity, do ordain and establish this Constitution for the United States of America.

fig. 5
Second place in the turtle race at Hundreds' 4th of July celebration

fig. 6
Memorabilia of West Virginia and American political campaigns

fig. 7
Wheeling's Festival of Lights each winter depicts national symbols as well as many other displays

fig. 8, right page
Celebration at the White House

fig. 9, far right page
Kids reading a pocket version of the Constitution during the Bicentennial celebration

X

Contents

THE CONGRESS OF THE UNITED STATES

THE PRESIDENT AND THE EXECUTIVE BRANCH

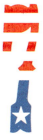

THE FEDERAL JUDICIARY

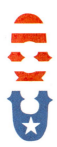

PAYING FOR THE FEDERAL GOVERNMENT

THE STATE OF WEST VIRGINIA AND ITS CONSTITUTION

THE POLITICAL PROCESS IN WEST VIRGINIA

THE WEST VIRGINIA LEGISLATURE

THE GOVERNOR AND THE EXECUTIVE BRANCH OF WEST VIRGINIA

THE WEST VIRGINIA JUDICIARY

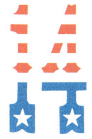

PAYING FOR OUR STATE GOVERNMENT

COUNTY AND MUNICIPAL GOVERNMENT IN WEST VIRGINIA

THE FEDERAL SYSTEM AT WORK IN WEST VIRGINIA

Introduction To Government

PREVIEW

The word "government" comes from Latin and Greek words meaning "to direct" or "to steer." *Government* is a word for the person or organization that directs or steers the public actions (political life) of a group of people. In the United States all Americans live under several governments. In this course, which is called "American Government," we will learn how our governments work. We will also learn what the people of West Virginia can do to make government work for them and for the good of all citizens.

In Chapter One we will answer these questions:
1. Why do we have government?
2. What are some different types of government?
3. What are the levels of government in the United States and West Virginia?
4. Why has government grown large and powerful in today's world?

Pronounce and discuss the meanings of the following words found in this chapter.

authority	embassy	prosecutor
citizen	environment	regulation
complicated	officials	representative
	organization	

Each chapter opens with a court house detail from a different county. Would you recognize your court house?

fig. 10, left page
Marion County Courthouse in Fairmont

fig. 11
United States Capitol dome

fig. 12
West Virginia capitol dome

SECTION ONE: THE IMPORTANCE OF GOVERNMENT

Why People Formed Governments. American government plays a big part in our lives. In our nation's Declaration of Independence, it is written:

> . . . all men are created equal, . . . they are endowed by their Creator with certain unalienable Rights, . . . among these are Life, Liberty and the pursuit of Happiness. . . . to secure these rights, Governments are instituted among Men . . .

Thus the founders of our country believed that government is needed to protect our rights.

Chief Cornstalk. Cornstalk was an able and brave leader of the Shawnee Indians during the time of the American Revolution. In a struggle for control of the Ohio Valley, he almost defeated the Virginians at the Battle of Point Pleasant (in present-day West Virginia) where the Kanawha River empties into the Ohio. Cornstalk signed a peace treaty with Virginia after the battle. However, as chief of a tribe, Cornstalk could not force all Shawnee men to follow his policy of keeping the peace. When a few Shawnees shot a Virginia hunter, Cornstalk and his son were murdered by some of the soldiers at Fort Randolph in Point Pleasant. This caused several years of warfare between the Shawnees and the Virginians.

Humans have lived with government for thousands of years. People formed governments before they invented writing. For this reason, we have no record of the first governments. We could imagine, however, a time when people lived free of government. There were no laws to obey and no policemen to enforce laws. Of course, there were no government services such as parks or schools. Humans were free to do what they wished, but they could not enjoy the safety and benefits that government provides its citizens.

A society that has no government is in a condition of anarchy. Living in anarchy would be the same as living in a state of nature without laws or rules. This might seem attractive in some ways, but very few of us would really like it. A famous English political writer, Thomas Hobbes, once described life in a state of nature as "nasty, brutish and short." He believed that without laws and officials to enforce the laws there would be much violence. The weak would be oppressed by the strong and aggressive. No one would ever feel safe if there was anarchy instead of government.

People may have formed government in order to protect themselves and their families. They may have formed government to help people cooperate with one another. For example, when humans had only simple weapons, it was possible for them to hunt large animals only if they worked closely together.

The Earliest Governments. The first governments were probably found among small groups of related people who formed *clans*. Long ago, people of Scotland, for example, were divided into hundreds of clans. In some cases, several clans joined together into larger groups called *tribes*. The Indians who lived in the eastern United States had formed many tribes before the Europeans arrived.

Clan and tribal governments were much simpler than the governments of modern nations. They did not have kings or presidents, written laws, or organized society. There were no soldiers, teachers, or tax collectors. Most clan and tribal governments were formed by the adult men who met in a council. The council elected a headman or chief to be the leader. However, the chief could not make decisions by himself. Many clans and tribes made rules or laws only when all of the council members were present and in agreement.

Today's Governments. Our society today is much more complicated than that of the Scottish clans or Indian tribes. We have more people living closely together than in the past, so it is not surprising that our governments have become more complicated. Today we expect government to do many things that people cannot do for themselves.

One of the major functions of government is to protect citizens and preserve their rights. Governments pass laws to make life safer and more pleasant. They also set punishments for those who break laws.

fig. 13
Cornstalk

They hire policemen, prosecutors, and judges to enforce the laws. Thus, we are not allowed to do everything we might want to do. We lose some freedom under a modern government, but we gain protection from the law.

For example, almost all governments have laws against stealing or murder. In addition, some governments do not allow factories to pollute streams or the air with toxic wastes. Governments may even make laws that keep us from hurting ourselves. West Virginia and many other states require people who ride motorcycles to wear helmets to protect their heads in case of an accident. Some states have passed laws that require motorists to wear seat belts in cars.

In addition to protecting our lives and property, modern governments offer many other services. A basic duty of many governments is to provide schools for public education. Governments also build highways and streets, airports and dams. Many operate public parks and forests for the benefit of all. Governments give help to the poor, and many provide medical care for some or all of the people.

REVIEW OF SECTION ONE:
1. Why did people first form governments?
2. How were tribes governed?
3. What are some of the activities or functions of modern governments?

fig. 14
School patrols act governmental by enforcing traffic regulations for younger schoolchildren

fig. 15
The bald eagle has been used to symbolize the best qualities of American products by their manufacturers.

SECTION TWO: TYPES OF GOVERNMENT

Government of Civilizations. When people in some parts of the world built cities, invented writing, and traded with each other, "civilization" was born. A civilization is too complex for clan or tribal government and needs larger and highly organized governments. Their rulers have more power than tribal chiefs. In a civilization, the laws are written, and a "game plan" is put in place to guide and direct society and the world in which the citizens live.

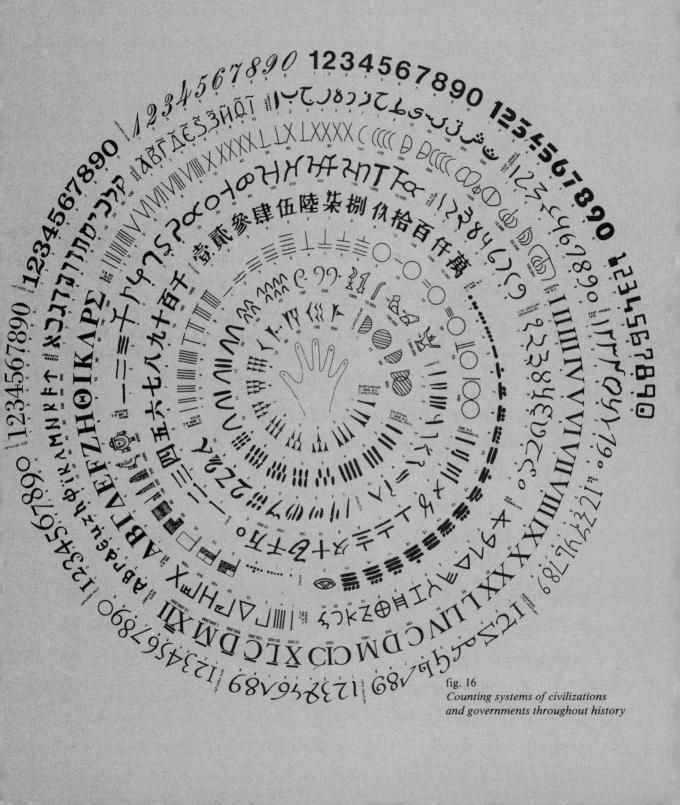

fig. 16
*Counting systems of civilizations
and governments throughout history*

fig. 17
Prime Minister Bhutto of Pakistan

Monarchy and Oligarchy. Since the first civilizations appeared about seven thousand years ago in Egypt and Mesopotamia (present-day Iraq), many types of government have been formed. One way to describe a government is by the number of people who may have the power to rule.

If a government is ruled by a single person, such as a king (or queen) or an emperor, it is called a *monarchy*. Monarchs are not elected. Instead, they inherit their thrones from their fathers or mothers. The king in ancient Egypt (who was called pharaoh) was thought to be a god. He owned all of the land in his kingdom, and he made all of the laws. There are not many monarchies today. Some countries, such as Great Britain, Sweden, and Japan, still have monarchs, but they no longer have power to rule. In fact, all three of these countries have democratic governments.

An *oligarchy* is a government that is ruled by a small group of people. In the past these oligarchs were frequently nobles who owned much of the land. Today oligarchies often are ruled by a few army generals who usually gain their power by force rather than by election. This has happened in Chile and Guatemala. In the Soviet Union and China, power is held by the leaders of the Communist Party. Elections for some offices may be held in their countries, but only Communist Party members were named on the ballot until recently. Many Communist governments in the world today are forms of oligarchy. However, beginning in 1989 important changes have occurred in several Communist countries in eastern Europe. Former Communist countries such as Poland and Hungary now permit non-Communist parties to take part in elections.

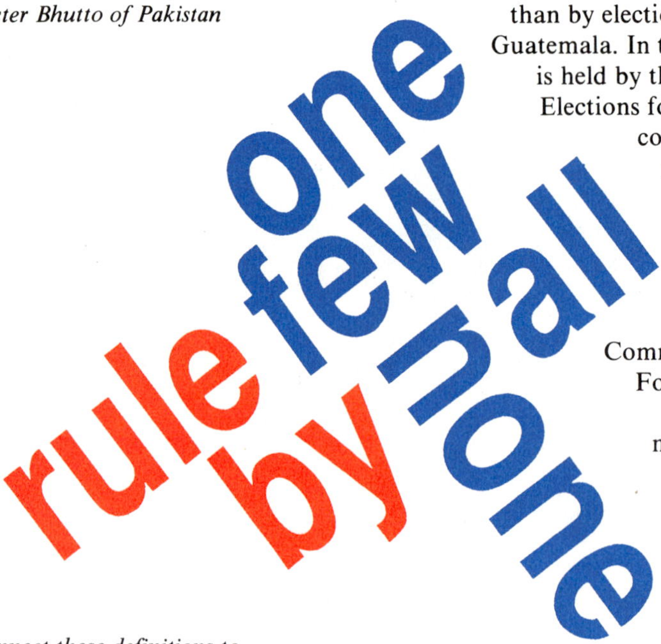

rule one few by all none

fig. 18
Can you connect these definitions to the type of government they represent?

Democracy. In a *democracy,* power is held by the people who elect public officials to represent them. These officials may be voted out of office in the next election. Democracies have more than one political party, and all voters have the opportunity to join a party. Democracies also allow freedom of thought and expression.

In many democratic nations, laws are made by elected representatives who meet in a *parliament.* The head of a parliamentary government, called a prime minister, is chosen by the members of parliament. England, Canada, Australia, and India are examples of parliamentary democracies.

In the United States, the national government is led by the president, who is elected by the voters. Laws are made by officials elected by the voters to *Congress.* The national government of the United States and some other countries, such as France, is called a presidential democracy.

No matter what their type, all governments must decide what regulations to establish and what services to provide. In addition, they must decide how money is to be raised to pay for government. These important matters may cause conflict, because people disagree. A successful government is able to settle conflict by peaceful means rather than by force. "We are a government of law" and not men.

Conflict in Government. In democracies there is much difference of opinion, because everyone is free to speak out, join a political group, or run for public office. There are many ways to take part in a democratic government and express an opinion. Some people favor increasing the size of the Army, Navy, and Air Force. They are opposed by those who want to cut the size of the military and spend taxes on something else. Some people urge their government to raise more money to improve schools. Others don't want to pay more taxes on their property, even though weaker schools may result.

The Need to Support Democracy. For a democracy to work, citizens must tolerate the views of others, and political leaders often must make *compromises.* This means that no person, group, or party can get its way on every issue. Democracies must serve the interests of the majority. However, they must also protect the rights and welfare of the minority.

Governing, especially in a democratic manner, is a difficult task. A democracy needs the help of all citizens in order to work well. Otherwise, a few people can use the power of government for their own benefit, and the public may be harmed.

Greece, the first democracy

North Korea, dictatorship

Chile, democracy

Cuba, communist dictatorship

Panama, democracy since 1989
fig. 19
All red, white and blue flags do not denote democracies.

Sometimes democratic governments have been overthrown by a few people or by a single *dictator*. Adolph Hitler was a dictator of Germany more than half a century ago. He was elected head of a democratic government. Soon after, he ended democracy and declared himself Germany's leader for life. His opponents were killed or jailed. Under Hitler, Germany attacked its neighbors and started the Second World War. Millions of people suffered because not enough citizens of Germany supported democracy.

Another example of a dictator was Joseph Stalin. He ruled the Soviet Union when Hitler ruled Germany. Stalin removed all of his rivals from the Communist Party, and no other parties were permitted. Many people were falsely accused of crimes. Thousands were imprisoned, and many were executed. Millions of ordinary people died, too, because of Stalin's harsh rule and mistakes.

In recent years, leaders in several countries have acted like dictators. This has happened in Argentina, Chile, Guatemala, Rumania, Zaire, North Korea, and others. In this course we will study how average Americans living in West Virginia can support democracy and protect their freedom.

REVIEW OF SECTION TWO:
1. What are several types of government in civilized societies?
2. Why is there conflict in democratic governments?
3. Why is democratic governing a hard task?

fig. 20
Adolph Hitler, German dictator

fig. 21
At the Yalta Conference during World War II are Winston Churchill, British prime minister, Franklin Roosevelt, U.S. president, and Joseph Stalin, Russian dictator

SECTION THREE: LEVELS OF GOVERNMENT IN THE UNITED STATES

Our Four Levels of Government. A good citizen knows how government works. For Americans it is important to learn about the different levels of government in which we all have a part. The United States has a national government, which is often called the *federal* government. The federal government has some authority over the whole nation. There are fifty states, including West Virginia, that have *state* governments. Within each state there are counties (parishes in Louisiana). The *counties* also have governments with local duties. Finally, there are thousands of cities and towns that have *municipal* governments.

fig. 22
Four levels of government

citizens

municipal

county

state

federal

Thus, all West Virginians live under at least three governments: the federal government, the state government of West Virginia, and their county government. About half of the people of West Virginia also live in municipalities and thus are subject to four levels of government.

The Federal Government. The federal government of the United States was formed by the American states in 1787. Representatives met in Philadelphia, Pennsylvania, to form a stronger central government for the good of all the states. In the Constitution of the United States they wrote the powers of the new federal government. The federal government was given complete control of foreign relations (dealings with other nations). No state may make a *treaty* with another nation, and only the federal government can regulate or tax trade from one state to another (*interstate commerce*). Only the federal government can declare war.

fig. 23
Some city ordinances say that a dog must be on a leash, but Scotty has found a way to beat the system.

States, Counties, and Municipalities. The states did not give all of their powers to the federal government. In fact, the Tenth Amendment to the Constitution allows the states to do anything that is not forbidden to them by the Constitution. State governments, including West Virginia's, have many duties. They enforce law and order. They also provide services such as the building and maintenance of highways, public colleges and universities, state parks, and mental health facilities.

West Virginia has fifty-five counties, each one having its own county government. The counties collect property taxes to support public schools and other services. They usually provide some police protection and public health services such as ambulances and clinics.

Municipalities often maintain a police force and a fire department. They may pave or repair city streets, collect garbage, and operate parks and swimming pools. Municipalities often pass ordinances to make life more pleasant. Some municipal ordinances prevent people from keeping farm animals in their yards.

The Federal System. Because there are four levels of government in the United States, we say that our government is *decentralized*. There are many government bodies rather than a single one. Our system of national, state, county, and municipal governments is called the *federal system*. In this course we will learn how each level of government affects us, and how they work together in a democratic way.

REVIEW OF SECTION THREE:
1. What are the levels of government in the United States?
2. How many governments do you live under?
3. Why do we say that government in the United States is decentralized?

SECTION FOUR: THE GROWTH OF MODERN GOVERNMENT

How the Federal Government Has Grown. Government in the United States has changed greatly in the past two hundred years. One of the biggest changes has been in the size of government. The federal government has grown especially large. After the Constitution was approved by the states in 1788, the nation's capital was located in Washington, D.C. At first Washington was a small town with less than four thousand residents. Only a few hundred people worked for the federal government. Today, Washington is a huge city that is the working place for tens of thousands of government employees. There are many federal government workers in other cities, too. In fact, there are more federal government workers outside Washington, D. C., than in our nation's capital.

Why the Federal Government Is Bigger. The federal government has grown partly because it now does many things that once were left to state and local governments. The federal government has passed laws to help citizens everywhere. For example, there are many federal safety rules for cars and trucks. It has helped to pay for thousands of miles of highways. There are federal laws to protect workers and to improve the environment. The federal government operates a social security program for most Americans. Many of these services used to be the responsibility of the state governments. Others were not done by government at any level.

Our federal government also is large because the United States is one of the world's largest and most important nations. The federal government defends the rights of Americans wherever they go in the world. The United States sends *ambassadors* abroad to represent its interests. The federal government also protects America with a large military force (the army, navy, air force, and marines). More than three million Americans are members of the armed forces.

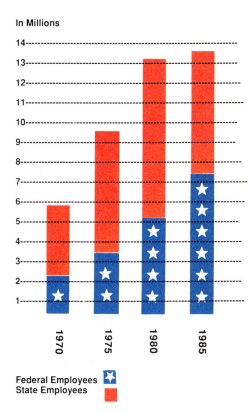

fig. 24
Growth in Government Employees

In Millions

Federal Employees ⭐
State Employees 🟥

fig. 25
All American citizens over the age of six get a Social Security card.

The Growth of Government around the World. The growth of government in the United States is not unusual. Everywhere in the modern world government has grown larger. In some countries, the national government has even more authority than our federal government. Big government is partly a result of modern times; there are more people, bigger businesses, and instant communication around the world. We know more about people in other counties and states, and we have more in common with them. Teenagers across the nation and around the world listen to the same top forty songs and attend rock concerts. They wear the same brand of jeans and shoes. For some events, such as the Olympic games, almost half of all humans watch the same television program.

fig. 26
These countries had democratic systems of government at the time this book was being printed. At the rapid rate things are changing in Europe even more democracies may soon be added. Can you identify them?

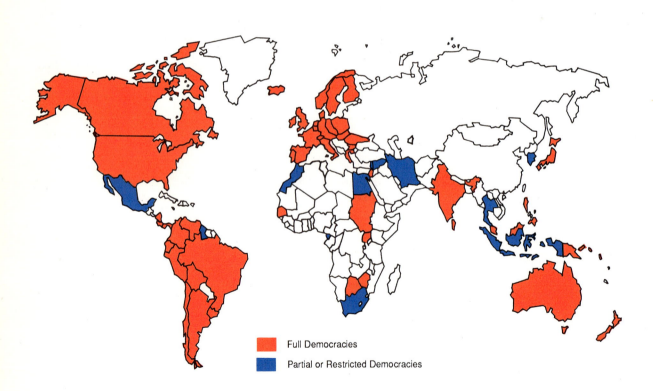

Full Democracies

Partial or Restricted Democracies

Democracies in the World

Bigger government in the United States also is related to the progress of democracy. At first only a minority of Americans (usually white men of means) had the right to vote or hold office. In time, all white men, then black men, women, and, finally, eighteen-year-olds won equal voting rights. Millions of active citizens have asked government to do more for the welfare of the people. When government meets these demands, it, of necessity, grows larger.

In West Virginia the same trend toward larger government can be seen. The state government has grown more than county or municipal governments have. For example, the West Virginia state government builds and repairs highways. Long ago, counties did most of the roadbuilding. Another major service of our state government is public higher education. State colleges and universities are much larger than in the past because more West Virginians now attend college.

fig. 27
Patriotic flour label from the S. George Company in Wellsburg, WV

REVIEW OF SECTION FOUR:

1. What has been one of the biggest changes in American government?
2. Why is the federal government much larger than it used to be?
3. Which level of government in West Virginia has grown most rapidly?

REFERENCES:

1. Fraenkel, Jack R., and Frank T. Kane. *Civics: Government and Citizenship.* Boston: Allyn and Bacon, Inc., 1983, pp. 2–10.
2. McClenaghan, William A. *Magruder's American Government.* Boston: Allyn and Bacon, Inc., 1983, pp. 2–14.
3. Wirt, Daniel, P. Allen Dionisopoulis, and Robert J. Gennette. *Our American Government and Political System.* River Forest, IL: Laidlow Brothers, 1983, pp. 12–47.

The Birth of American Liberty and Government

PREVIEW

To take part in democracy, we must know how our government is organized and how it works. It will help us if we study the early history of our country. This chapter will describe some of the exciting events that led to the birth of the United States. Learning about these will help us to understand why early American leaders created a new government, one of the first democracies in the world.

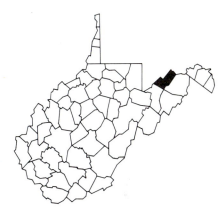

In Chapter Two we will answer the following questions:

1. Why did the American colonists rebel against England and declare the United States to be a free nation?
2. Why do Americans (and many other people) consider the Declaration of Independence to be so important?
3. What was the first government of our new nation? Why did it fail?
4. What document describes our national government and how it should work?
5. How were disagreements about the best form of government settled at the Constitutional Convention?

Pronounce and discuss the meanings of the following words found in this chapter.

anniversary
convention
delegate
European
exports

impose
petitions
provisions
repealed
tyrant

fig. 28, left page and above
Mineral County Courthouse in Keyser

fig. 29
Early Colonization of America

France
Verrazano, 1524 ———
Cartier, 1534 - - - -

England
Frobisher, 1576 - - - -
Drake, 1579 ———
Cabot, 1497 •—•—•

Spain
Columbus, 1492, 1493, 1498, 1502 ———
Vespucci, 1497 •—•—•
Balboa, 1513 – – –

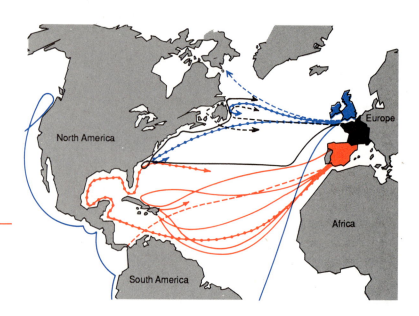

fig. 30
Symbol for the 1976 Bicentennial of the American Revolution

SECTION ONE: THE COLONIAL EXPERIENCE

The year 1976 was very special to Americans. It was the two-hundredth birthday of the United States. Millions of people across the country took part in parades and ceremonies to honor our nation's birth. In 1987 we celebrated again, this time the two-hundredth *anniversary* of our Constitution. Why do Americans celebrate events in our past? How did those events occur? For answers we must look back to a time when our nation did not exist.

Europeans Come to America. Five centuries ago Christopher Columbus discovered America by accident while trying to sail from Spain to Asia. After the discovery, several European countries sent men to America to explore and claim the land. Spanish, English, French, Dutch, and Swedish settlers established colonies in what is now the United States. A *colony* is a settlement in one land ruled by a government in another land.

The Europeans argued about which country should own parts of America. These disputes often led to wars. By 1763, after many years of fighting, England won control of all land east of the Mississippi River. England ruled thirteen colonies in this part of America.

Conflict between England and Her American Colonies. It was difficult for England to rule colonies three thousand miles away. It

took many weeks for ships to sail across the Atlantic Ocean. Therefore, England allowed each colony to form its own local government. The English government set some rules for all; however, the settlers made most of their own decisions. They became accustomed to doing things their own way.

fig. 31
Celebrating the Bicentennial of the United States Constitution

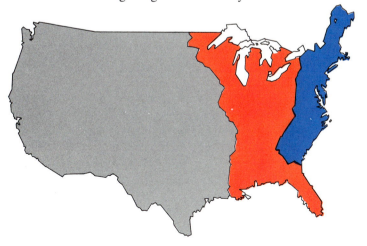

fig. 32
English Colonies in America

Before the French and Indian War

After the French and Indian War

fig. 33
Early American flags exhibited in the Navy Museum

fig. 34
Advertising of the early 1900s in West Virginia, as well as the rest of America, celebrated our founding through naming of family business.

After 1763, England paid more attention to the colonies. The English had just won a long and costly war with the French, part of which had been fought in America. As a result of the war, some of the English colonies gained new land. England tried to tax the Americans to help pay for the cost of the war. The English government also passed laws to force the colonies to trade only with England.

Many colonists opposed the new taxes and trade laws. They wanted to trade with other countries. They said that the taxes were unfair, because the colonists had no part in the government of England. Their slogan was "No taxation without representation!"

The colonists tried many forms of protest. They held public meetings and signed *petitions,* which were sent to England. They formed groups that tried to prevent Americans from buying products from England. Many disobeyed the trade laws. A few colonists used violence against English tax collectors.

In 1775 England finally *repealed* most of the new taxes. However, this came too late for many colonists. They were angry that England kept soldiers in American towns to enforce the law. Some of the soldiers were even attacked with sticks, stones, and snowballs. Many of the American colonists were ready for freedom from England.

REVIEW OF SECTION ONE:
1. Which European country controlled all land east of the Mississippi River by 1763?
2. How were the American colonies treated by England before 1763?
3. Why did the American colonists become upset with England after 1763?
4. In what ways did the colonists protest the actions of England between 1763 and 1775?

SECTION TWO: REVOLUTION AND INDEPENDENCE

The Colonies Revolt against England. In September 1774, leaders from most of the colonies met in Philadelphia, Pennsylvania. This group was called the *First Continental Congress.* It met to consider what should be done about the problems with England. Most who attended the meeting did not want to separate from the mother country. However, they wanted the English government to know that they would not stand for unjust laws.

After much debate, the Congress sent a Declaration of Rights to the king of England. The Declaration protested the unfair treatment of the colonies by England. The Congress also asked Americans not to trade with England until the colonies were treated better. Before the Congress *adjourned* (ended the meeting), the delegates planned another meeting for May 1775.

Before the *Second Continental Congress* met, fighting broke out. English soldiers had marched to Concord and Lexington in Massachusetts, where they had been fired upon and driven back by American volunteers. The Congress now prepared to fight a war against England. George Washington was made commander of a colonial army. The *American Revolution* was under way.

fig. 35
King George III

fig. 36
Battle of Bunker Hill

fig. 37
This portrait of Thomas Jefferson by Francois Jacques Dequevauvillier was made in 1824 and is housed in the National Portrait Gallery in the Smithsonian Institution.

fig. 38
Signing of the Declaration of Independence

fig. 39, right page
This Declaration of Independence engraving by James Barton Longacre was made in 1818 and is housed in the National Portrait Gallery in the Smithsonian Institution.

The Declaration of Independence. The Second Continental Congress declared the American colonies to be free of English rule. It appointed five men to write a statement, which was called the *Declaration of Independence*. The chief author of the Declaration was Thomas Jefferson of Virginia, whose work was approved by the Congress on July 4, 1776. Today the Fourth of July is our most important national holiday.

The Declaration of Independence announced to the world that the colonies were forming a new nation to be named the United States of America. The Declaration listed many of the complaints that had led the Americans to rebel. It claimed that King George III of England was a *tyrant* who had failed to protect American rights. The Declaration also stated some basic American beliefs about the purpose of government. As Jefferson wrote:

> We hold these truths to be self-evident, that all men are created equal, that they are endowed by their Creator with certain unalienable Rights, that among these are Life, Liberty and the Pursuit of Happiness — That to secure these Rights, Governments are instituted among Men, deriving their just Powers from the Consent of the Governed, that whenever any Form of Government becomes destructive of these Ends, it is the Right of the People to alter or to abolish it, and to institute new Government. . . .

fig. 39

fig. 40
*Dress of enlisted men in the
Revolutionary War*

Americans believe that all humans have certain rights, including the rights of life and liberty. Governments are formed by the people. If a government fails to protect basic rights, the people may change it or do away with it.

The Declaration of Independence stated that the king had failed to protect American rights. It declared the English government to be illegal in America. The Congress now set out to create a new government that would have the support of the American people. The United States government would protect their rights.

The Revolutionary War. England did not accept the Declaration of Independence. The United States had to fight a long war to win independence. This was called the *Revolutionary War*. England sent many ships and soldiers to put down the revolt. Some Americans opposed independence and backed England, and people on both sides suffered. Many American cities and towns were held by the English army. The American army under George Washington won some battles but also lost some.

France became an American ally during the war. The French gave money and arms to the United States, and the French navy joined the fight against the English navy. In England, some people opposed the government's war. They favored giving independence to the Americans. In 1781 England gave up, and the United States won the Revolutionary War. A treaty was signed that recognized the United States as a free nation.

REVIEW OF SECTION TWO:
1. What body led the colonies during the American Revolution?
2. What reasons does the Declaration of Independence give for the revolt against England?
3. What does the Declaration of Independence say is the major purpose of government?
4. What nation helped the United States win independence?

fig. 41
Sheet music, 1840

SECTION THREE: THE ARTICLES OF CONFEDERATION

The Continental Congress Creates a Government. During the Revolutionary War, the Second Continental Congress served as our national government. It was the only body that represented all of the states. (The colonies became states after independence was declared.) Members of the Congress wanted a better form of government. In 1777 they drew up a new plan called the *Articles of Confederation.* The Articles were not approved by all of the states until the end of the war in 1781.

The new national government was very weak, because at that time the states wanted as much freedom as possible. Most Americans feared strong central government. They had fought a war to free themselves from the powerful government of England. Under the Articles, the United States was a *confederation* (a loose alliance of independent states).

The Articles established a small and simple national government. Laws were made by a Congress with only one house. The legislature of each state elected representatives to Congress. Every state had one vote in Congress, regardless of its size or population. The new government had no president and no national courts of law. Only the states had courts.

Published by SAM.L CARUSI Baltimore

fig. 42
*The Providence, replica of a 1778
trading vessel in the colonies*

fig. 43
Independence Hall, Philadelphia

The Articles of Confederation gave some powers to Congress. Only Congress could handle relations with foreign countries and declare war or make peace. Only Congress could borrow money, set up a postal system, and settle disputes among the states. Congress also could build a navy and appoint top army officers. However, the American army was made up of volunteer soldiers sent by the states.

Weaknesses of the Articles of Confederation. The American government under the Articles of Confederation was very weak. When England had tried to tax Americans and control their trade, revolution broke out. Therefore, the Articles did not allow Congress to *impose* taxes or regulate trade. Congress could raise money only by borrowing from other countries or asking the states for grants. Other nations refused to lend, because the United States already owed too much money. None of the states gave as much money as Congress needed. As a result, Congress was not able to pay the nation's debts or to carry out any programs.

The economy of the United States was weak because Congress could not regulate trade or commerce. Each state could make its own trade treaties with other nations, and some states refused to trade with other states. Most states taxed goods from other states. This raised prices, so people bought less. Fewer goods were produced, and there were fewer jobs.

The national government was also weak because it could not easily pass new laws. Under the Articles, nine states had to vote for a bill before it became law. To *amend* or change the Articles, all thirteen states had to approve the change.

It was hard to enforce national laws under the Articles. The American government had no president or king in charge of carrying out laws, and there were no national courts. If someone broke a national law, the state courts were supposed to handle the case. However, the courts in most states were not willing to enforce national laws.

The Articles of Confederation Fail. Many Americans grew unhappy with the government under the Articles of Confederation. Finally, in 1787 Congress called for a meeting in Philadelphia to improve the Articles. Every state except Rhode Island sent delegates. However, these men soon gave up trying to change the Articles. Instead, they decided to draw up a completely new plan of government. The result of their work was called the *Constitution of the United States.*

REVIEW OF SECTION THREE:
1. What is a confederation?
2. What were the Articles of Confederation?
3. In what ways was the government of the United States weak under the Articles of Confederation?
4. How did a weak national government under the Articles harm the welfare of America?

THE CRADLE OF LIBERTY.

fig. 44
Centennial print by Currier & Ives entitled "Cradle of Liberty," 1786

fig. 45
Washington presiding over the 1787 Convention

fig. 46
Signing the Constitution

fig. 47
Wigs worn for formal occasions for this period were sometimes made for the individual wearing it, and so tight that the wearer had to shave his head to get it on.

SECTION FOUR: WRITING THE CONSTITUTION

The Constitutional Convention. The meeting that produced the Constitution was called the *Constitutional Convention.* The Convention met from May 25 to September 17, 1787, in Independence Hall in Philadelphia. That is the building where the Declaration of Independence had been signed.

Fifty-five *delegates* attended the Constitutional Convention. Some, such as George Washington, had been important during the Revolutionary War. Washington was famous and well respected, so the delegates chose him unanimously to preside over the Convention. Many other delegates held important public positions in state governments.

These delegates were not only important leaders in their states but were also well educated. Many knew the histories of other countries that had tried to improve their governments. They had learned useful lessons about politics from their experience under English rule. They also understood the weaknesses of the Articles of Confederation. It is fortunate that they were so well prepared to write a new constitution, for a difficult task faced them.

The Delegates Agree on Many Points. The meetings of the Constitutional Convention were held in secret. This allowed the delegates to express their views freely. The delegates were protected from outside interference, because the public did not know what issues were being debated. It was not until many years later that the public learned what happened during the Convention. James Madison, a delegate from Virginia, kept a complete written record of the meetings. His notes were not published until 1840, four years after his death. Madison was the last surviving member of the Convention.

Because of Madison's notes we know that the delegates agreed on many things at the beginning of the Convention. They agreed that the national government must have more power than it had under the Articles but at the same time must not be too powerful.

The delegates also felt the government should be organized in a new way. Congress was the only governmental body under the Articles. The Convention decided that the new government should have three branches or divisions: the executive, the legislative, and the judicial. However, the delegates also wanted to make sure that none of the three branches could become too strong.

Perhaps most important, the delegates agreed that the new government must be *representative*. In a representative form of government, the voters elect public officials, who are then representatives of the people. Representative government was a popular idea among the delegates, but they disagreed over who should be allowed to vote and to hold public office.

Compromises in the Constitution. Madison's records tell us of several points of disagreement in the Constitutional Convention. The most lengthy arguments were about representation in Congress and the control of trade. Following many weeks of debate, the delegates settled their differences by making compromises.

How the states would be represented in Congress was one of the most difficult questions facing the Convention. Delegates from the larger states wanted the number of Congressional representatives from each state to be based on population. Delegates from the smaller states were afraid their states would have little influence if representation were based on population. They wanted each state to have the same number of representatives in Congress.

fig. 48
Articles of Confederation, 1777

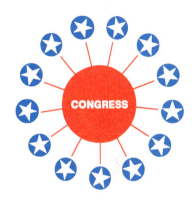

fig. 49
Constitution of the United States, 1787

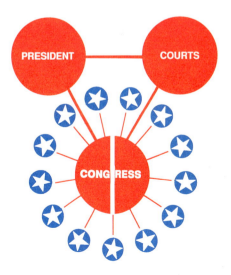

The conflict over representation was settled by an agreement known as the *Great Compromise*. The delegates decided that Congress should have two houses rather than one, which would be called the Senate and the House of Representatives. In the Senate each state would have two representatives. In the House of Representatives each state would be represented according to the size of its population. The Great Compromise gave the delegates from both the larger and smaller states part of what they wanted.

Support in Western Virginia for the Constitution. Most of the people living in western Virginia (present-day West Virginia) backed the American cause during the Revolutionary War. Soldiers from western Virginia fought in many important battles of the Revolution. Three western Virginians, Horatio Gates, Charles Lee, and Adam Stephen, were generals in the American army. Many western Virginians gave food, clothing, and other supplies to American troops. Western Virginians also helped the American cause by defending the frontier against the Indian allies of England.

The Indian tribes that helped England during the Revolutionary War did not give up when England surrendered to the Americans. Indian attacks continued against settlements in western Virginia. Western Virginians were dissatisfied with the national government under the Articles of Confederation, for it was too weak to end the Indian threat. For this reason almost all western Virginians favored the Constitution. They believed it would create a government strong enough to defeat the Indians.

The support among western Virginians for the new government was rewarded in 1794 when President Washington sent the army to fight the Indians. Led by General Anthony Wayne, the federal troops defeated the Indians in Ohio. After that defeat, the Indians were no longer a threat to western Virginia. Wayne County, West Virginia, was named for General Wayne.

The Great Compromise did not settle all of the arguments about representation. Another question was whether or not slaves would be counted as part of a state's population. Delegates from the southern states, where there were many slaves, wanted them to be counted, for their states would then have more members in the House of Representatives. Delegates from the northern states, where there were few slaves, did not want slaves to be counted.

The agreement reached by the delegates is called the *Three-Fifths Compromise*. It provided that each slave would be counted as three-fifths of a person in determining the population of a state. Thus, both sides received part, but not all, of what they wanted. The Three-Fifths Compromise is no longer part of the Constitution, because slavery was abolished in the United States in 1865.

The Convention also compromised on the regulation of *commerce,* or trade.

Many delegates felt that the national government must have the power to regulate trade, but the southern delegates were afraid to give the government that power. The southern states exported large amounts of agricultural products such as cotton to other countries. Buying and selling slaves was also an important business in the South. Southern delegates were afraid that if Congress had the power to regulate commerce it might tax *exports* and interfere with the slave trade. *The Commerce and Slave Trade Compromise* settled the problem. Congress would be given the power to regulate commerce but would not be allowed to tax exports. In addition, Congress could not interfere with the slave trade for a period of twenty years.

The three compromises explained above were among the most important ones in the Constitution. However, many other compromises had to be reached so that a majority of delegates would accept it. Probably no one delegate was completely satisfied with the finished document. But all of the delegates realized they had to sacrifice some of the things they wanted if the Convention was to succeed.

By September 1787 the delegates had agreed on what should be included in the Constitution. On September 17 the Convention met for the last time to approve the finished work. Forty-two delegates were present, and thirty-nine approved the Constitution by signing it.

The Struggle over Ratification. The Constitutional Convention had completed the task of designing a new government for the United States. However, the Constitution could not go into effect until nine of the thirteen states had *ratified* (approved) it. Each state would select delegates and hold a special convention to vote on the Constitution.

On September 28, 1787, copies of the Constitution were sent to the state governments. Soon copies of the document were read throughout the country. As people became familiar with the *provisions* of the Constitution, they began to divide into two groups. Those in favor of the Constitution were called *Federalists.* Opponents were known as *Antifederalists.* Both groups printed pamphlets, wrote letters to newspapers, and held rallies to win people to their side.

The Federalists argued that the Constitution should be approved because the United States needed a strong federal government. They pointed out that the country had suffered from weakness under the Articles of Confederation. If the Constitution was not approved, warned the Federalists, the United States would probably split into thirteen separate nations.

The Antifederalists disliked nearly everything about the Constitution. However, they were most concerned about the amount of

fig. 50
This engraving of General Anthony Wayne by Benjamin Tanner in 1797 resides in the National Portrait Gallery in the Smithsonian.

fig. 51
Samuel Adams

power given to the national government and the lack of a *bill of rights*. They feared that the states would have too little power and the national government would have too much power. They were also afraid that a strong national government might take away the liberties Americans had won in the Revolution. The Antifederalists argued that without a list or bill of rights the people would have no way to protect their freedom.

The bitter struggle between the Federalists and Antifederalists lasted for several months. The Federalists began to gain support after they agreed to add a bill of rights to the Constitution. In December 1787 the state conventions of Delaware, Pennsylvania, and New Jersey voted in favor of ratification. Seven more states gave their approval by June 1788, and in May 1790 Rhode Island became the last state to accept the Constitution.

In 1987 Americans celebrated the two-hundredth anniversary (bicentennial) of the Constitution. They recognized that the delegates who met in 1787 had produced a truly remarkable document. The system of government that they established has worked very well. Under it democracy has grown, and the liberties of the American people have been protected.

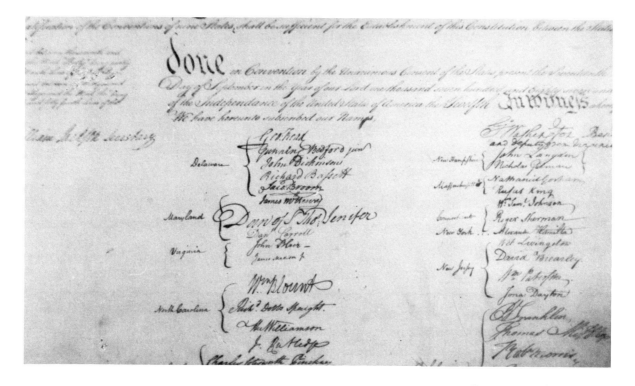

fig. 52, far left page
John Hancock

fig. 53, left page
Patrick Henry

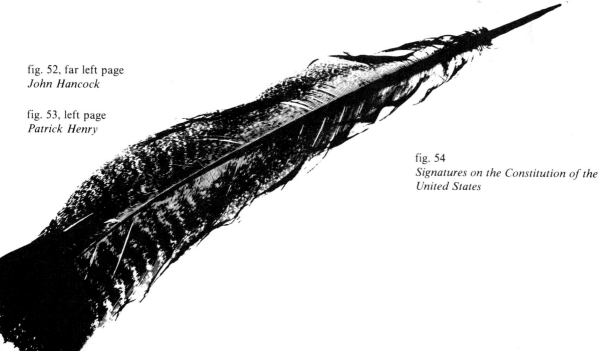

fig. 54
Signatures on the Constitution of the United States

fig. 55

fig. 56
State money from the bank of Charleston, Virginia

COMPARING THE GOVERNMENTS UNDER THE ARTICLES OF CONFEDERATION AND THE CONSTITUTION

Articles of Confederation	Constitution of the U.S.
States have a great deal of power. The national government has little power.	States have some power, but the national government is given many important powers.
No president or chief executive carries out laws.	A president heads the government and carries out laws.
Only state courts exist. There is no system of national courts.	Courts exist at both the national and state level.
A one-house Congress is responsible to the state legislatures.	A two-house Congress is responsible to the people.
Congress has no power to tax.	Congress has the power to tax.
Congress cannot regulate trade.	Congress can regulate trade.
Laws must be approved by nine of the thirteen states.	Laws may be passed by a majority of both houses of Congress.
No national currency exists. Each state coins its own money.	Only the national government can coin money.
Congress cannot establish a national army. Each state has its own troops.	Congress can establish an army and navy.
Amendment of the Articles requires approval of all the states.	Amending the Constitution requires the approval of three-fourths of the states.

SYMBOLS OF THE UNITED STATES

A *symbol* is something that stands for or represents something else. For example, the cross is a symbol of Christianity and $ is a symbol for the dollar. Symbols remind us of the things they represent.

All nations have symbols. They remind people of important beliefs and special events in their nation's history. However, national symbols are not very effective unless people understand their meaning. The United States has several symbols. You see some of these symbols nearly every day, but you may not know what they mean. The material which follows will help you understand the meaning of some of our symbols.

The American Flag. The most important symbol of our country is the flag. For that reason it is seen almost everywhere. It is flown over schools and government buildings. Many churches display the flag, and millions of Americans fly the flag outside their homes on certain holidays. The flag appears on the shoulder patches of some policemen, on bumber stickers, window decals, lapel pins and in many other places. But what does this familiar symbol mean? Why does it have stars and stripes? Why is it red, white and blue?

fig. 57

One of the original flag designs with 13 stars and stripes and the Great Seal

In 1777, during the Revolutionary War, the Continental Congress adopted the first American flag. The members of Congress decided that the flag of the new nation would have 13 red and white stripes and 13 white stars on a blue field. The 13 stripes and 13 stars were symbols for the 13 states which declared their independence from England. The three colors of the flag are also symbols. Red stands for courage, white for purity and blue for vigilance (watchfulness), perserverance (persistence) and justice.

Our flag is a symbol which is meant to remind us of beliefs and events that all Americans should remember. It should remind us of the brave people of the 13 colonies who founded the United States and those who have served the nation with courage since that time. It should help us remember that the pursuit of justice and the vigilance and perserverance of the American people were, and still are, important to the well-being of our country. Above all, the flag should remind us of the many freedoms Americans enjoy.

The American flag, the Statue of Liberty, the Great Seal and the bald eagle are important symbols of our country. However, they are not the only ones. The Liberty Bell and Uncle Sam are also famous American symbols. Do some research to find out more about them. Try to think of other American symbols. See if you can find out how they became national symbols and what they mean.

fig. 58

REVIEW OF SECTION FOUR:

1. How do we know so much about what happened at the Constitutional Convention if the meetings were held in secret?
2. What were the major points of agreement among the delegates to the Constitutional Convention?
3. What were the most important points of disagreement among the delegates? How were these disagreements settled?
4. What points were made by supporters and opponents of the Constitution during the struggle for ratification?
5. Name six popular symbols of the United States, and explain the major purpose of national symbols.

Can you describe the national symbols used in the design of these products? Did you notice which hand Ms. Liberty has in the air?

fig. 59
Flour sack label

fig. 60
Patriotic fan

REFERENCES:
1. Davidson, James W., and Mark H. Lytle. *The United States: A History of the Republic.* Englewood Cliffs, N.J.: Prentice-Hall, 1986: pp. 100–165.
2. Patrick, John J., and Richard C. Remmy. *Lessons on the Constitution.* Boulder, Co.: Social Science Education Consortium, Inc., 1985: pp. 39–110.
3. Risjord, Norman K. *Representative Americans: The Colonists.* Vol. 1, Lexington, Mass.: D.C. Heath Co., 1981.

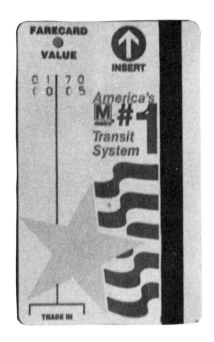

fig. 63
Fare card for the Metro subway in Washington, DC

fig. 61
James Montgomery Flagg recruitment poster of 1917

fig. 62
Wood engraving

The Constitution
of the United States

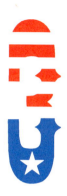

PREVIEW

The Constitution of the United States begins with these words:

> We the People of the United States, in order to form a more perfect Union, establish Justice, insure domestic Tranquility, provide for the common defense, promote the general Welfare, and secure the Blessings of Liberty to ourselves and our Posterity, do ordain and establish this Constitution for the United States of America.

The first sentence of the Constitution is called the *preamble*. It is a very short introduction that lists the goals or purposes of the new government. What do the goals listed in the preamble mean?

"to form a more perfect Union" - The new system of government should bring the states closer together.

"establish Justice" - The government should make sure that all Americans are treated fairly by the laws and the courts.

"insure domestic Tranquility" - The government should keep the peace within the United States.

"provide for the common defense" - The government should defend the United States against enemy nations.

"promote the general Welfare" - The government should help meet the needs of all the people.

"secure the Blessings of Liberty to ourselves and our Posterity" -The government should protect our freedom both now and in the future.

fig. 64, left page and above
Hampshire County Courthouse in Romney

fig. 65

The authors of the Constitution worked to design a system of government that could achieve these goals. This chapter will show how the goals in the preamble have been reached.

In Chapter Three we will answer the following questions:

1. What are the principles of government in our Constitution?
2. What are the three major parts of the Constitution?
3. What are the purposes of the preamble, the articles, and the amendments?
4. What is the Bill of Rights?
5. What changes have occurred in our federal system since 1787?

Pronounce and discuss the meaning of the following words found in this chapter.

accused	traditions
customs	Union
denied	unstated
evidence	vital
goals	witnesses

fig. 66
Signing of the Bill of Rights

SECTION ONE: THE BASIC PRINCIPLES
OF THE CONSTITUTION

The Constitution of the United States is the world's oldest written plan of government. After two centuries it is still supported strongly by Americans. This is partly because the Constitution is based on principles, or basic rules of government, that most of us accept.

The Principle of Popular Sovereignty. One of our Constitutional principles is *popular sovereignty.* This means that our government was created and approved by the people and not just by a king or a small group. In other words, the people are *sovereign,* or dominant, because all political power really belongs to them.

The men who wrote the Constitution believed that popular sovereignty is important. There are many statements in the Constitution that show this. Because the people are sovereign, we have representative government. Many of our public officials are elected by the people and are responsible to the people for their actions.

fig. 67
Thomas Paine

fig. 68
This mezzotint of Benjamin Franklin done in 1793 resides in the National Portrait Gallery in the Smithsonian.

The Principle of Limited Government. Another basic rule in the Constitution is the principle of *limited government*. Delegates to the Constitutional Convention wanted the federal government to be stronger than the government under the Articles of Confederation. However, they did not want it to be as powerful as England's government. Therefore, the Constitution limits the national government. It states what the government may do and what it may not do.

The Principle of Federalism. One problem the Constitutional Convention faced was how to make the federal government stronger without making the states too weak. The principle of federalism gave

fig. 69

Enumerated Powers (Powers of the Federal Government)	Concurrent Powers (Powers Shared By Federal and State Governments)	Reserved Powers (Powers of State Governments)
To regulate foreign trade and interstate commerce	To provide for the health and welfare of the people	To establish local governments
To conduct foreign relations	To make and enforce laws	To conduct elections
To coin money	To collect taxes	To regulate trade within the state
To establish post offices	To borrow money	To provide for public education
To issue copyrights and patents	To establish courts	To build highways
To establish naturalization laws	To charter banks	To incorporate businesses
To establish standards of wieghts and measures		To protect public safety
To admit new states and govern American territories		To issue licenses
		To determine the qualifications of voters

fig. 70

it a solution. *Federalism* is a system that splits power between the national government and the state governments.

Under the federal system our national, or federal, government may make and enforce laws that affect the whole nation. For example, interstate commerce and national defense are concerns of the federal government. The powers of the federal government are written in the Constitution. They are known as *enumerated* (listed) or *delegated* powers.

State governments also have certain powers that are not listed in the Constitution. Instead, the Tenth Amendment grants to the states or the people all powers not given to the federal government or not denied to the states. These are called *reserved* powers because the Tenth Amendment reserves or keeps them for the states. State governments deal with matters that affect only the people inside their borders. They support school systems, conduct elections, employ police, and provide many other services.

fig. 71

Separation of Powers in Government Branches

Some powers are shared by the federal and state governments. These are known as *concurrent* powers. Both levels of government may levy taxes, borrow money, establish courts, and punish criminals.

The federal system has worked well. The federal government is strong but not all-powerful. The states also have certain powers, and some powers are shared by both levels of government.

The Principle of Separation of Powers. Another principle in the Constitution is *separation of powers*. This means that each branch or part of the federal government has some power that the other branches do not have. The power to rule is split up, which helps to limit the power of the federal government.

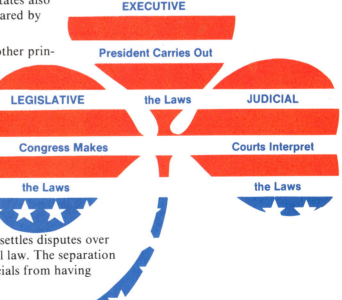

There are three branches in the federal government. The *legislative branch* (Congress) makes laws. These laws are enforced or carried out by the *executive branch* (the presidency). The *judicial branch* (the courts) settles disputes over the law and punishes those who break federal law. The separation of powers keeps any official or group of officials from having too much power.

The Principle of Checks and Balances. The Constitution also keeps one branch of government from being more powerful than the others. This comes from the principle of *checks and balances.* The Constitution gives each branch powers that it can use to check, or limit, the powers of the other branches. This helps make the three branches equal and their power in balance.

For example, Congress passes laws, but the president can *veto,* or reject, laws passed by Congress. The president, however, would have too much power if he could stop laws by himself. So the Constitution gives Congress a way to check the power of the president. Congress can *override,* or cancel, a veto. If two-thirds of the members of both houses vote to do this, the law then goes into effect. Although Congress can get around a veto, it is not easy to get enough votes to do so.

The diagram in the text shows how each branch of government can check the powers of the other two branches. We will learn more about how the principle of checks and balances works in later chapters.

REVIEW OF SECTION ONE:
1. What are five major principles of government in the U.S. Constitution?
2. How is representative government a part of the principle of popular sovereignty?
3. What is the federal system of government?
4. How does the principle of checks and balances limit the power of the federal government?

fig. 72

fig. 73
President Reagon in the Oval Office

fig. 74 THE CONSTITUTION OF THE UNITED STATES 43

The President checks the power of the courts by appointing federal judges and granting pardons.

EXECUTIVE BRANCH

The President checks the powers of Congress by vetoing laws, calling special sessions, recommending laws, appealing to the people, making foreign policy and appointing federal officials.

The Federal courts check the power of the President by declaring actions of the executive branch unconstitutional.

JUDICIAL BRANCH

The Federal courts check the power of Congress by declaring laws passed by Congress unconstitutional.

System of Checks and Balances

Congress checks the power of the Federal courts by rejecting the appointees to the courts, impeaching and removing judges, and creating new courts.

LEGISLATIVE BRANCH

Congress checks the power of the President by overriding vetos, rejecting treaties and presidential appointments, controlling funding for the executive branch, and impeaching and removing the President

SECTION TWO: THE ARTICLES OF THE CONSTITUTION

The Constitution has three major parts. The preamble states the goals of the Constitution. It is followed by the main body of the Constitution, which has seven *articles*. The third part is made up of twenty-six amendments that have been added since 1787.

The Constitution is a plan of government for the United States. The seven articles are the heart of that plan. They state how our government is organized and how it should function.

This section of the chapter describes each of the seven articles. Read the summary of Article I. Then use a copy of the Constitution and read the full text of the article. Do the same with the other six articles. We will learn more about some of the articles in later chapters.

Article I. Article I of the Constitution created the legislative branch of the federal government. The legislative branch is called Congress. It has two houses, the Senate and the House of Representatives. The major duty of Congress is to make the national laws. Article I is the longest of the seven articles. It describes who may serve in Congress and how they are elected. It explains what powers Congress has and how it should function.

Article II. The executive branch of the national government was created by Article II. The executive branch carries out the laws passed by Congress. Article II provides for only two members of the executive branch, the president and the vice president. Over the years, more executive offices have been added through laws passed by Congress.

Article III. Article III created the judicial branch of the national government. The judicial branch is made up of a Supreme Court and other courts that Congress has established. The judicial branch settles disputes about the meaning of laws and punishes lawbreakers.

Article IV. Article IV sets forth how the states and the federal government must cooperate. It requires that each state respect the rights of citizens from other states. For example, a marriage performed in West Virginia is legal in all other states. Article IV also requires states to return escaped criminals or persons accused of crimes to the state in which the crime was committed. It explains how new states can be admitted to the Union. It also guarantees that the federal government will protect the states from foreign enemies or violence within their borders.

fig. 75
The Executive Branch
(President Bush in the White House)

Article V. Article V explains how the Constitution may be *amended* or changed. The amendment process is difficult. Thousands of amendments have been proposed since 1789, but only twenty-six have been added.

There are two ways an amendment can be proposed: (1) Congress may propose an amendment if two-thirds of both houses vote to do so. (2) The legislatures of two-thirds of the states may ask for a national convention to propose an amendment. The second method has never been used.

After an amendment has been proposed, it must be *ratified* (approved) by three-fourths of the states. The proposed amendment can be ratified either by (1) state legislature or (2) special state conventions. All but one of the amendments have been ratified by state legislatures.

fig. 76
*The Judicial Branch
(Supreme Court Building)*

fig. 77

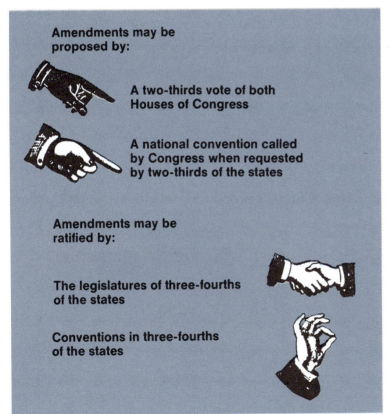

Amendments may be proposed by:

A two-thirds vote of both Houses of Congress

A national convention called by Congress when requested by two-thirds of the states

Amendments may be ratified by:

The legislatures of three-fourths of the states

Conventions in three-fourths of the states

fig. 78
Freedom of assembly

fig. 79
Freedom of speech

Article VI. Article VI states that the new government would honor all debts and contracts of the old government. It also requires that federal and state officials promise to support the Constitution. In addition, it forbids the use of religious qualifications for federal offices.

Article VI has another important rule. The states may not pass laws that conflict with the Constitution or federal laws. The Constitution and the laws of the United States are the supreme law of the land. Thus, in cases of conflict, state law must be set aside and the Constitution or federal law must be obeyed.

Article VII. The last article states that the Constitution would go into effect after nine states approved it.

REVIEW OF SECTION TWO:
1. The first three articles of the Constitution created what parts of the federal government?
2. What is the major duty of each branch of the federal government?
3. How can the Constitution be amended?
4. According to Article VI, what is the supreme law of the United States?

SECTION THREE: THE BILL OF RIGHTS

The third major part of the Constitution is made up of twenty-six amendments. The first ten are called the *Bill of Rights.* They were added to the Constitution in 1791. The Bill of Rights is a very important part of the American tradition of liberty. For that reason, we will look at the first ten amendments separately.

You remember that one reason the American colonists revolted against England was to protect their rights. Guarding the rights of the people was a major goal of the authors of the Constitution. The seven articles included ways to limit the power of government and protect individual rights. However, many people insisted on adding a bill of rights to the Constitution.

The First Amendment. The First Amendment protects five rights needed in a free country. One of these is *freedom of religion.* During the colonial era people could not always worship freely. The First Amendment lets Americans worship as they choose, even if they choose not to practice religion. Government may not set up an official church or use taxes to support a church.

The First Amendment also protects *freedom of speech* and *freedom of the press*. The right to express any idea is vital in a democracy. However, there are limits to our right to speak and write. We do not have the right to make statements about people that we know are not true. Nor do we have the right to say false things that might hurt others as a result. For example, a person does not have the right to shout "fire" in a crowded room. This could cause harm to people as they try to escape.

Two other rights in the First Amendment are *freedom of assembly* and *freedom of petition*. Freedom of assembly allows us to meet with others in a peaceful manner. The government cannot deny people the right to gather even when they want to protest some act of the government. We also have the right to bring our *grievances,* or complaints, to our elected officials. Freedom of petition allows us to tell officials how we feel about public issues.

fig. 80
Freedom of religion

fig. 81
Freedom of the press

fig. 82
Freedom of petition

fig. 83
*Early American with musket,
Pt. Pleasant Park*

The Second Amendment. The Second Amendment gives states the right to have an armed *militia,* or force of volunteer soldiers. The new United States did not have a large army. Each state had a militia that could be used in case of war. Members of militias always had to use their own weapons. Many Americans wanted the new federal government to permit state militias and allow people to own weapons. That is the purpose of the Second Amendment.

The Third Amendment. The Third Amendment protects us from having to give housing to soldiers during peacetime. The English government had sometimes forced colonists to take in soldiers. Americans did not want the government to have such power.

The Fourth Amendment. The Fourth Amendment prevents the government from unfairly searching or taking property. The police can search or seize property only if they have a *search warrant,* which must be issued by a judge. A search warrant gives the reason for a search and describes the place to be searched and the property to be seized. Judges cannot issue a search warrant unless they think that a search will lead to evidence of a crime.

The Fifth Amendment. The Fifth Amendment protects those accused of a crime. It does so in several ways. First, a person cannot be tried for a serious crime unless he or she has been *indicted* (charged) by a *grand jury.* Grand juries do not decide whether a person is guilty or innocent. They determine whether there is enough evidence to hold a trial.

The Fifth Amendment lists other protections, too. It keeps the government from trying a person more than once for the same crime. It cannot force people to give evidence that could be used against them. The government may not take a person's life, liberty, or property without *due process of law.* This means that a person cannot be punished unless found guilty of a crime in a fair trial.

The last part of the Fifth Amendment protects property rights. The government has the power to take private property for public use. This is known as the power of *eminent domain.* However, the government must pay a fair price for property it takes.

The Sixth Amendment. The Sixth Amendment also protects those accused of crimes. It guarantees them a speedy and public trial before a fair jury. Members of the jury must come from the area where the crime occurred. The person on trial must be told what he or she is accused of doing. The accused also has the right to have a lawyer, to hear and question witnesses, and to call his own witnesses.

The Seventh Amendment. The Seventh Amendment deals with conflicts between people or between people and the government. Courts not only try those accused of crimes, but they also settle disputes about such things as money or property. Those involved in most *civil* (noncriminal) cases may choose to have a jury rather than a judge settle their case.

The Eighth Amendment. The Eighth Amendment keeps courts from setting fines or *bail* too high. Most people arrested for crimes do not want to stay in jail until their trial. If they do not seem dangerous, a judge can free them on bail, or money the accused must leave with the court. This helps assure that he or she will show up for trial.

The Eighth Amendment also denies courts the right to punish people in a cruel or unusual manner. The meaning of cruel and unusual punishment is not completely clear. For that reason, people disagree about it. For example, some people believe that the death penalty is cruel and should not be allowed. Others disagree and support the death penalty.

The Ninth Amendment. The Ninth Amendment gives Americans rights that are not even listed in the Constitution. For example, the Constitution does not include the right to marry or to have children. It does not mention the right to privacy or the right to travel around the country. The Ninth Amendment protects our unstated rights.

The Tenth Amendment. The Tenth Amendment gives other rights to the states and to the people. Any power not given to the federal government is given to them unless the Constitution bars it. The state governments have *reserved powers,* because the Tenth Amendment reserves them for the states.

fig. 84
Commemorative stamp for the 200th anniversary of the Bill of Rights in 1989

fig. 85
Freedom of Expression

REVIEW OF SECTION THREE:

1. What is the Bill of Rights in the U.S. Constitution?
2. What rights are protected by the First Amendment?
3. How does the Fourth Amendment protect Americans from unfair search and seizure?
4. How are people accused of committing a crime protected by the Fifth, Sixth, and Eighth Amendments?
5. Why are the Ninth and Tenth Amendments important safeguards against the power of the federal government?

fig. 86
Indiana Company claim

SECTION FOUR: THE GROWTH AND DEVELOPMENT OF THE CONSTITUTION

Amendments 11-26. Sixteen amendments have been added to the Constitution since the Bill of Rights was adopted. Many of the amendments have helped make our country more democratic. The chart below states their most important features and shows when each was ratified.

West Virginia and the Eleventh Amendment. In 1768 the English government and several Indian tribes signed the Treaty of Fort Stanwix. In one part of the treaty the Indians gave up their claims to a large tract of land, including most of present-day West Virginia. Another part granted 2,862 square miles of land to a group of merchants from Philadelphia. This land was located in the northwestern part of our state. At that time this area was called Indiana.

Colonial Virginia would not allow the merchants to have Indiana. The dispute lasted many years. After the Revolutionary War, the merchants tried but failed to persuade the U.S. government to support their claim to Indiana.

When the Constitution took effect, the merchants took their case to the United States Supreme Court. Virginia's representatives in Congress proposed amending the Constitution so that a state could not be sued by citizens of another state. They won in 1798 when the Eleventh Amendment was added to the Constitution. The Supreme Court then dismissed the Indiana case. Thus, it was a dispute over land in what is now West Virginia that led to the Eleventh Amendment.

Rights Given by the Amendments. Half of the amendments added to the Constitution since 1791 give more rights to some or all Americans. The *Thirteenth Amendment,* ratified after the Civil War, ended slavery. However, it was not until the *Fourteenth Amendment* was passed in 1868 that black Americans were made citizens. The Fourteenth Amendment also required the states to treat all citizens equally and fairly.

Five amendments have been added to the Constitution in order to give *suffrage,* or the right to vote, to more people. In many states, only white males over twenty-one were allowed to vote. As you can see in the chart in the text, black men gained the right to vote with the *Fifteenth Amendment* in 1870. After a long struggle, women won the right to vote with the *Nineteenth Amendment* of 1920. The *Twenty-*

fig. 87
*13th
Amendment*

fig. 88
Belva Lockwood, suffragette

fig. 89, *Political cartoon against suffrage*

fig. 90
Susan B. Anthony, suffragette

third Amendment let the people of Washington, D.C., vote for president and vice president. Before 1961 they could vote only for city officials. The *Twenty-sixth Amendment* reduced the voting age to eighteen in 1971.

Although the Fifteenth Amendment gave blacks the right to vote, several states passed laws to keep them from voting. For example, some states required all voters to pay a *poll tax* in order to vote. Many blacks and some whites could not afford the tax. In 1964 the *Twenty-fourth Amendment* ended the use of poll taxes in national elections.

The *Seventeenth Amendment,* ratified in 1913, did not increase the number of votes. However, it did give the voters more power. Until 1913, United States senators were chosen by state legislatures. Many senators did not represent the people very well, because they were not elected by the people. The Seventeenth Amendment made our government more representative by letting the people elect their senators.

Other Ways Government Has Changed. The amendment process is the basic way of updating the Constitution and changing our system of government, but it is not the only way. Changes also are made by acts of Congress, the president, and the federal courts. Our system of government also is influenced by custom and tradition.

Congress may make all laws necessary and proper to carry out its powers. We say that Congress has *implied powers.* They are implied, because they are not described exactly. For example, there is nothing written about highway traffic between the states. The authors of the Constitution did not know about modern cars, trucks, and interstate highways. However, Congress does have the power to regulate interstate commerce. It has used the implied powers in the Constitution to make traffic laws such as the sixty-five-miles-per-hour speed limit.

One way in which presidents have changed our government is by appointing leaders to the *president's cabinet.* Cabinet members are the heads of the different departments of the federal government. The Constitution does not mention the cabinet.

The federal courts have changed government, too. The courts have the duty to *interpret* (decide the meaning) of the Constitution. Sometimes the courts have changed their interpretations, and this has changed our laws.

fig. 91
Lucy Stone, reformer

fig. 92
Geraldine Ferarro, Democratic running mate of Walter Mondale, became the closest woman to the office of president since women gained the right to vote.

National Portrait Gallery photos

This 1880 photograph of Belva Lockwood, a suffragette, was made by Benjamin Falk and now resides in the National Portrait Gallery in the Smithsonian.

This photograph of Susan B. Anthony (another reformer) by Theodore Marceau in 1989 is also in the National Portrait Gallery.

This daguerreotype of Lucy Stone, reformer, was made about 1805 and also is housed in the National Portrait Gallery.

AMENDMENTS TO THE CONSTITUTION
ADDED SINCE 1791

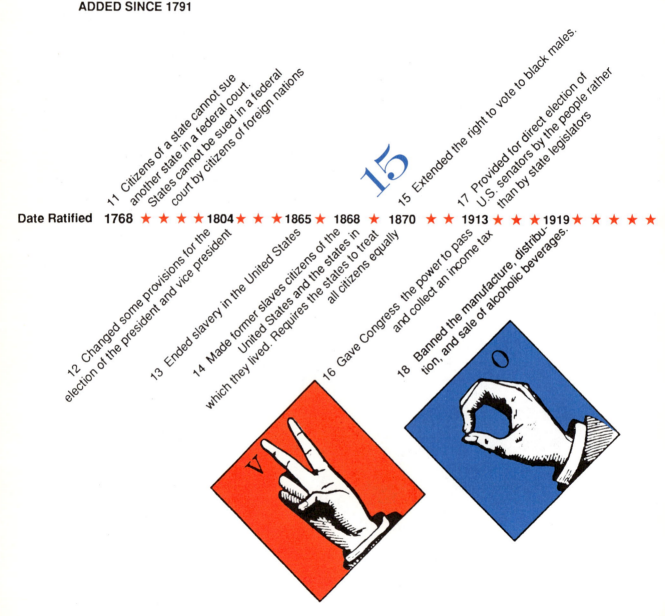

11 Citizens of a state cannot sue another state in a federal court. States cannot be sued in a federal court by citizens of foreign nations

15

15 Extended the right to vote to black males.

17 Provided for direct election of U.S. senators by the people rather than by state legislators

Date Ratified   1768 ★ ★ ★ ★ 1804 ★ ★ ★ 1865 ★ 1868 ★ 1870 ★ ★ 1913 ★ ★ ★ 1919 ★ ★ ★ ★ ★ ★

12 Changed some provisions for the election of the president and vice president

13 Ended slavery in the United States

14 Made former slaves citizens of the United States and the states in which they lived. Requires the states to treat all citizens equally

16 Gave Congress the power to pass and collect an income tax

18 Banned the manufacture, distribution, and sale of alcoholic beverages.

19 Extended the right to vote to women

21 Repealed the Eighteenth Amendment. Alcoholic beverages were legal once again.

22 Limited the number of times a person can be elected president to two.

24 Banned the use of poll taxes in federal elections.

★ ★ ★ ★ 1920 ★ ★ ★ 1933 ★ ★ ★ 1951 ★ 1961 ★ ★ ★ ★ 1964 ★ ★ ★ 1967 ★ ★ ★ 1971 ★ ★ ★

20 Changed the dates upon which terms of office for Congress and the president and vice president begin

23 Gave the right to vote for president and vice president to residents of the District of Columbia

25 Explained how the president will be replaced should he die, resign, or become disabled.

26 Lowered the voting age to eighteen in all federal, state, and local elections.

fig. 93
*Sign language illustrates
"VOTE." Amendments 15, 19, 23, 24,
and 26 all affect the right to vote.*

Some changes come from customs or traditions that develop over the years. For example, the role of political parties grew by tradition. They were not described in the Constitution, and no law was passed by Congress to form them. However, political parties are very important in our government. They choose people to run for political office, and they work for laws on issues that they support.

One reason that the Constitution has worked so well is that it has allowed government to change. The authors did not try to make rules for every matter. As time has passed and democracy has grown, our government has done many new things. Our country is very different from the United States of two hundred years ago. We are lucky that these changes could be made without breaking the Constitution.

fig. 94
School girls at "A Celebration of Citizenship" day in Washington, DC

REVIEW OF SECTION FOUR:

1. What groups of Americans gained the right to vote through amendments to the Constitution?
2. How did the Seventeenth Amendment make our government more representative?
3. What is responsible for the many changes that have occurred in our system of government since the Constitution was written in 1787?
4. What are implied powers? Why does Congress rely so much on its implied powers?

REFERENCES:

1. Faber, Doris, and Harold Faber. *We the People: The Story of the United States Constitution since 1787.* New York: Scribners, 1987.
2. Mabie, Margot. *The Constitution: Reflections of a Changing Nation.* New York: Henry Holt, 1987.
3. Patrick, John J., and Richard C. Remy. *Lessons on the Constitution.* Boulder, Co.: Social Science Education Consortium, Inc., 1985.

fig. 95
Jesse Jackson, who ran a close second for Democratic candidate for president in 1988

THE FIRST COLORED SENATOR AND REPRESENTATIVES.
In the 41st and 42nd Congress of the United States.

fig. 96
This lithograph of the first black Congressmen made in 1872 by Currier and Ives, includes seated from left to right: Hiram Revels, Benjamin Turner, Josiah Walls, Joseph Rainey, R. Brown Elliot, and standing, left to right: Robert DeLarge and Jefferson Long. The portrait resides in the National Portrait Gallery in the Smithsonian.

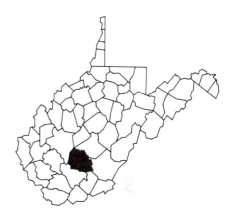

The Role of the Citizen
in American Government

PREVIEW

We have learned how the United States Constitution set up a representative federal government. With the Bill of Rights and its other amendments, the Constitution also gives us many rights. Among these is the right to take part in government. Adult citizens may run for public office and vote for elected officials. Citizens of all ages may state their views on public issues. These rights are necessary for democracy. However, for democracy to work well citizens must use their rights.

In Chapter Four we will answer the following questions:
1. What are the responsibilities of a citizen?
2. How do political parties contribute to our democracy?
3. What is the role of public interest groups in government?
4. How do we elect federal officials?

Pronounce and discuss the meanings of the following words found in this chapter.

ballot	politician
caucus	public
contribution	register
election campaign	testify
nominate	tolerance

fig. 97, left page and above
Fayette County Courthouse in Fayetteville

SECTION ONE: RESPONSIBILITIES OF CITIZENSHIP

fig. 98
Lincoln with son Tadd

fig. 99
Uncle Sam still wants you!

Our Rights Are Our Duties. In his famous address at Gettysburg, Pennsylvania, in 1863, President Abraham Lincoln expressed the American belief in democracy. He described our government as one "of the people, by the people, for the people." Our right to take part in government is also our duty. If the people are not active citizens, then government cannot be democratic.

A basic duty for an adult is to vote in public elections. Too many Americans do not care enough to vote. However, voting alone is not enough. There are many other ways for a citizen to support our democratic society. Students can take part, too, even though they cannot vote until they reach age eighteen.

Keeping Informed. An important responsibility of Americans is to be informed about government. We must know how our government works. We must know who our public officials are. We must learn about important public issues. We should know what officeholders and candidates think about the issues. It doesn't mean much to vote if we don't know what we are voting for or against.

For students, a part of good citizenship is being a good student. In school we study the basic workings of government. Other social studies classes help us learn our history and geography. This knowledge also informs us about public life. Hard work in all of our subjects, including math, science, and language, helps us know about the world in which government acts. We also learn how to think properly and express our thoughts. That helps us when we think about and discuss public issues.

The *mass media* are good sources of information about government. The media include newspapers, magazines, radio, and television. The media give us news about affairs and public people. They report on the actions of Congress, the president, the federal courts, and other government bodies. They inform us about election campaigns.

The media are also used to influence *public opinion*. Political candidates and officeholders advertise their good points in the media. They try to convince us to vote for them and support them. We can sometimes listen to public addresses by politicians on radio and see them on television.

The owners of the media try to influence how their audience thinks. They present *editorials* or statements for or against certain officials or viewpoints. Editorials often help us to think about issues. This helps us form our own opinions.

fig. 100
Where the man on the street gets his say

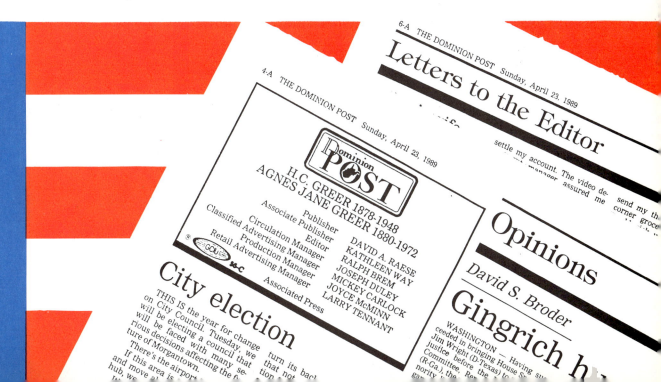

figs. 101-105
On October 7, 1989, approximately 250,000 citizens from most states marched to the Mall in front of the Capitol in Washington, DC, to tell the government that they wanted some serious attention given to the homeless problem in America. Young and old alike joined in the effort, and celebrities such as Sugar Ray Leonard, Jesse Jackson, Tracy Chapman, and many others spoke to the huge crowd.

Community Life. Citizens can also contribute by taking part in community life. A good citizen cares about the welfare of his town or county. There are many organizations that try to improve local life and help people. Some of these, such as the Girl Scouts, the Explorers, 4-H clubs, and others, are especially for young people.

Some organizations are made up of people who want to take part in political affairs. *Political parties* play an important role in government, and any citizen may join a political party when he or she is old enough to vote. Adult citizens may also run for election to a public office. They are often active members of political parties. *Public interest groups* are also political organizations. They are made up of people who work for some public goal or concern. We will study more about political parties and interest groups in the next two sections of Chapter Four.

Tolerance and Understanding. As citizens in a democracy we are responsible for being informed and taking part in public affairs. We have the right to form our own opinions. We have the right and duty to express our views. We can join groups that seek to influence government or improve our communities.

There is another aspect of democracy that we must defend. Everyone has the right to take part. In a democracy many different opinions are expressed. There is always conflict between those who favor one side of an issue and those who favor the other side. We are all protected when the rights of everybody are defended.

Thus, we have a duty to respect the thoughts and opinions of others. It is important that we *tolerate* or accept those who disagree with us. We should try to understand why others think and believe the way they do. Tolerance and understanding help democracy work well.

West Virginia made a good contribution, with five busloads of people coming from Morgantown alone.

ethics

Ethics in Government. As you have learned, the United States has a democratic government. During most of our nation's history that form of government has worked very well. A major reason for its success is the support it has received from the American people. Americans have supported their government because they trust and respect it. Without that trust and respect, popular support for our government would weaken, and it would no longer work so well.

People trust and respect their government for many reasons, but one of the most important ones is the behavior of their political leaders. We expect our leaders at every level of government to do what is best for the people who elected them. We do not expect them to misuse their power by being dishonest and immoral. As representatives of the people, it is important that they behave in an *ethical* way. That means obeying the laws and being honest and moral. When political leaders fail to behave ethically, public support for our government weakens. If it happens too often, people begin to mistrust their leaders and lose respect for their government.

Most public officials are honest and work very hard for their constituents. Like other Americans, they are deeply bothered when some officials behave unethically. They know that such behavior weakens our democracy. Because of the growing concern about ethics in government, Congress and many state legislatures have recently passed ethics laws. The West Virginia Legislature passed such a law in 1989. Ethics bills are intended to make officials aware of the kinds of behavior that the public considers unethical. They also provide for the punishment of officials who violate ethics laws.

As citizens we are also responsible for ethics in our government. We must take enough interest in politics to help ensure that ethical people are elected to office. We must support those in Congress and our state

fig. 106
This photograph of cartoonist and political conscience of his day Thomas Nast, was made by Sarony about 1878. It can be seen in the National Portrait Gallery in the Smithsonian.

legislature who want to pass stronger ethics laws. We must also insist that unethical public officials be removed from office. By doing these things we help strengthen our democracy.

REVIEW OF SECTION ONE:

1. Why does democracy depend on active citizens?
2. What are several responsibilities of citizenship?
3. How do the mass media inform citizens about public affairs?
4. How can young people be active citizens?
5. Why is tolerance important to democracy?
6. Why is it important to our democracy that public officials behave ethically?

fig. 107
Nast cartoon fingering Boss Tweed, mayor of New York, and his cohorts

DEM★CRAT

SECTION TWO: POLITICAL PARTIES AND THE CITIZEN

What Is a Political Party? Political parties are organizations of citizens who join together to influence government. Their members agree on many issues. Together they try to win elections for their members and make government work for their goals.

In the United States today we have two major political parties, the Republican Party and the Democratic Party. Millions of Americans have joined, or *registered,* as Republicans or Democrats. However, it is not necessary to join a political party. Some Americans are independents. Independents are not members of any political party.

How American Political Parties Developed. When the United States government was formed after the American Revolution, there were no political parties. When the Constitution was written, nothing was included about political parties. Some early American leaders, such as President George Washington, thought that parties would be harmful. Parties might divide Americans and weaken our nation. However, political leaders found it necessary to join with others to accomplish their goals. In time, they formed political parties.

The first American political parties were the *Federalist Party* and the *Democratic-Republican Party.* Federalists wanted a strong national government. Democratic-Republicans opposed the Federalists. They wanted state governments to have more power than the federal government.

fig. 108
Republican clip-ons

fig. 109
Donkey (Democrat) and elephant (Republican) long stood as party symbols.

REPUBLICAN

Today the Federalist Party does not exist. It was eventually replaced by the *Republican Party*. The Democratic-Republican Party became the *Democratic Party*.

The Two-Party System. During most of our history the United States has had two major political parties. All of our presidents elected since 1860 have been either Democrats or Republicans. For this reason, we say that we have a *two-party political system*.

Some democracies, such as Italy, have more than two major parties. They are called *multi-party systems*. Countries ruled by a small oligarchy or a single dictator usually have only one political party. These are *one-party systems*. Some one-party nations hold elections and claim to be democratic. However, real democracy must give the voters a choice between the party in power and the party or parties out of power.

Although the United States has a two-party political system, there are a number of small parties. These are called *third parties*. They usually appeal only to a small number of people. Some third parties in America today include the American Independent Party, the Communist Party, the Libertarian Party, and the Socialist-Labor Party.

fig. 110
1904 campaign poster

INDEPENDENT

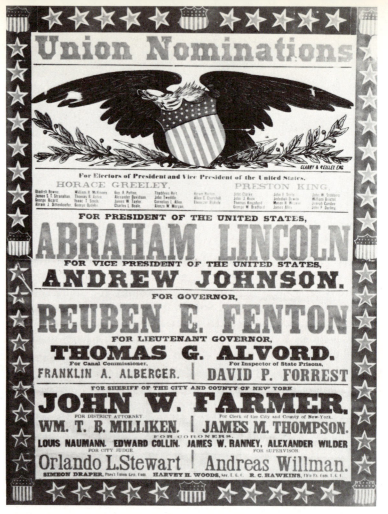

fig. 111
1861 campaign poster

fig. 112
The Black Panther political party was originally started in Lowndes, Alabama, in 1964 to allow blacks to vote their own candidates into office. At the beginning of the civil rights movement, this predominantly black county was governed totally by white officials. The new party allowed blacks to run for and be elected to offices, which would otherwise have been more difficult in the whitedominated Republican and Democratic parties of that time.

Sometimes third parties have influenced the major parties and have changed our government. This was true of the Populist Party almost a century ago. The Populist Party appealed to millions of farmers and workers. It asked for public regulation of railroad companies, direct election of United States senators, and other changes. These reforms were later enacted by the major parties.

A third party could grow popular and become a major party. The Republican Party began in 1854 as a third party. It opposed the spread of slavery in the United States. Many Americans agreed with that view, and the Republicans became a major party by 1860. Their nominee, Abraham Lincoln, was elected president.

How Parties Are Organized. The members of American political parties are ordinary citizens. Millions of people have *registered* as Democrats or Republicans. However, most of the work of the parties is done by *activists,* those people who actively participate in running the parties.

The major parties are organized on national, state, and local levels. The national party structure is made up of a national committee, which consists of a man and a woman from each of the fifty states, plus the District of Columbia and the territories. The national committee elects one person as national chairman. There are also state party committees and local committees, such as the county executive committees in West Virginia.

How the Parties Function. Political parties want to win elections, and they act in several ways to reach their goals. One function is to select the candidates whom the party will try to elect. A party's candidates are *nominated* in a primary election or in a party meeting such as a *caucus* or convention.

fig. 113
1976 convention souvenir

fig. 114
Convention premonitions

fig. 115

*Stars 'n stripes forever in
Ravenswood, WV*

Parties also raise money to help pay for election campaigns. They sell tickets to dinners and receptions, and telephone and write to party members, asking for contributions. Parties also look for volunteer workers to help raise money and work in election campaigns. There are many party jobs that young people can do. They can pass out campaign literature, telephone voters, and baby-sit while voters go to the polls to vote.

When parties meet in conventions before election campaigns, they usually write a *party platform*. The platform is a statement of party beliefs and goals. It helps inform voters what the party stands for and what its candidates will try to do if they are elected to office.

REVIEW OF SECTION TWO:
1. What are political parties and who are their members?
2. What were the first American political parties and when did they begin?
3. Why do we say that the United States has a two-party political system?
4. What do American political parties do?

SECTION THREE: POLITICAL INTEREST GROUPS

What Is an Interest Group? Citizens can take part in the political process by supporting a political candidate. They can also join a political party. Parties need contributions of money and work from volunteers. Party members may seek election to party committees and as delegates to conventions. Another way in which citizens can participate in public affairs is by joining a *political interest group*.

Interest groups are organizations that try to influence government policy and public opinion. They are sometimes called pressure groups, because they use pressure from their members to accomplish their goals. Interest groups are different from political parties. They do not nominate their own candidates for an election. More important, they work for just a few goals. They do not have a platform that makes statements about all the major public issues.

Some interest groups have only one major aim. They are called *single-issue interest groups*. An example is the National Rifle Association, which is interested mainly in preventing Congress and state legislatures from enacting laws to regulate the ownership of guns.

Types of Interest Groups. There are thousands of public interest groups. Some interest groups are formed only for the purpose of political action. Common Cause, for example, is a citizen group that supports laws to ensure fairness and honesty in government. Other groups, such as the Veterans of Foreign Wars (V.F.W.), have some political aims, but they are also social organizations. The V.F.W. supports legislation to help veterans of the armed forces and also operates clubs for its members.

There are many business interest groups that try to influence government for the benefit of businesses. One of the largest national business groups is the United States Chamber of Commerce. The Chamber of Commerce is also organized in every state and in many local communities. In West Virginia, the West Virginia Coal Association is another important business interest group. It represents the coal companies operating in West Virginia.

There are also interest groups that ask government to help workers. These are mainly labor unions. On the national level, the largest labor organization is the American Federation of Labor–Congress of Industrial Organizations, or the A.F.L.-C.I.O. It is an alliance of dozens of national labor unions. In our state, the West Virginia

fig. 116
Nonverbal freedom of speech

fig. 117
Special interest group

AMERICAN LEGION
POST #1
of WHEELING, W.V.
THE OLDEST POST IN THE U.S.

We are the People

POST N°1
Oldest Post in U.S.

Federation of Labor is a part of the A.F.L.–C.I.O. One labor union that is very important in West Virginia is the United Mine Workers of America (U.M.W.A.). Most of the coal miners of West Virginia belong to the U.M.W.A.

Some interest groups are concerned about social issues such as civil rights, prayer in schools, and abortion. The National Association for the Advancement of Colored People (N.A.A.C.P.), the National Organization of Women (N.O.W.), and the National Right to Life Organization are examples of this type of interest group.

You can see that just about everyone (workers, business people, teachers, veterans, women, minorities, and others) is represented by one or more interest groups. Many such groups are looking for volunteers to help them.

fig. 118, left page

The American Legion of Wheeling expresses its patriotism through thousands of names, which create a Liberty motif

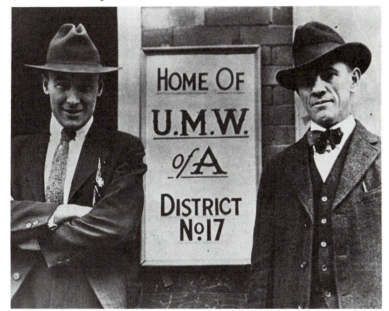

fig. 119
Special interest group

fig. 120

fig. 121
Old wood engraving of our favorite uncle

fig. 122
Social interest group

How Do Interest Groups Operate? Interest groups work in many ways to meet their goals. Almost all of them raise money. Members pay dues to support interest groups. Appeals for money are sent through the mail to millions of Americans. Interest groups ask their members to vote and work for candidates whom they *endorse* or support. They encourage members to make contributions to these candidates.

Interest groups cannot give money directly to candidates or political parties. However, they form *political action committees* (PACs), which do donate money. Interest groups often buy advertisements in the mass media to state their views and influence public opinion. Public officials pay close attention to public opinion.

Interest groups try to influence what laws are enacted and carried out by governments. Many groups employ *lobbyists,* paid representatives of interest groups. Lobbyists are called this because many of them meet lawmakers in the lobbies of capitol buildings and city halls. Lobbyists present the views of their organizations to officials, and speak, or *testify,* before legislative committees. They sometimes help write bills that would meet their goals if enacted. Lobbyists often invite public officials to dinners, receptions, ball games, and other social events.

fig. 123
Special Interest Groups

Pros and Cons of Interest Groups. Interest groups are controversial. Some believe that they do more harm than good. Since interest groups represent particular views, the public good might suffer if a few powerful interest groups had their way. Interest groups might *bribe,* or illegally pay, public officials to do favors for them.

Others think that interest groups are a useful part of the political process. Interest groups help officials understand how laws and regulations affect their members. No congressman in Washington, D.C., could keep up with the thousands of bills that are introduced every year. Lobbyists help provide them with useful information.

The federal government and most states have passed laws to regulate interest groups. Lobbyists must register and state what groups they represent. Candidates must list all sources of money given to their election campaigns. Many citizens believe that these rules are too weak to work well. They think that some interest groups have too much political influence.

REVIEW OF SECTION THREE:
1. What is a political interest group?
2. Can you name several types of interest groups?
3. What do lobbyists do?
4. Why do some people believe that interest groups are harmful?

fig. 124
*Lawn ornament
found near Parsons*

SECTION FOUR: THE ELECTION PROCESS

Why We Have Elections. One of the easiest and most important acts of citizenship is voting. Every citizen who is eighteen years or older may vote in the United States. Before voting it is necessary to register, however. Laws differ from one state to another, but generally it is easy to become a registered voter. In Chapter Ten we will learn how to register and vote in West Virginia.

We have elections in order to choose officials for our federal, state, and local governments. In some elections candidates for offices on all levels of government appear on the ballot. In other elections, especially for city or town offices, only local candidates are chosen.

fig. 125

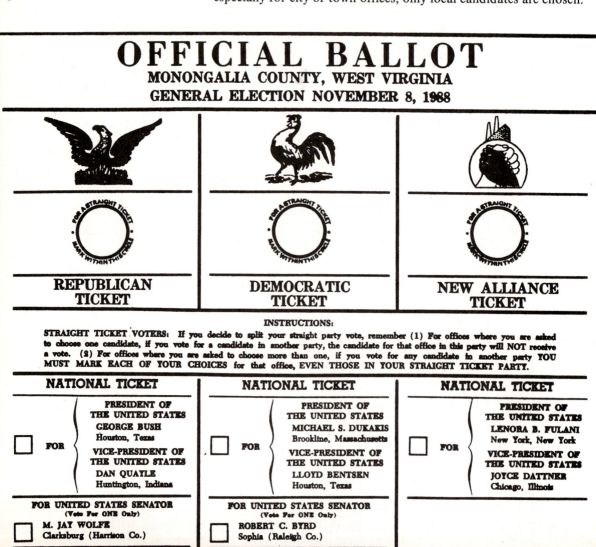

OFFICIAL BALLOT
MONONGALIA COUNTY, WEST VIRGINIA
GENERAL ELECTION NOVEMBER 8, 1988

REPUBLICAN TICKET	DEMOCRATIC TICKET	NEW ALLIANCE TICKET

INSTRUCTIONS:

STRAIGHT TICKET VOTERS: If you decide to split your straight party vote, remember (1) For offices where you are asked to choose one candidate, if you vote for a candidate in another party, the candidate for that office in this party will NOT receive a vote. (2) For offices where you are asked to choose more than one, if you vote for any candidate in another party YOU MUST MARK EACH OF YOUR CHOICES for that office, EVEN THOSE IN YOUR STRAIGHT TICKET PARTY.

NATIONAL TICKET	NATIONAL TICKET	NATIONAL TICKET
FOR PRESIDENT OF THE UNITED STATES GEORGE BUSH Houston, Texas VICE-PRESIDENT OF THE UNITED STATES DAN QUAYLE Huntington, Indiana	FOR PRESIDENT OF THE UNITED STATES MICHAEL S. DUKAKIS Brookline, Massachusetts VICE-PRESIDENT OF THE UNITED STATES LLOYD BENTSEN Houston, Texas	FOR PRESIDENT OF THE UNITED STATES LENORA B. FULANI New York, New York VICE-PRESIDENT OF THE UNITED STATES JOYCE DATTNER Chicago, Illinois
FOR UNITED STATES SENATOR (Vote For ONE Only) M. JAY WOLFE Clarksburg (Harrison Co.)	FOR UNITED STATES SENATOR (Vote For ONE Only) ROBERT C. BYRD Sophia (Raleigh Co.)	

Elections are also used to let citizens make certain public decisions. We sometimes vote for or against an amendment to our state constitution. We also vote on *levies* (special property taxes) to support schools, libraries, parks, and other services.

To elect officials, there are two types of elections. In a *primary election,* voters choose the *nominees* of the political parties. In a *general election,* voters decide which party's nominee will win each office.

Primary Elections. Primary elections are held several months before a general election. The dates of primary elections differ from state to state. In West Virginia, the primary election is held on the second Tuesday in May in years during which there is a general election.

fig. 126

In most states primary elections are open only to voters who are registered party members. Elections for party members only are called *closed primaries.* In West Virginia, the Republican and Democratic parties hold closed primary elections. Republicans can vote only in the Republican primary election, and Democrats can vote only in their party's primary election. A few states have *open primaries.* This means that registered independents and party members may choose to vote for the candidates of any one party they choose.

Before primary elections candidates try to persuade party members that they would make the best nominees. In most states the candidate who receives the largest number of votes for an office becomes the party nominee. Most party members want to have strong people to represent them. In the general election their nominees will face the nominees of other parties and independent candidates.

Parties also use primary elections to choose party leaders. Members of many state and local party committees are elected in the primary. Delegates to the *national convention* of each party are also elected in some primary elections. The national conventions are large meetings held every four years during which the candidates for president and vice president are nominated and the party platform is written.

fig. 127
1988 hopefuls

Other Ways to Nominate Candidates. In some states the primary election is not used to choose party nominees. In Iowa and South Carolina, for example, some candidates and party offices are chosen in many small caucuses. Other candidates may be chosen in statewide meetings called *state conventions*.

General Elections. General elections for federal officers are held at the same time in every state. Many states also use the same general election to choose state officials. The date for general elections is the Tuesday after the first Monday of November of even-numbered years.

For weeks before a general election, candidates *campaign* for office. Now they try to persuade all voters to support them, not just members of their own party. The political parties work hard to raise

fig. 128
Jimmy Carter campaigning in 1976

fig. 129
Reagan for re-election in 1984

fig. 130
Eisenhower in 1953

money and elect their nominees. As we have seen, public interest groups are very active in election campaigns. They give money and work for candidates whom they think will help them.

The election campaign is an exciting time for active citizens. They may volunteer to help the party and the candidates of their choice. Many will have the chance to meet candidates at campaign *rallies*. Even the presidential nominees try to visit every state during an election campaign. Often there are debates between candidates that are shown on television. Finally, on election day citizens may cast their votes. Every voter plays a role in defending democracy and freedom.

Electing the President. The most important political official in the United States is the president. When the president is elected every four years, more citizens vote than in years when there is no election for president. Presidential election years include 1992 and 1996, and every four years thereafter.

fig. 131
Hoover in 1929

Running for president is hard work. The campaign to win a party's nomination begins many months before the general election. Candidates must build a team of supporters and raise several million dollars. Most strong candidates have political experience. Many have served in Congress, while some have been governors of their states. They must be popular to succeed. Only Republicans and Democrats have been elected president since 1860. No woman, no black, and no Hispanic has been elected president. Before 1960, when John F. Kennedy was elected, no Roman Catholic had ever won our highest office.

How the West Virginia Primary Election Helped Make a President.

In the presidential primary election of May 1960, West Virginians helped decide who would be the next president. This was unusual, because West Virginia is a small state. More often, elections in the large states are important.

In 1960 Senator Hubert Humphrey and Senator John F. Kennedy were the leading candidates for the Democratic nomination. Because Kennedy was a Roman Catholic, many people believed that he could not win in West Virginia. Only about 5 percent of our state population is Roman Catholic.

Both candidates campaigned hard in West Virginia. John F. Kennedy traveled to the poorest sections of our state. He said that if elected, he would help the poor people of our region.

Many West Virginians liked Kennedy. When he won the state Democratic primary, it showed that most Protestants would not oppose a Catholic because of his religion. Partly as a result, Kennedy won the Democratic nomination and the general election. He was the youngest person elected president of the United States.

Presidential candidates campaign to win delegates in every state. They need delegates to vote for them in the national party conventions. Some states hold primary elections to choose delegates to the national convention. Other states hold caucuses or state conventions.

The first caucuses are held in Iowa in the February before a general election. The first primary election is held in New Hampshire later in February. Early in March many states, including most states in the South, hold a primary election for presidential candidates called *"Super Tuesday."* West Virginia holds its primary election on the second Tuesday of May. The last presidential primaries are held in California and New Jersey on the first Tuesday in June. All of these dates are subject to change by acts of the state legislatures of the states named.

Each candidate tries to win a majority of the delegates who attend the national party convention. The Democratic National Convention is usually held in July. The party's presidential nominee must win the votes of more than two thousand delegates from all the states and territories of the United States. The Republican National Convention is usually held a few weeks later in the summer. The votes of more than eight hundred Republican delegates are needed to win the party's nomination.

After convention delegates nominate their candidate for president, they nominate one for vice president. They usually vote for a person selected by their presidential nominee. In 1984 the first woman was nominated by a major party for the vice presidency. The Democratic presidential nominee, Walter Mondale, picked Geraldine Ferraro as his *running mate.*

The general election campaign begins in August and lasts until election day in early November. The candidates try to make speeches in every state. They must raise millions of dollars more to pay for advertising, campaign materials, travel, and staff members. The presidential nominees usually face one another in televised debates. Finally, on election day, millions of voters make their choice.

We usually know who won the election a few hours after the polls close. However, when we vote for president and vice president, we actually choose *electors* from our state who will meet in the *Electoral College* in December. Each state sends a number of electors equal to its number of members in both Houses of Congress. West Virginia has four members in the House of Representatives and two in the United States Senate, a total of six. Since the addition of the Twenty-third Amendment to the Constitution, Washington, D.C., which is not a state, sends three electors.

fig. 132
Kennedy in West Virginia in 1960

The electors from each state cast their votes for the candidate who won the most popular votes in their state. The vote of the Electoral College is not official until it is declared in Congress on the following January 6th. The president and vice president take their offices on January 20th.

Members of Congress are also federal officials who are nominated and elected by the voters. Congress has both United States senators and members of the United States House of Representatives. Two senators are elected from each state. The number of representatives from a state depends on the size of its population. We will study more about congressmen in Chapter Five.

fig. 133
Roosevelt in 1933

REVIEW OF SECTION FOUR:

1. How do political parties choose their nominees for office?
2. What is the difference between primary elections and general elections?
3. What kind of people usually run for president of the United States?
4. What do the national party conventions do during an election year?
5. What does the Electoral College do?

fig. 134

Electoral Votes Based on the 1980 Census

REFERENCES:

1. Corbin, Carole Lynn. *The Right to Vote: Issues in American History.* New York: Watts, Franklin, Inc., 1985.
2. La Raus, Roger, and Richard C. Remy. *Citizenship Decision-Making: Skills, Activities and Materials.* Menlo Park, CA: Addison-Wesley Publishing Co., 1977.
3. Modl, Thomas, ed. *America's Elections: Opposing Viewpoints.* St. Paul, MN: Greenhaven Press, Inc., 1988.

fig. 135
Taft in 1909

fig. 136
Adlai Stevenson in 1953
Eisenhower in 1953, before smoking was a public and political risk

fig. 137
This plate commemorates the presidents through Jimmy Carter. When do you think it was made?

The Congress of the United States

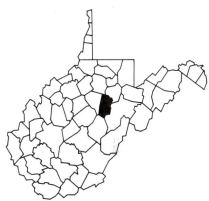

PREVIEW

The authors of the Constitution placed a great deal of emphasis on Congress. Article I, which created Congress, is the longest article in the Constitution. The organization and functions of Congress are described in much greater detail than those of the executive and judicial branches. The Constitution also grants Congress most of the powers given to the national government.

Congress is so important because it has the power to make the nation's laws. Therefore, the lives of all Americans are affected in many ways by the acts of Congress. We should all learn how Congress is organized and how it works. This will help us understand why active citizens care about who is elected to Congress. We will also know how citizens can influence the decisions of Congress.

In Chapter Five we will answer these questions:
1. How many members are there in the House of Representatives and in the Senate?
2. What determines the number of members each state has in the House of Representatives and in the Senate?
3. What qualifications must be met by representatives and senators?
4. Who are the leaders of the House of Representatives and the Senate, and how are they selected?
5. What are the legislative and nonlegislative functions of Congress?
6. Why are Congressional committees so important?
7. How does a bill become a law?

Pronounce and discuss the meanings of the following words found in this chapter.

circumstances	procedure
disbanded	proposed
enumerated	qualifications
introduced	vacancy
presiding	versions

fig. 138, left and above
Upshur County Courthouse in Buckhannon

SECTION ONE: THE STRUCTURE OF CONGRESS

The Congress of the United States is a *bicameral* legislature. This means it is made up of two houses — the Senate and the House of Representatives.

The House of Representatives. The House of Representatives has 435 members. The number of members each state elects to the House depends on the size of its population. California, the state with the most people, has 45 members, or seats, in the House. West Virginia has 4 seats.

Every ten years the federal government takes a *census* (counts the population). Congress uses census figures to determine how many seats in the House each state is to have.

fig. 139

House of Representatives Delegation Based on 1980 Census

Members of the House are elected in general elections held in November of each even-numbered year. All representatives serve two-year terms of office. There is no limit on the number of terms they may serve.

The qualifications for serving in the House are stated in the Constitution. One must be at least twenty-five years old. He or she must have been a citizen for at least seven years. A representative also must live in the state from which he or she is elected.

After every census each state legislature is required to divide its state into *congressional districts.* A state has one district for each seat in the House of Representatives. West Virginia has four seats in the House, so it must be divided into four congressional districts. Each district must contain about the same number of people. The voters of a district elect one member of the House of Representatives.

fig. 140
Senator John D. Rockefeller IV

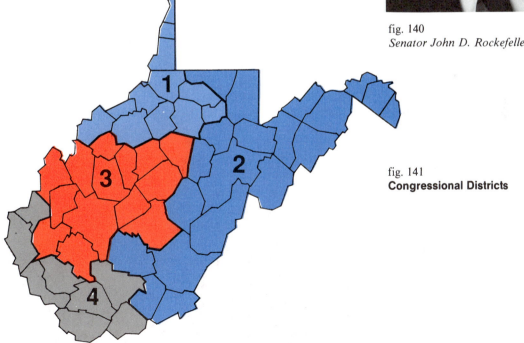

fig. 141
Congressional Districts

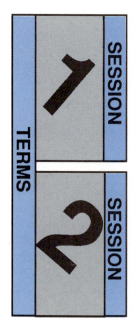

fig. 142

The Senate. The Senate is much smaller than the House of Representatives. All states, large and small, have two senators. The Senate now has one hundred members, and that number will not change unless more states are added to the Union or unless the Constitution is amended.

Senators are elected for terms of six years. There is no limit on the number of times a senator can be elected. Elections for senators are held at the same time as elections for members of the House. However, only one-third of the Senate is elected every two years. Senators are elected in statewide elections. They represent all the people of a state rather than the people of one district.

The Constitution sets slightly higher qualifications for senators than for representatives. A senator must be at least thirty years old and must have been a citizen for at least nine years. Senators also must be residents of the states from which they are elected.

Terms and Sessions of Congress. Each *term* of Congress lasts for two years. New terms begin on January 3 of every odd-numbered year. There are two regular *sessions,* or meetings, of Congress during each term. One session is held during each year of the term. The length of a session is determined by the amount of work Congress faces. Today the workload is so great that Congress stays in session most of the year.

Congressional Leaders. Congress is a large body, and it must deal with many difficult issues. It has to be well organized to carry out its duties effectively. The Constitution requires members of the House of Representatives to choose a presiding officer. It says that the vice president of the United States shall preside over the Senate. The Senate also must select one of its members to preside when the vice president is absent.

Near the start of each term of Congress, the Democratic and Republican members of each house hold *party caucuses.* During these meetings the Democrats and Republicans of each house select their party leaders.

The political party that has the most members in the House of Representatives is called the *majority party.* The other political party is known as the *minority party.* The Senate also has majority and minority parties. Both parties want to have the largest number of members in each house. The majority party is able to select the key officers of Congress.

fig. 143
Vice President Dan Quayle presides over the Senate.

The most powerful figure in Congress is the *speaker of the House,* who presides over the House of Representatives. The speaker is elected by members of the House but always from the majority party. The members of the majority party of the House agree in their party caucus who the speaker will be. This ensures that the party's choice will be elected when the entire House votes on the speaker.

No member can speak in the House without the speaker's permission. The speaker enforces rules of procedure and keeps order. In addition, the speaker decides which committees will consider proposed laws, and he appoints members to certain committees. The speaker can do many things to help pass laws favored by his party or to defeat proposals his party opposes.

The vice president of the United States is the presiding officer of the Senate. However, the vice president cannot take part in Senate debates and may vote only when there is a tie. The vice president generally does not attend meetings of the Senate because he has other

THE CONGRESS OF THE UNITED STATES   fig. 144

	House of Representatives	**Senate**
Number of Members	435 Representatives	100 Senators
Basis of Appointment	Number of Representatives elected by each state determined by size of state's population	Two Senators from each state
Length of Term	Two years	Six years
Required Age	At least 25 years old	At least 30 years old
Citizenship	U.S. Citizen for at least seven years	U.S. Citizen for at least nine years
Residence	Resident of state where elected	Resident of state where elected

duties to perform. When the vice president is absent, the *president pro tempore* (president for the time being) presides over the Senate. The president pro tempore is elected by the Senate and is always a leading member of the majority party.

In addition to presiding officers, each house of Congress has other important leaders. These leaders, however, are not mentioned in the Constitution. In fact, they are party leaders rather than officers of Congress. They are selected by party caucuses and are not voted on by all the members of the House or the Senate.

Robert C. Byrd. *For two decades Robert C. Byrd of West Virginia has been one of the most powerful members of the United States Senate. He was first elected to the Senate in 1958 and has been re-elected five times. Senator Byrd has been a senator longer than any other person from West Virginia. He has also held more legislative offices than any other West Virginian. Before going to the Senate, he served in both houses of the West Virginia legislature and in the United States House of Representatives.*

Senator Byrd has been a leader of the United States Senate. He was Democratic party whip for six years and minority leader for four years. He was elected majority leader in 1977 and held that position until the Democrats lost control of the Senate in 1980. In 1986, Senator Byrd was again elected majority leader. In 1988 he gave up his position as majority leader to become chairman of the powerful Appropriations Committee. The positions held by Senator Byrd have enabled him to influence much of the legislation passed by the Senate in recent years.

During their caucuses the Democratic and Republican members of the House choose a party leader and a party whip. The same procedure is followed in the Senate. The leaders of the majority party in both the House and Senate are known as the *majority leaders*. Those selected by the minority party are called *minority leaders*. The majority and minority leaders do everything they can to gain support for proposed laws favored by their party.

Party whips are selected in the same way as party leaders. They assist the leader of their party. The main task of whips is to persuade party members to vote as their leader wants on proposed laws. They also see that members of their party are present for important votes.

REVIEW OF SECTION ONE:

1. What is a bicameral legislature?
2. What determines the number of seats each state has in the House of Representatives?
3. How many senators does each state have?
4. What are the qualifications for representatives and senators?
5. What are the duties of the speaker of the House, the president pro tempore of the Senate, majority leaders, minority leaders, and party whips? How are people selected for these positions?

SECTION TWO: THE FUNCTIONS OF CONGRESS

Legislative Functions. The authors of the Constitution knew that the legislative branch of the federal government would be very powerful. Therefore, they carefully listed the powers Congress does and does not have. They wished to make sure that Congress could pass needed laws but not laws that threaten our liberty. The powers of Congress described in the Constitution are known as *enumerated* or *delegated powers*. They give Congress authority to pass laws in the following areas:

Finance. The Constitution requires Congress ". . . to pay the debts and provide for the common defense and general welfare of the United States . . . ". Therefore, Congress has the power to pass tax laws to raise money for these things. It may also pass laws to let the government borrow and print money.

Commerce. Congress can regulate commerce among the states and with other nations. It uses this power to pass laws to control imports. Congress also prevents some American goods from being sold abroad. Power over interstate commerce allows Congress to regulate many activities. These include the production of goods, radio and television programs, and the operations of trucking and bus companies, airlines, and railroads.

fig. 145
Senator Robert Byrd

Foreign Relations. The president is primarily in charge of relations with foreign nations. However, Congress can regulate foreign trade. It also has the power to declare war on other nations.

War Powers. Several of the enumerated powers deal with war and national defense. Only Congress can declare war. It passes laws to raise and govern the armed forces. Congress also can govern state militias during national emergencies.

Judicial Powers. Congress may establish federal courts below the level of the Supreme Court. Chapter Seven describes those courts. Congress also passes laws that set the punishments for counterfeiting, treason, piracy, and *felonies* (serious crimes) committed at sea.

Governing Powers. Congress manages the land and buildings owned by the federal government. The District of Columbia and territories such as Puerto Rico, Guam, American Samoa, and the Virgin Islands are governed by laws passed by Congress. Congress also regulates national parks and forests, military bases, and federal buildings.

Postal Powers. Only Congress can establish post offices. Congress has used this power to pass many postal laws. There are federal laws against preventing mail from being delivered or using the mail to commit a crime.

fig. 146

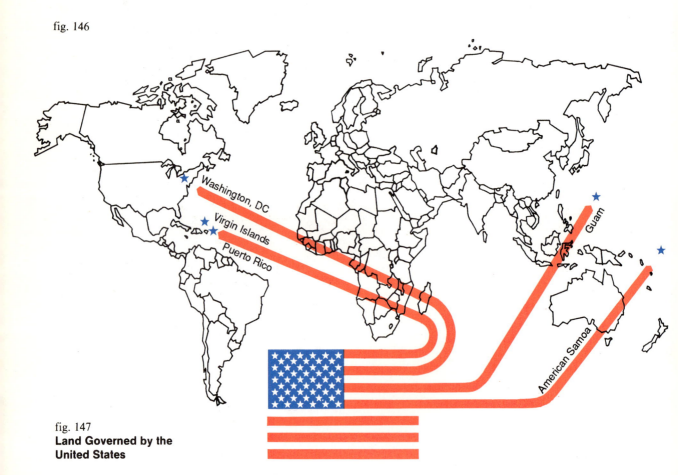

fig. 147
Land Governed by the United States

The Statue of Liberty

One of the most familiar symbols of the United States is the Statue of Liberty. The enormous copper statue, which is over 50 yards high, stands on Liberty Island in New York Harbor.

The Statue of Liberty was a gift from France to the United States to honor the 100th anniversary of American independence. The statue was built in France. It was then taken apart and shipped to the United States. It was opened to the public in 1886.

The statue is a woman who represents liberty. She is wearing a long robe and a crown with seven spikes. In her right hand she is holding a burning torch high above her head. In her left hand is a law book inscribed with the date July 4, 1776. Broken chains, symbolizing the end of the tyranny, lie at her feet as she steps forward to enlighten the world.

In 1903 a poem entitled "The New Colossus" was inscribed on a tablet at the base of the statue. The poem was written by Emma Lazarus, and it helps explain the meaning of the Statue of Liberty. The last part of the poem says:

fig. 148
Liberty is honored in a float at the Buckwheat Festival in Kingwood, WV

> "Give me your tired, your poor,
> your huddled masses yearning to breathe free,
> The wretched refuse of your teeming shore,
> Send these, the homeless, tempest-tost to me,
> I lift my lamp beside the golden door!"

For many years millions of immigrants poured into the United States from Europe. Most of them came to New York on ships. The Statue of Liberty was one of the first things the immigrants saw as they entered the harbor. This important symbol of freedom still welcomes thousands of immigrants and visitors to our country.

fig. 149
New York claims this American symbol.

fig. 150
Naturalization ceremony, 1940s

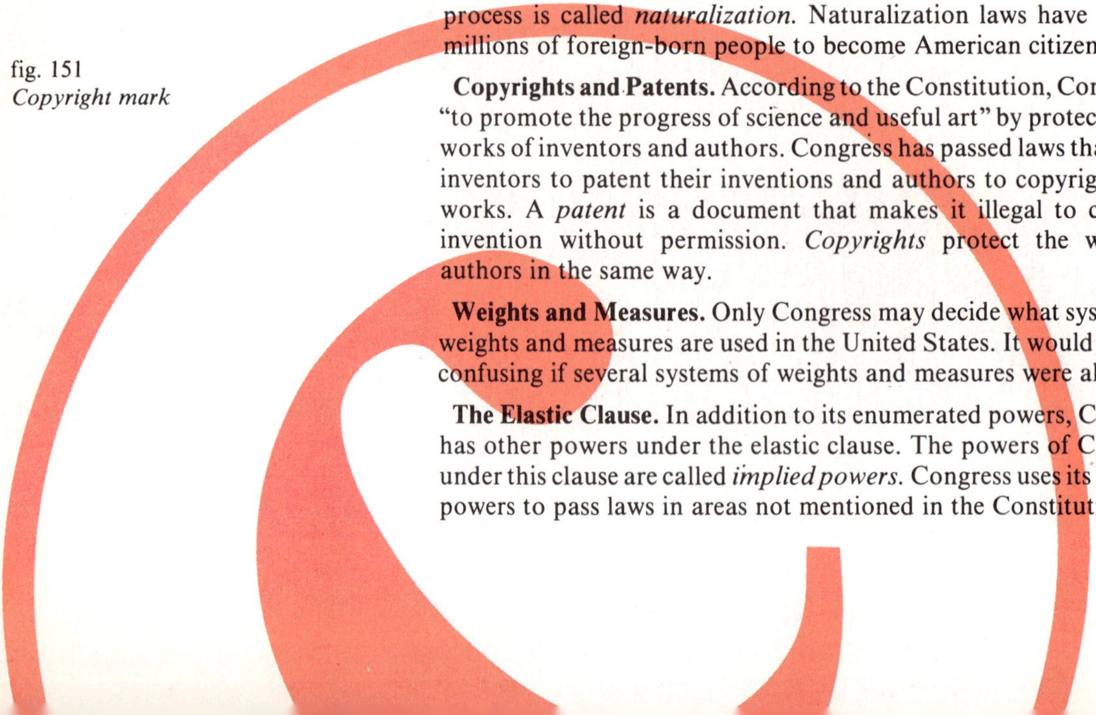

fig. 151
Copyright mark

Naturalization. Congress may establish a process by which people from other nations can become citizens of the United States. This process is called *naturalization*. Naturalization laws have allowed millions of foreign-born people to become American citizens.

Copyrights and Patents. According to the Constitution, Congress is "to promote the progress of science and useful art" by protecting the works of inventors and authors. Congress has passed laws that allow inventors to patent their inventions and authors to copyright their works. A *patent* is a document that makes it illegal to copy an invention without permission. *Copyrights* protect the work of authors in the same way.

Weights and Measures. Only Congress may decide what systems of weights and measures are used in the United States. It would be very confusing if several systems of weights and measures were allowed.

The Elastic Clause. In addition to its enumerated powers, Congress has other powers under the elastic clause. The powers of Congress under this clause are called *implied powers*. Congress uses its implied powers to pass laws in areas not mentioned in the Constitution.

Nonlegislative Functions. Although the major duty of Congress is to make the nation's laws, it has several other important roles:

Electing the president and vice president. Under special circumstances, Congress would decide who will be president and vice president. If no candidate gets a majority of electoral votes, the House of Representatives picks the president. The Senate chooses the vice president when no candidate receives a majority of electoral votes.

Proposing Amendments. Congress may propose amendments to the Constitution by a two-thirds vote in each house. It may call a national convention to propose an amendment at the request of two-thirds of the state legislatures.

Approving Appointments. Many of the president's appointments to the executive and judicial branches must be approved by a majority of the Senate.

Confirming Treaties. Two-thirds of the Senate must approve treaties with other nations. The president negotiates treaties, but the Senate must accept them before they can go into effect.

Conducting Investigations. Congress has the power to conduct investigations. Investigations can provide information to help Congress make new laws or change existing laws.

Impeachment and Trial. The Constitution grants Congress the power to accuse high federal officials of crimes against the nation and to put them on trial. The House may *impeach,* or bring charges against, government officials such as the president and federal judges. If a majority of the House agrees with the charges, the accused must resign from office or stand trial in the Senate. The Senate hears the evidence against the accused and questions witnesses. A two-thirds vote of the senators who are present is needed for conviction. If convicted, the official is removed from office.

fig. 152
Andrew Johnson was impeached February 24, 1868. This lithograph, produced by the J.H. Bufford company in 1864, resides in the National Portrait Gallery in the Smithsonian.

fig. 153
Richard Nixon, nearly impeached in 1974, resigned from office. Gerald Ford became president to finish his term.

fig. 154

fig. 155

Helping Constituents. Members of Congress spend a great deal of time helping their *constituents*. Constituents are the people who are represented by congressmen. People write or call their senators and representatives for many reasons. Sometimes they try to influence how their congressmen will vote on a bill. Some complain about a law or an official. At other times people want some type of help from the government. Congressmen often try to meet their requests.

Limits on the Powers of Congress. Although Congress is strong, its powers are not unlimited. The Constitution limits the authority of Congress in several ways. Article I, Section 9 lists certain powers denied to Congress. Congress cannot suspend, or set aside, the *writ of habeas corpus* except during invasions or rebellions. All persons accused of crimes have the right to a writ of habeas corpus. A writ of habeas corpus is a court order requiring that the accused be brought before a court to determine if there is enough evidence to hold the person for trial.

Congress may not pass *bills of attainder* or *ex post facto laws*. A bill of attainder is a law that sentences a person to punishment without a trial. A law that makes illegal an action taking place before the law was passed is called an ex post facto law.

Article I, Section 9 also denies Congress the power to tax goods being sent to other countries or shipments of goods that cross state lines. Congress may not pass any trade law that would help one state more than another. Congress cannot withdraw money from the treasury without passing a law.

Other parts of the Constitution also limit the powers of Congress. The system of checks and balances helps prevent Congress from becoming too powerful, as does the Bill of Rights. Congress may not pass any law that violates the Bill of Rights.

REVIEW OF SECTION TWO:

1. The enumerated powers of the Constitution give Congress authority to pass laws on what types of matters?
2. How does the elastic clause allow Congress to stretch its legislative powers?
3. What are the nonlegislative functions of Congress?
4. How does the Constitution limit the powers of Congress?
5. Why did France give the United States the Statue of Liberty? Why do you think it was placed in the New York harbor?

fig. 156
Powers of Congress

DELEGATED

- To collect taxes
and pay the debts
of the US
-To regulate foreign
and interstate
commerce
-To borrow money
-To establish
naturalization laws
-To coin money
-To punish counter-
feiters, traitors,
piracies and felonies
on the
high seas
-To establish
post offices
-To grant patents
and copyrights
-To regulate weights
and measures
-To establish courts
below the level of
Supreme Court
-To govern the District
of Columbia, US
territories, and federal
lands and buildings
-To declare war
-To raise, maintain and
govern the armed forces
of the United States
-To govern state militia
during emergencies

NONLEGISLATIVE

-To elect the President
and Vice President
when no candidate
receives a majority of
electoral votes
-To propose amend-
ments to the
Constitution
-To approve Presidential
appointments
(Senate only)
-To confirm treaties
(Senate only)
-To conduct
nvestigations
-To impeach federal
officials (House only)
-To try impeached
officials (Senate only)

IMPLIED

-To make all laws necessary
and proper to carry out the
enumerated or delegated
powers

POWERS OF CONGRESS

SECTION THREE: THE COMMITTEE SYSTEM OF CONGRESS

The Importance of Committees. Thousands of *bills,* or proposed laws, are introduced in Congress every term. No member of Congress could consider every bill. Therefore, Congress uses a committee system to deal with bills. Most of the work of Congress is done in committees, and committees usually decide which bills will become laws.

fig. 157

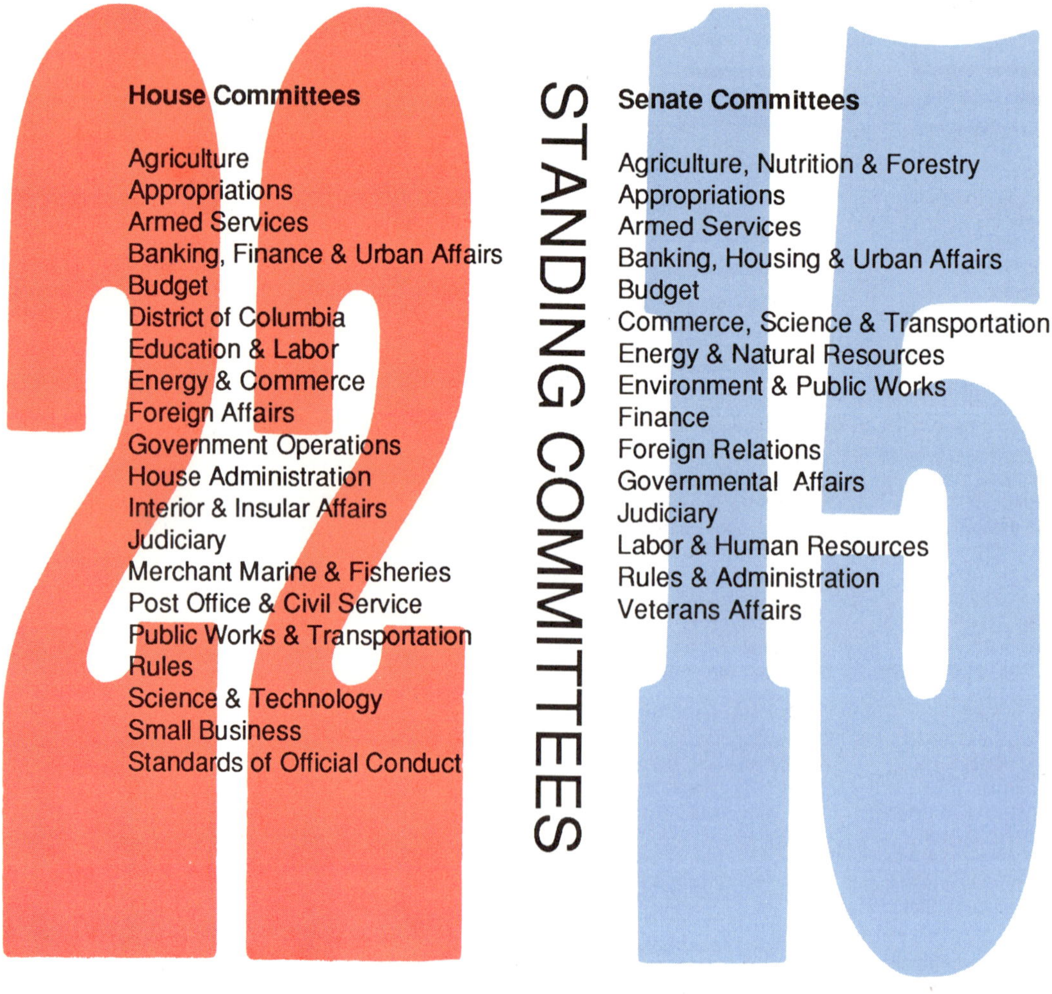

STANDING COMMITTEES

House Committees

Agriculture
Appropriations
Armed Services
Banking, Finance & Urban Affairs
Budget
District of Columbia
Education & Labor
Energy & Commerce
Foreign Affairs
Government Operations
House Administration
Interior & Insular Affairs
Judiciary
Merchant Marine & Fisheries
Post Office & Civil Service
Public Works & Transportation
Rules
Science & Technology
Small Business
Standards of Official Conduct

Senate Committees

Agriculture, Nutrition & Forestry
Appropriations
Armed Services
Banking, Housing & Urban Affairs
Budget
Commerce, Science & Transportation
Energy & Natural Resources
Environment & Public Works
Finance
Foreign Relations
Governmental Affairs
Judiciary
Labor & Human Resources
Rules & Administration
Veterans Affairs

Types of Committees. There are several types of Congressional committees. The most important is the *standing committee*. Standing committees are permanent. There are twenty-two in the House and fifteen in the Senate. Each standing committee is responsible for a special area of concern. The chart in the text lists the standing committees. Bills introduced in either house of Congress are sent to the proper standing committee in that house. For example, a bill introduced in the House that would affect schools would be assigned to the Committee on Education and Labor. That committee would study the bill and recommend what the House should do with it.

Another type of Congressional committee is the *select committee*. A select committee is a temporary body for dealing with a special problem. Both houses appoint select committees from time to time. Most select committees investigate social problems or government officials accused of breaking the law. Select committees recommend to Congress ways of dealing with these matters.

Congress also has *joint committees*. They are made up of members of both houses. Some are select committees, but most joint committees are permanent. They deal with matters such as defense and taxes that both houses must work on together. By working together, each house saves time.

Conference committees are another type made up of members of both houses. They have only one purpose. The House and the Senate often approve different versions of the same bill. When this happens, a conference committee is formed to work out a compromise. This is necessary, because a bill cannot become a law unless both houses pass the same version of a bill.

Committee Membership. All members of Congress serve on committees. As the House of Representatives is large, most representatives serve on only one standing committee. However, he or she also may be assigned to select and joint committees. Senators usually serve on at least two standing committees. They also sit on select and joint committees.

Both political parties have members on all standing committees. However, the number of Democrats and Republicans on each is not equal. Instead, membership is equal to the proportion of seats each party has. For example, if Democrats hold 60 percent of the seats in the House, they will hold 60 percent of the seats on House standing committees. The same is true of the Senate. Therefore, the majority party controls much of the committee work.

fig. 158
Committees of Congress

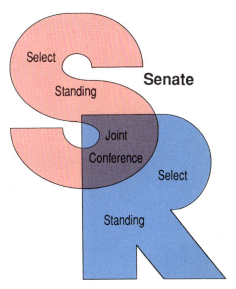

Senate

House of Representatives

Some standing committees are more important than others. The House Appropriations Committee decides how billions of dollars of public money should be spent. It is more important than the House District of Columbia Committee, which considers bills that would affect only the nation's capital. Congressmen always want to serve on major committees.

Not every member can serve on the most important committees. How then are assignments made? Both parties have a *committee on committees* in each house of Congress. These committees recommend members of their party for seats on the standing committees. The party caucus reviews the recommendations and makes assignments. Those who have been in Congress the longest and who are loyal to the party tend to get the assignments they want.

Committee Chairs. Because most of the work of Congress is done by committees, the people who lead them are very important. The head of a congressional committee is the *committee chair* or *chairperson.* Chairpersons are powerful, because they control the work of the committee and have much influence on its decisions.

For many years, committee chairs were picked on the basis of *seniority,* or length of service. The member of the majority party who had served longest on the committee became the chairperson. This was known as the *seniority system.* Many members of Congress disliked the seniority system. They felt that the senior member was not always the best qualified person. During the early 1970s Congress changed its method of selection. Chairpersons are now chosen by the caucus of the majority party. They are often, but not always, senior members of a committee.

REVIEW OF SECTION THREE:
1. Why are Congressional committees so important?
2. What is the major function of each type of Congressional committee: standing committees, select committees, joint committees, and conference committees?
3. What determines how many members each political party will have on a standing committee?
4. How are members of Congress assigned to committees?
5. How are committee chairs selected?

SECTION FOUR: HOW BILLS BECOME LAWS

Although Congress has many other duties, its major task is making laws. Members of Congress spend most of their time dealing with thousands of bills introduced in every session. This flood of bills comes from many sources. Any citizen can ask a congressman to introduce a bill in Congress. Lobbyists who work for interest groups often want new laws. The president always has a program that requires new laws. Members of Congress also seek to pass laws. However, only a few hundred bills become laws each year. The process of getting a bill passed is long and difficult.

We can learn this process by tracing the route a bill must follow through Congress. We will begin with the introduction of a bill in the House of Representatives.

Introducing a Bill. Most bills can be introduced in either house of Congress. *Revenue bills,* however, must begin in the House of Representatives. A revenue bill would raise money, or revenue. Bills that would change federal taxes are revenue bills.

First, bills are *drafted,* or written, by a representative or a committee. After the bill has been drafted, it is introduced by a member of the House. The representative writes his or her name on the bill and places it into the *hopper,* or bill box. The clerk of the House gives a number to each bill as it comes in. HR505 would be the 505th bill introduced in the House during a term. The clerk also gives the bill a title. The bill is then sent to the Government Printing Office. Printed copies of the bill are given to members of the House and other interested people.

Committee Action. The speaker of the House decides which standing committee will receive the bill. Usually this is a routine matter.

A committee can treat a bill in several ways. Sometimes the entire committee will consider the bill, but often it is assigned to a subcommittee. It is easier to pass a bill if the full committee deals with it. A subcommittee may recommend that a bill be rejected. Even if a subcommittee approves the bill, the full committee may oppose it. Many bills die in committee and are never sent to the House for a vote.

When a committee decides to consider the bill, it may hold a *public hearing.* People who are for or against the bill are invited to appear as witnesses. Witnesses may be government officials, experts on the

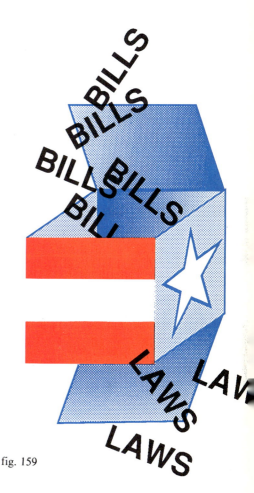

fig. 159

fig. 160

fig. 161

subject of the bill, interested citizens, or lobbyists working for an interest group.

After the public hearing, the committee has a few choices. It may let the bill die, approve it, amend it, or write a new bill. Very few bills are approved by committees in their first form. Almost all approved bills are amended in some way. If the committee approves the bill, it goes to the entire House.

Action on the House Floor. Bills sent back to the House by committees are placed on the House calendar. The calendar lists bills in the order in which the House will consider them.

When a bill comes before the entire House, it is debated and discussed. The House Rules Committee decides how much time will be allowed for debate. Debate can be stopped any time a majority of the House votes to do so.

House members may offer amendments to bills during discussion. Each amendment offered must be voted on. Any amendments approved are added to the bill. After the bill has been considered, members of the House vote on it. The bill passes if a majority of members present vote to approve it. However, the bill is not yet a law. It must also be passed by the Senate.

Senate Action on a Bill. When a bill passed by the House arrives in the Senate, it will be handled much as it was in the House. It will be introduced and given a number preceded by the letter S. The bill will then be assigned to a standing committee. If the committee recommends passage of the bill, it will be returned to the Senate for debate.

A major difference between the House and the Senate is the way each debates a bill. The Senate does not limit the time for debating a bill. Senators may speak as long as they like. In fact, they sometimes talk for hours to prevent a vote on a bill that they oppose.

Using long speeches to delay voting is known as *filibustering*. Filibusters have been used to delay the passage of some bills for years. Debate in the Senate can be limited only by a vote known as *cloture*. Cloture requires that three-fifths of the Senate vote to limit debate. This rarely happens.

The Conference Committee. If the Senate passes the same bill approved by the House, the bill goes to the president. However, both houses seldom pass identical bills. Therefore, the differences must be worked out. A bill passed by the House and then the Senate goes back to the House. The House is asked to accept the Senate's bill. If the House agrees, the Senate bill is sent to the president.

Usually, the differences have to be settled by a conference committee. The conference committee works on the bill until a compromise is reached. The new bill is then sent to both houses for approval.

Presidential Action. After both houses of Congress pass the same version of a bill, the president must consider it. The president has ten days either to sign the bill into law or to veto it. The president vetoes the bill by sending it back to Congress, explaining his reasons for not signing. The bill can still become law if Congress *overrides* the president's veto. This takes a vote by a two-thirds majority in both houses. It is hard to get that many votes and override a veto.

A third choice for the president is to keep the bill for ten days without acting. If Congress is still in session at the end of ten days, the bill becomes law without the president's signature. If, however, Congress has adjourned within ten days, the bill dies. This type of veto is called a *pocket veto*.

fig. 162
President Reagan signing a bill into law

fig. 163

HOW A BILL BECOMES A LAW

The bill is introduced by a Representative and given a title and number

The bill is assigned to the proper committee by the Speaker of the House.

The committee chair may assign the bill to a subcommittee. Public hearings are held. The committee may amend, rewrite or approve the bill. However, most bills die in committee. If the committee approves the bill or an amended version, it is placed on the House calendar.

The bill is read, debated and voted on by the entire House. The bill may be amended at this point. If the bill is not approved by the House, it dies. If it is approved, it is sent to the Senate.

The bill is given a number and assigned to the proper committee by the presiding officer.

The committee chair may assign the bill to a subcommittee. Public hearings are held. The committee may amend, rewrite or approve the bill. However, most bills die in committee. If the committee approves the bill or an amended version, it is placed on theSenate calendar.

The bill is read, debated and voted on by the entire House. The bill may be amended at this point. If the bill is not approved by the Senate, it dies. If the Senate approves the same version approved by the House, the bill is sent to the President. If the Senate approves a different version, the bill is sent to a conference committee.

The conference committee compromises on a single version of the bill. If both houses approve the revised bill, it is sent to the President.

The President signs or vetos the bill or lets it become law without his signature. Congress can override the veto by a two-thirds vote of both houses.

We have seen that the legislative process is long and difficult. A bill must go through many steps to become a law, and it can be killed at every step. However, making our laws is a major responsibility. The long process that Congress must follow helps prevent passage of unneeded or poorly written laws.

REVIEW OF SECTION FOUR:
1. Where do ideas for new laws come from?
2. What are the steps by which a bill becomes a law?
3. Why are conference committees often necessary?
4. How can a bill become a law if the president does not sign it?
5. What is a pocket veto?

REFERENCES:
1. *The Congress: Perspectives on Representation in American Government.* Arlington, VA: Close Up Foundation, 1987.
2. *Power in Congress: Who Has It, How They Got It, How They Use It.* Washington: Congressional Quarterly, 1987.
3. Wirt, Daniel, P. Allen Dionisopoulis, and Robert J. Gennett. *Our American Government and Political System.* River Forest, IL: Laidlaw Brothers, 1983: pp. 254–317.

fig. 164
The West Virginia delegation to the House of Representatives

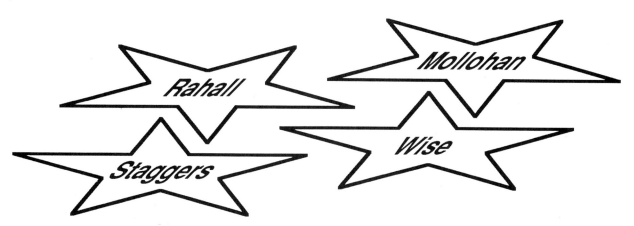

This was the West Virginia delegation to the House of Representatives in 1989. After the 1990 census is tabulated, it is predicted that we will lose one delegate because of our loss in population. Have any of these delegates changed since 1989?

The President and the Executive Branch

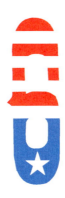

PREVIEW

The Constitution gives the executive branch a very large task. The president and other executive officials must carry out and enforce the nation's laws.

We have seen that Congress passes thousands of laws. Our lives are affected when the executive branch carries out those laws. For example, if you eat school lunches, you are using a program supported by the Department of Agriculture. The mail you send or receive is delivered by the Postal Service. Both agencies are part of the executive branch. We will discover many other ways in which its activities affect us.

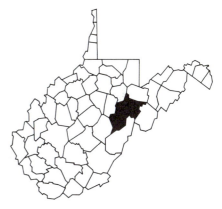

In Chapter Six we will answer the following questions:
1. What are the qualifications for a president?
2. How long is the president's term of office? How many terms may a president serve?
3. If both the president and vice president die or leave office, who becomes president?
4. What are the major powers and duties of the president?
5. What agencies and departments help the president carry out his duties?
6. What is the president's cabinet?

Pronounce and discuss the meanings of the following words found in this chapter. You may need to use a dictionary.

ceremonial	minorities
correspond	processing
foreign policy	succession
immigration	supervise
lawsuits	territories

fig. 165, left page and above
Randolph County Courthouse in Elkins

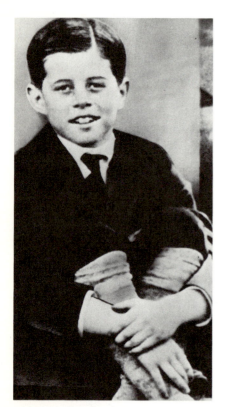

fig. 166
John F. Kennedy, Jr., as a boy

fig. 167
President Kennedy

SECTION ONE: THE PRESIDENCY

The president of the United States heads the executive branch of the federal government. The president is the most powerful official in our country and the only one who represents all of the American people. The United States is a rich and powerful nation. Therefore, the president is one of the most important leaders in the world.

Qualifications. The Constitution set only three qualifications for the presidency. The president must be a native-born American. He or she must be at least thirty-five years old and have been a resident of the United States for at least fourteen years. However, over the years several customs and traditions concerning the president have developed. The Constitution does not say the president must be white, or male, or a member of the Democratic or Republican party. But all presidents have been white men, and since the Civil War all have been either Democrats or Republicans. Customs and traditions do sometimes change. No Catholic was ever elected until John F. Kennedy became president in 1960. Women and members of racial minorities now hold many important political offices. The presidency is no longer completely out of their reach.

Term of Office. The president's term of office is four years. Until passage of the Twenty-second Amendment in 1951, there was no limit on the number of terms a president could serve. It was customary for presidents to serve only two terms until Franklin Roosevelt ran for a third term in 1940. Roosevelt was elected president four times. The Twenty-second Amendment was passed to restrict presidents to two terms in office.

Replacing the President and Vice President. The president is a very important figure in our nation. What if something should happen to the president? Who would step into the position? That is an important question, for the presidency is a dangerous, pressure-filled job. Ten presidents have been shot at, and four have died from gunfire. Four other presidents have died while in office. Several were so ill at times that they could not perform their duties. One president, Richard Nixon, resigned.

The original Constitution stated that the vice president would replace the president if he should die, resign, or be removed from office. The Constitution gave Congress the power to decide who should step in if both the president and vice president died or left office. In 1947 Congress passed a law that fixed the order of presidential succession. According to that law, the speaker of the

House is to become president if both the president and vice president die or leave office. The officials who are next in line for the presidency are shown on the chart in the text.

The 1947 law did not take care of all the problems. Who would become vice president if the vice president moved up to the presidency? What would be done if the president became seriously ill? In 1967 the Twenty-fifth Amendment was adopted to answer those questions. Now, if a president is replaced by a vice president, the new president can choose someone to become vice president. Both houses of Congress must approve the choice. The Twenty-fifth Amendment also says that the president must notify the leaders of Congress if he becomes too ill to carry out his duties. The vice president becomes acting president until the president recovers.

REVIEW OF SECTION ONE:
1. What qualifications for the presidency are set by the Constitution?
2. How long is the president's term of office? How many terms may a president serve?
3. Who takes over the presidency if the president dies, leaves office, or becomes seriously ill?

fig. 168   *President Kennedy's funeral following his assassination in 1963*

fig. 169
Order of Succession

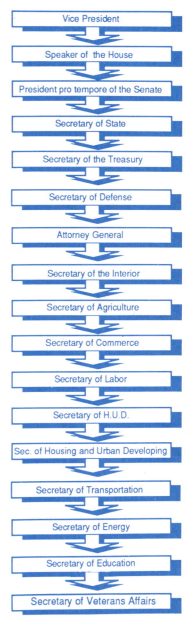

Vice President

Speaker of the House

President pro tempore of the Senate

Secretary of State

Secretary of the Treasury

Secretary of Defense

Attorney General

Secretary of the Interior

Secretary of Agriculture

Secretary of Commerce

Secretary of Labor

Secretary of H.U.D.

Sec. of Housing and Urban Developing

Secretary of Transportation

Secretary of Energy

Secretary of Education

Secretary of Veterans Affairs

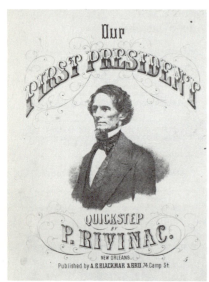

fig. 170

The only president in this land, not of the United States was Jefferson Davis of the Confederacy. This 1861 sheet music depicting him resides in the National Portrait Gallery in the Smithsonian.

Fig. 171

President Reagan as chief executive, signing legislation against child abuse

SECTION TWO: THE POWERS AND DUTIES OF THE PRESIDENT

The authors of the Constitution did not want any branch of the federal government to be too powerful. They were very concerned about the executive branch. They did not want the president to be as strong as their old enemy, the king of England. The Constitution gave the president powers allowing him to be effective. However, these powers are also limited.

The United States has changed a great deal since 1787. Today it is a much larger country with different needs and problems. Because of these changes, the duties and powers of the presidency have grown. Modern presidents are expected to be involved in practically every aspect of our nation's political life. We will look at several of the powers and duties of the president to understand the importance of the office.

Chief Executive. The president heads the executive branch and is called the *chief executive*. As chief executive, the president must see that the thousands of laws passed by Congress are put into effect and enforced.

The president faces an enormous task. He cannot do the job without a great deal of help. Many executive departments and agencies have been formed to help the president.

The president appoints his top officials with the approval of the Senate. The president may also remove most of the officials he appoints. The power to appoint and remove top officials in the executive branch is important. As he is directly responsible for how well the huge executive branch works, the president must have good people in leading positions.

As chief executive, the president also must write and send the federal budget to Congress. After Congress approves the budget, the president must see that the money is spent properly.

Chief Legislator. Although Congress is the legislative branch, the president has a role in making laws. The Constitution requires the president to inform Congress of the condition of the nation and to suggest new laws. The president does this in several ways. In late January he delivers a *State of the Union* message to Congress. Each year the president also sends Congress his ideas about the budget and a report on the nation's economy. Messages on other subjects are sent by the president to Congress from time to time. In all of these messages and reports the president recommends new laws.

The most important legislative power the president has is the veto. As we have learned, the president can prevent a bill from becoming a law by vetoing it. Even though Congress may override the president's veto, it is hard to do. Presidents have vetoed more than 2,400 bills passed by Congress. Fewer than one hundred vetoes have been overridden.

fig. 172
President Bush as chief diplomat with Prime Minister Margaret Thatcher

Chief Diplomat. The president has several powers and duties that make him our nation's *chief diplomat*. The president may make *treaties* with foreign countries. Treaties are written agreements between two or more nations. Treaties made by the president must be approved by the Senate.

The president appoints officials to represent the United States in foreign countries. He decides whether or not new foreign governments will receive *recognition* from the United States. Recognition means the United States will accept representatives of the new government and have diplomatic relations with it.

Being our nation's chief diplomat is a big part of the president's job. He must meet with or correspond with many leaders from other nations. Sometimes he must travel outside the United States and improve our relations with foreign nations.

fig. 173
President Truman as commander in chief

fig. 174
President Reagan as Chief of State with former presidents Ford, Carter, and Nixon

Commander in Chief. The president is the commander of our armed forces. He appoints our highest ranking military officers. Major military decisions are often made by the president. President Truman, for example, had to decide whether the atomic bomb would be used against Japan in the Second World War. Only Congress can declare war. However, the president has authority to send American troops to trouble spots. If Congress does not approve such actions, the president must bring back the troops within sixty days. The president may also use federal troops or state militias to deal with riots or other emergencies.

Chief of State. The Constitution does not require the president to act as the *chief of state,* or ceremonial head, of our government. However, Americans expect this of the president. As a result, he spends much of his time greeting important visitors to the United States and presiding over ceremonies.

Judicial Powers and Duties. The president has several judicial powers and duties. He appoints all federal judges with the approval of the Senate. He may grant *reprieves* and *pardons.* A reprieve is an order that postpones a sentence. It gives a convicted person time to appeal to a higher court or to gather new evidence. A pardon frees a person who has been convicted or accused of a crime. The president may also *commute,* or reduce, a sentence.

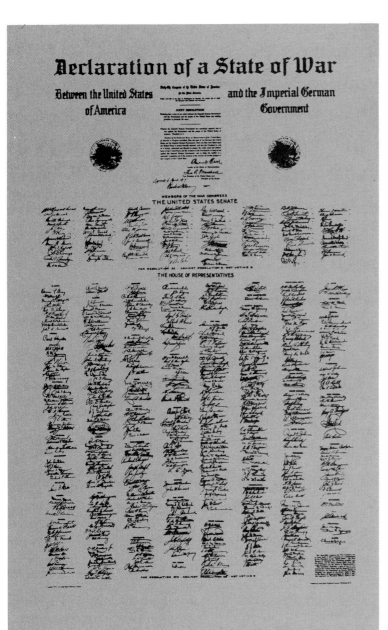

fig. 175
President Roosevelt as commander in chief during World War II

fig. 176
Declaration of War against Germany approved by all members of Congress

fig. 177
The Capitol on Inauguration Day

fig. 178
President John Adams, 1797 – 1801
This silhouette of John Adams resides in the National Portrait Gallery in the Smithsonian.

Party Leader. The president is also the leader of his political party. As party leader, he chooses the national chairperson of the party. He also helps the party raise money and often makes campaign speeches for members of his party who run for Congress.

REVIEW OF SECTION TWO:
1. Why is the president called the chief executive?
2. What is the State of the Union message?
3. What are the president's duties as chief diplomat? As commander in chief?
4. What judicial powers does the president have?

SECTION THREE: THE EXECUTIVE OFFICE AND THE EXECUTIVE DEPARTMENTS

The president's duties are so great that he must have a great deal of help. For this reason, the executive branch is very large. It has far more employees than the other two branches combined. The employees of the executive branch are organized into three major divisions. These divisions are the Executive Office of the President, the executive departments, and the independent agencies. We will study the Executive Office and the executive departments in this section. Independent agencies will be covered in the last section of this chapter.

The Executive Office of the President. The president relies on the help of many different advisers. In 1939 Congress created the *Executive Office of the President* to provide the president with the help he needed. The Executive Office is made up of several agencies that are shown on the chart in the text. The heads of these agencies report only to the president.

fig. 179
This silhouette portrait of John Quincy Adams, grandson of John Adams, also resides in the National Portrait Gallery in the Smithsonian.

The *White House Office* employs the president's closest advisers and several hundred experts in various fields. The president's doctor and press secretary are part of the White House Office. The people who serve in the White House Office have many different tasks. Some work with Congress and other departments of the executive branch. They also make the president's appointments, plan his trips, write his speeches, and provide him with information. The press secretary answers reporters' questions and gives statements to the mass media.

Other agencies in the Executive Office of the President have very special roles. For example, the National Security Council advises the president about how to keep the nation secure. The Council of Economic Advisers deals with the economy.

The vice president also works in the Executive Office. The Constitution does not assign many duties to the vice president. For many years vice presidents did very little. However, most recent presidents have given their vice presidents many jobs. The vice president often fills in for the president at ceremonies or gives speeches. Some vice presidents have represented the president in meetings with foreign leaders. Several have attended meetings of the president's cabinet and such groups as the National Security Council.

The Executive Departments. Most work in the executive branch is done by the fourteen executive departments. When George Washington was president there were only three executive departments. However, as the federal government grew, Congress created new departments.

Each department takes care of a specific area. For example, the Department of Defense defends the United States while the Department of Education is concerned with schools.

The head of each department is appointed by the president with the approval of the Senate. Thirteen department heads are called *secretaries*. The head of the Department of Justice, the attorney general, is the only department head who is not called a secretary. The fourteen heads of executive departments make up the *president's cabinet*. Most presidents meet often with their cabinet. Cabinet members discuss policy with the president and give him information and advice. Therefore, cabinet members have two important jobs. Each supervises an executive department, and each serves in the cabinet.

The following is a list of each executive department and its functions. The dates indicate the year in which a department was formed.

The Department of State (1789) was one of the first executive departments. The secretary of state is usually the president's main adviser on foreign affairs. State Department officials help the president decide what policies to follow when dealing with other nations. The department also carries out the president's foreign policies.

The State Department sends officials of the United States to most parts of the world. The chief representatives are called *ambassadors*. They are the heads of United States embassies in foreign capitals. The

The West Virginian Who Ran for President. Did you know that a West Virginian was once nominated for the presidency by the Democratic Party? His name was John W. Davis. Davis was born in Clarksburg and was a lawyer there from 1897–1913. He served in the West Virginia legislature and the United States House of Representatives. Davis became one of President Woodrow Wilson's most trusted advisers. In 1913 President Wilson appointed him solicitor general of the United States. The solicitor general is a leading official in the Department of Justice. The president rewarded Davis again in 1918 by appointing him ambassador to Great Britain.

The Democrats had trouble choosing their presidential candidate in 1924. Delegates to the Democratic National Convention voted 103 times before John W. Davis was selected. However, in the general election he was defeated by Calvin Coolidge. Following his defeat, Davis became a well-known lawyer. He argued more cases before the United States Supreme Court than any other lawyer ever has. He died in 1955.

ambassador and staff handle American affairs in the country in which they are located.

The Department of the Treasury (1789) has three major functions. First, it advises the president on economic policy. For example, the department might recommend that taxes be raised or lowered. Second, it collects taxes, pays the nation's debts, and produces postage stamps, paper money, and coins. The third function is handled by the *Secret Service.* The Secret Service enforces laws against counterfeiting. It also protects the president and vice president and their families, visiting heads of state, and presidential and vice-presidential candidates.

The Department of Defense (1947) is in charge of the armed forces. It organizes, trains, and equips our military forces. It operates military bases at home and abroad. It is also in charge of the academies that train our military officers.

The Department of Justice (1870) enforces federal laws. The *Federal Bureau of Investigation* (F.B.I.) is part of the department. It investigates most violations of federal laws. Other divisions enforce civil rights, tax, drug, and immigration laws. Justice Department lawyers prosecute those who break federal laws. They also defend the United States in court when lawsuits are brought against it. The department also operates federal prisons.

fig. 180
John W. Davis

The Department of the Interior (1849) supervises the use of our natural resources. The department handles programs to conserve water and protect land, timber, minerals, fish, and wildlife. It also manages millions of acres of land owned by the government, as well as national parks, monuments, historic sites, and scenic areas. In addition, it supervises Indian reservations and our overseas territories.

The Department of Agriculture (1862) has many programs to help farmers produce more food and sell their crops. It also provides loans to farmers and promotes soil conservation and animal disease

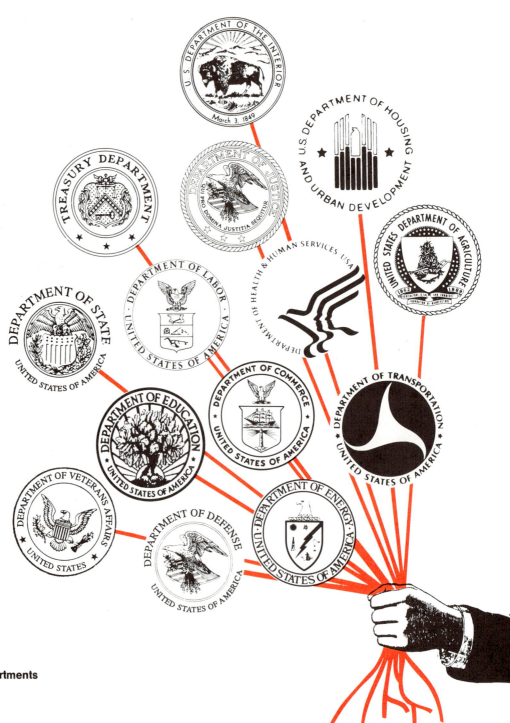

fig. 181
The Executive Departments

control. The Forest Service division manages national forests and does research on woodlands. The department also helps consumers by inspecting food processing plants to see that their products are safe to eat. The food stamp program, which helps the needy buy food, is run by the Agriculture Department. The department also supports school breakfast and lunch programs.

The Department of Commerce (1903) was created to encourage trade in the United States and exports to other nations. It provides information and other help to American businesses. Other duties include taking the census, setting official weights and measures, issuing patents, and operating the National Weather Service. The Commerce Department also promotes the American merchant fleet.

The Department of Labor (1913) serves American workers. It provides information on working conditions and jobs. It also enforces laws on wages, pension plans, child labor, worker safety, and aid to unemployed and injured workers. The department also operates several job training programs.

The Department of Health and Human Services (1953) was the Department of Health, Education, and Welfare until 1979. In that year, a separate Department of Education was created. A major responsibility of this department is the social security program. This program helps support the aged and some needy people. The department also has programs to help the handicapped and people addicted to alcohol and drugs. The Public Health Service, a part of this department, is charged with the control of diseases. It also helps support hospitals and other health care facilities.

The Department of Housing and Urban Development (1965) helps cities deal with problems such as slums and poor housing. It gives home loans to low-income families and finances housing projects for the elderly and handicapped. HUD also makes grants to cities to help them rebuild run-down urban areas.

The Department of Transportation (1967) works with the states to develop a safe and modern system of transportation. The department has several divisions. The Highway Administration, the Railroad Administration, and the Aviation Administration make grants to states to promote better roads, railways, and airports. The Urban Mass Transportation Administration helps cities with mass transit systems such as subways and bus lines.

The Department of Energy (1977) develops ways to conserve energy and find new sources of energy. It oversees the use of nuclear and

fig. 182
WVU's Personal Rapid Transit System for travelling between the three campuses was built as a project of the Department of Transportation

hydroelectric power as well as oil and gas pipelines. The department also enforces federal laws on the production and sale of oil, gasoline, and natural gas.

The Department of Education (1979) does a great deal to assist the nation's school systems. It provides information on many aspects of education and makes grants to improve schools.

The Department of Veterans Affairs (1989) is the newest executive department. It provides many services to Americans who have been in the armed forces. For example, it is responsible for the payment of pensions to some veterans. The department also administers many hospitals that help veterans with their medical problems.

fig. 183
Executive Offices

EXECUTIVE OFFICES OF THE PRESIDENT

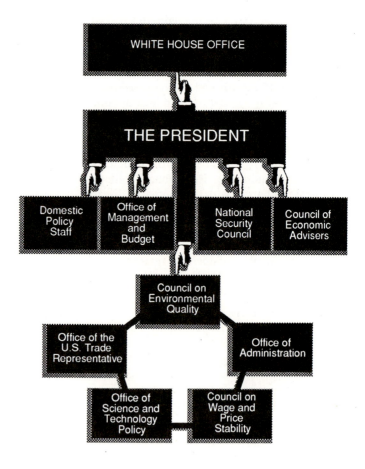

WHITE HOUSE OFFICE

THE PRESIDENT

Domestic Policy Staff

Office of Management and Budget

National Security Council

Council of Economic Advisers

Council on Environmental Quality

Office of the U.S. Trade Representative

Office of Administration

Office of Science and Technology Policy

Council on Wage and Price Stability

In Chapter One we read about the growth of modern government. The executive branch of our federal government is a good example of such growth. In 1789 only a few hundred people worked in the executive branch. The executive branch now employs over two and one-half million people. Some Americans think that the federal government has grown too much. Others believe that the federal government must be large enough to deal with many national issues.

REVIEW OF SECTION THREE:

1. What is the purpose of the Executive Office of the President?
2. What are some of the functions of the White House Office?
3. Who sits on the president's cabinet? How are they selected? What are their duties?
4. Describe the work of three executive departments.

SECTION FOUR: THE INDEPENDENT AGENCIES

Some tasks of the executive branch are very specialized. They cannot be done easily by either the Executive Office or the executive departments. Therefore, Congress has created nearly two hundred independent agencies to perform those duties.

fig. 184
Jon McBride, an astronaut from West Virginia, wore this helmet as a test pilot for NASA. It can be seen in the Cultural Center Museum in Charleston.

The heads of independent agencies are appointed by the president and approved by the Senate. The terms of most agency heads are rather long. Some are as long as fourteen years. Long terms ensure that no president can appoint all the leaders of these agencies. In addition, agency heads cannot be removed by the president. Congress set up this system so that independent agencies would be free of political pressure.

There are three types of independent agencies: independent executive agencies, independent regulatory commissions, and government corporations.

Independent Executive Agencies. Most of the independent agencies are known as *independent executive agencies.* Some, such as the General Services Administration and the National Aeronautics and Space Administration, have thousands of workers and large budgets. Others, such as the American Battle Monuments Commission, are very small. Whatever their size, all were formed to do specific tasks. For example, the Office of Personnel Management hires most of the people who work in federal agencies. The General Services Administration buys supplies for the federal government and builds and cares for government buildings. The National Aeronautics and Space Administration runs the space program.

fig. 185
Barges on the Ohio River

The Independent Regulatory Commissions. Congress has created twelve commissions to regulate several economic and scientific activities. These *independent regulatory commissions* have the power to enforce federal laws. The commissions also make rules that have the force of law. These rules must be obeyed just as a law must be obeyed. Each commission employs people who are well trained for their jobs.

The first regulatory commission was the Interstate Commerce Commission. It was created by Congress in 1887 to regulate railroads. Today it also regulates buses, trucks, and barges that carry goods across state borders. The chart in the text shows other concerns of independent commissions.

Government Corporations. About sixty independent agencies are *government corporations.* They are businesses owned by the federal government. Most provide goods or services that Americans want but businesses don't want to supply. The best-known government

1913 Federal Reserve System
(7 members - 14 year terms)
Regulates the banking system, the money supply and the use of credit.

1934 Securities and Exchange Commission
(5 members - 5 year terms)
Enforces laws against dishonest investment practices and regulates the selling of stocks and bonds.

1935 National Labor Relations Board
(5 members - 5 year terms)
Settles labor disputes, enforces labor relations laws, and remedies unfair labor practices.

1887 Interstate Commerce Commission
(11 members - 7 year terms)
Licenses, fixes rates, and regulates interstate carriers on highways, railroads and waterways.

1914 Federal Trade Commission
(7 members - 7 year terms)
Enforces laws against unfair business practices, price fixing and false advertising.

1934 Federal Communcations Commission
(7 members, 7 year terms)
Licenses and regulates radio and TV satellite communication systems, and interstate telephone and telegraph services.

corporation is the United States Postal Service. Another is Amtrak, which operates passenger trains.

REVIEW OF SECTION FOUR:

1. Why is there a need for independent agencies?
2. What is the difference between an independent executive agency and an independent regulatory commission?
3. Why have government corporations been created?

REFERENCES:

1. Close Up Foundation. *The Presidency: Perspectives on Presidential Power.* Arlington, VA: Close Up Foundation, 1987.
2. White House Historical Association. *The Presidents of the United States of America.* Washington: White House Historical Association, 1987.
3. Wirt, Daniel, P. Allen Dionisopoulis, and Robert J. Gennett. *Our American Government and Political System.* River Forest, IL: Laidlaw Brothers, 1983, pp. 209–53.

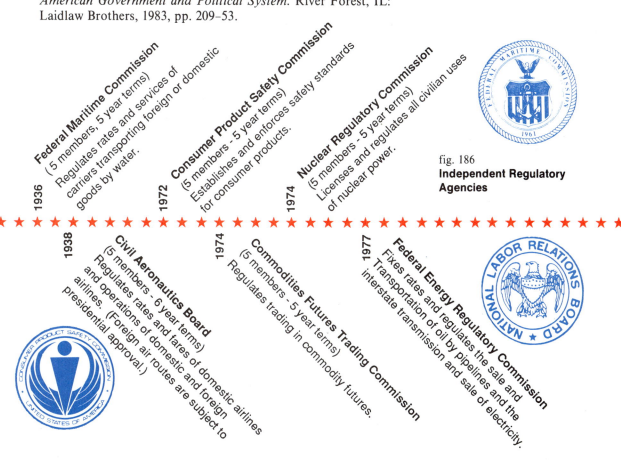

Federal Maritime Commission
(5 members, 5 year terms)
Regulates rates and services of carriers transporting foreign or domestic goods by water.
1936

Consumer Product Safety Commission
(5 members - 5 year terms)
Establishes and enforces safety standards for consumer products.
1972

Nuclear Regulatory Commission
(5 members - 5 year terms)
Licenses and regulates all civilian uses of nuclear power.
1974

fig. 186
Independent Regulatory Agencies

Civil Aeronautics Board
(5 members - 6 year terms)
Regulates rates and fares of domestic airlines and operations of domestic and foreign airlines. (Foreign air routes are subject to presidential approval.)
1938

Commodities Futures Trading Commission
(5 members - 5 year terms)
Regulates trading in commodity futures.
1974

Federal Energy Regulatory Commission
Fixes rates and regulates the sale and Transportation of oil by pipelines and the interstate transmission and sale of electricity.
1977

The Federal Judiciary

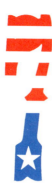

PREVIEW

The judiciary is the third branch of the federal government. Congress and the executive branch do not handle all tasks. After laws are made and carried out, someone must settle disputes about the laws. There must also be a way to deal with persons who break federal laws.

The federal courts, which make up the judicial branch, are in charge of these tasks. They try people accused of crimes. They see that the laws are applied equally and fairly to all Americans. The federal courts protect rights given us by the Constitution. We depend on the judiciary, and we should learn how the courts work.

In Chapter Seven we will answer these questions:
1. How does our federal system of laws work?
2. What is the difference between criminal and civil law?
3. What is equal justice under the law?
4. What are the different types of federal courts?
5. How are federal judges selected?
6. How many justices are on the Supreme Court?
7. What is the power of judicial review, and why is it important?
8. How does the Supreme Court protect and expand constitutional rights?

Pronounce and discuss the meanings of the following words found in this chapter. You may need to use a dictionary.

civilian	probation
custody	segregation
discrimination	strategy
disputes	unanimously
emphasizes	violations

fig. 187, left and above
Ritchie County Courthouse in Harrisville

fig. 188
The Parthenon, the orginial architectural model for many of our government buildings

SECTION ONE: THE AMERICAN LEGAL SYSTEM

The Functions of Law. When many people live together they have disputes and conflicts. Life would be very unpleasant if there were no peaceful way to settle conflict. We would never feel safe if everyone could do as he or she wanted. Government helps to control our behavior by making and enforcing laws.

A *law* is a rule that states how people are to behave. Laws define what we may or may not do. Our laws are based on what most Americans think is right or wrong.

Our legal system has several functions. One is to help settle disputes between people. When people disagree about money and other matters, courts use the law to decide who is right.

A second function is to protect people against harm. Many laws prohibit, or ban, harmful acts and provide punishment for criminals.

Another large role of American law is to protect our rights from violations by the government. We have learned that the Constitution, the supreme law of the land, puts many limits on government.

Criminal and Civil Law. We have both criminal and civil laws. *Criminal laws* define crimes such as murder and robbery. They also set punishments for criminals. As crime harms everyone, our criminal laws protect all citizens. The federal government has passed some criminal laws, but most are passed by state governments.

Civil laws deal with disputes between people or between citizens and the government. Civil cases between people may be disputes over such things as property lines, contracts, divorce, and highway accidents. Sometimes the government is in a civil case. However, most civil cases are between people.

The Role of Courts. Another big job of the courts is to interpret, or explain, the meaning of laws. The meaning of some laws is not always clear. Congress may pass laws that are not explained in great detail.

The laws on social security are a good example. They do not state every case in which a person would receive social security benefits. The Social Security Administration sets most of the rules about who may get benefits. A person who is denied benefits may go to a court. The court will first have to interpret the meaning of the social security laws. It will then decide whether or not the person should have the benefits.

Federal courts also hear cases about the Constitution. They must interpret the meaning of some part of the Constitution before such cases can be decided.

Equal Justice under the Law. Our legal system will work well only if we think that it is fair. The goal of our laws is to provide equal justice for all. This means that no one is excused from obeying the law, and everyone is treated fairly.

Our Constitution gives many rights to all Americans. These include the right to fair and equal treatment by the courts. The Constitution even protects people accused of crimes. No matter who is accused, his or her life, liberty, or property cannot be taken away without a fair trial.

Courts sometimes make mistakes. Therefore, our legal system allows those who think that they did not get a fair trial to appeal their cases. An *appeal* is a request to have a court decision reviewed by a higher court. If a higher court decides that the accused was treated unfairly, it can order a new trial.

REVIEW OF SECTION ONE:
1. Why are laws necessary? What is a law?
2. What are the functions of law in the United States?
3. What is the difference between criminal law and civil law?
4. What are the functions of courts?
5. What is meant by equal justice under the law?

fig. 189
An early engraving of the symbol for blind justice

fig. 190
The Supreme Court building in Washington, DC

SECTION TWO: THE FEDERAL COURT SYSTEM

In our federal structure of government we have two separate court systems. In this chapter we will read about the federal, or national, courts. The state courts will be described in Chapter Thirteen.

Article III of the Constitution created the federal judicial branch. It is made up of the federal courts, which apply and interpret national laws. Article III provided for one federal Supreme Court, but it also gave Congress the right to form other federal courts.

The Jurisdiction of Federal Courts. Article III of the Constitution also states the *jurisdiction* of federal courts. Jurisdiction refers to the type of cases a court may hear. Federal courts have jurisdiction only in the following cases:

A violation of the Constitution, laws, or treaties of the federal government.

Cases involving ships on the high seas or the coastal waters of the United States.

Disputes between states, between a state and a citizen of another state, between citizens of different states, between an American citizen and a foreign citizen or government, or between a state and a foreign citizen or government.

Cases involving the United States government.

Cases involving representatives of foreign governments in the United States or representatives of the United States government in foreign nations.

District Courts. There are three types of federal courts: district, appellate, and special courts. The United States District Courts are the federal trial courts. Each state has at least one district court, as do the District of Columbia and Puerto Rico. Large states may have as many as four districts. There are ninety-one district courts today. Each court has at least one judge but may have twenty or more.

District courts are courts of *original jurisdiction.* This means that most federal cases begin, or originate, in a district court. District courts handle about 90 percent of all federal cases. They hear and decide both criminal and civil cases.

District courts are the only federal courts in which jury trials are held. Grand juries in district courts decide whether there is enough evidence to hold accused persons for trial. Petit juries decide the guilt or innocence of the accused.

Appellate Courts. If someone wants to appeal the decision of a federal court, he or she may go to an appellate court. Sometimes an appellate court will also hear an appeal from a state court case or a federal agency decision. There are two levels of *appellate courts.*

The first level is made up by the United States Courts of Appeals. They were created by Congress in 1891 to help reduce the work of the Supreme Court. There are twelve United States Courts of Appeals. Each court has from three to fifteen judges.

The courts of appeals do not have original jurisdiction. Therefore, no case begins in a court of appeals. Its duty is to hear and decide upon appeals. The judges do not retry cases. Their job is to look for legal errors made during the original trial. They review the records of the trial and hear the arguments of lawyers for both sides. If a majority of the judges decide that serious mistakes were made, they will ask that the case be retried. If they decide that the trial was fair, they will uphold the lower court decision.

fig. 191
Judicial Circuits of the United States Courts of Appeals

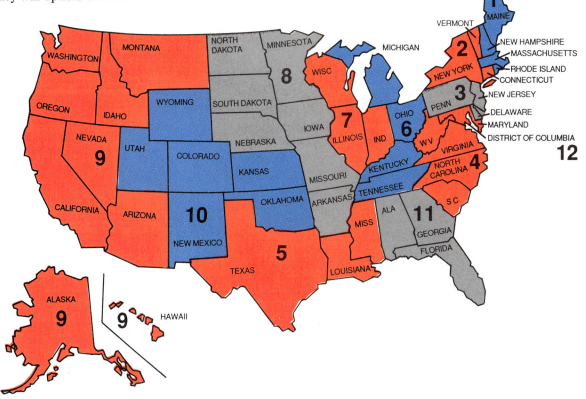

fig. 192
A statue of blind justice located on the Randolph County Courthouse, Elkins, WV

The second level of federal appellate courts is the Supreme Court. It is the highest court in the United States. Some decisions by courts of appeals will be taken to the Supreme Court. All of its decisions are final. We will study the Supreme Court in the next section of this chapter.

Special Courts. In addition to district and appellate courts, there are several special federal courts. Congress created them to deal with special types of cases.

The *United States Claims Court* hears claims against the federal government. For example, the government can take property needed for a highway or some other public use. However, the owner of the property may not be happy with the amount of money offered for the property. He or she can take the case to the claims court. There are sixteen judges on the claims court.

The *United States Tax Court* was formed in 1969 to deal with cases between taxpayers and the federal government. The court has nineteen judges. One judge hears and decides each case.

The *Court of International Trade* hears disputes about federal taxes on imported goods. Businesses sometimes disagree with the government about the amount of tax they must pay on imports. The Court of International Trade decides who is correct. The court has nine judges. Three judges hear and decide each case.

The *Court of Appeals for the Federal Circuit* was created in 1980. It hears appeals from the United States Claims Court and the Court of International Trade. It also settles disputes over patents. The court has twelve judges.

Territorial courts have been set up in Guam, the Virgin Islands, and the Northern Mariana Islands. These territories belong to the United States. Their courts handle the same type of cases as district and state courts.

The *Court of Military Appeals* hears appeals from military courts. Members of the armed forces are tried by military courts when accused of breaking military regulations. The judges of military courts are military officers. However, the Court of Military Appeals has three civilian judges. Decisions of the Court of Military Appeals are final.

Federal Judges. Federal judges preside over all of the courts in the federal judicial system. The president appoints all federal judges. They must be approved by the Senate before taking office.

Most federal judges are appointed for life. This means they stay as judges until they resign or die in office. They may be removed only by impeachment. Lifetime terms keep judges from being removed for decisions that the president or Congress does not like. The only federal judges with shorter terms are those who serve on some of the special courts.

The judges hear cases and make sure that proper court procedures are followed. All federal courts have other employees who work for the court. For example, at least one United States magistrate, United States attorney, and United States marshal work in each district court.

fig. 193
Justice Sandra Day O'Connor receiving her oath of office

fig. 194
1989 Issue

Magistrates issue warrants, decide if accused persons should be brought before a grand jury, and set bail for those who are to be tried.

United States attorneys prosecute persons charged with breaking federal laws. They also defend the government in civil cases.

Marshals make arrests, find witnesses, and keep accused persons in custody. In addition to these officials, district courts also hire clerks, court recorders, probation officers, and secretaries.

REVIEW OF SECTION TWO:

1. What is meant by jurisdiction?
2. What are the three types of federal courts?
3. How do district courts and courts of appeals differ?
4. Name two special courts and describe the type of cases they receive.
5. How are federal judges selected? Why are most judges appointed for life?

fig. 195
Federal Court System

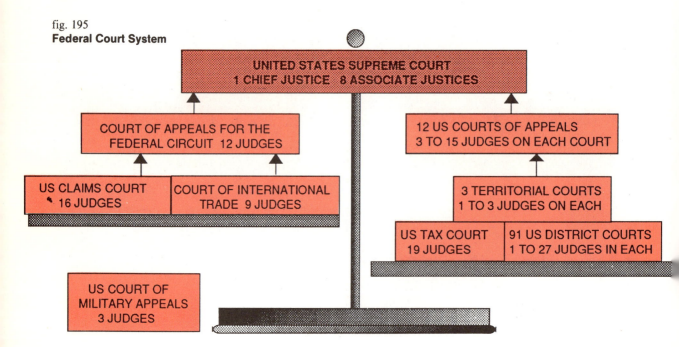

SECTION THREE: THE UNITED STATES SUPREME COURT

As our nation's highest court, the United States Supreme Court deserves special attention. Its decisions cannot be appealed. It has the last word in any case involving the Constitution, federal laws, or treaties. The Supreme Court is made up of one chief justice and eight associate justices. Congress determines the number of justices. All justices are appointed by the president for life. The president also decides who will be chief justice. The Senate must approve each justice.

Unlike other federal courts, the Supreme Court has both original and appellate jurisdiction. It has original jurisdiction in cases involving foreign nations and disputes between states or between a state and the federal government. However, such cases are not very common. Most Supreme Court cases are appeals from lower federal courts or the highest state courts.

The Supreme Court and Judicial Review. The most important power of federal courts, except the special courts, is judicial review. It allows a court to decide if the acts of a government are permitted by the Constitution. If a federal court says "no" to a law, it cannot go into effect. The same is true if a court rules that the president or a governor has done something unconstitutional. Of all the federal courts, the Supreme Court uses the power of judicial review most often.

The Constitution does not state that federal courts have the power of judicial review. However, in 1803 the Supreme Court ruled that the courts have this power. The Court made this decision in the case of *Marbury v. Madison.*

Marbury v. Madison was a result of the bitter election of 1800. In that election the Federalist Party lost the presidency to Thomas Jefferson. During his last days in office, President John Adams appointed many Federalists to jobs. He appointed William Marbury as a justice of the peace. By mistake the paper, or commission of office, for Marbury was not delivered. When President Jefferson took office, he ordered Secretary of State James Madison not to deliver the commission. Marbury then went to the Supreme Court. He argued that the Judiciary Act passed by Congress in 1789 gave the Court power to force Madison to deliver his commission.

The entire Supreme Court voted against Marbury. Chief Justice John Marshall said that part of the Judiciary Act of 1789 was unconstitutional. He ruled that the Judiciary Act gave the Court some powers that were unlawful. Since that time federal courts have had the power of judicial review.

The Supreme Court in Action. Each year more than four thousand lower court decisions are appealed to the Supreme Court. The Court cannot review all of these cases. The justices must decide which cases will be heard. Four of the nine justices must vote to accept a case before it will be heard. The Court usually hears fewer than two hundred cases each year.

fig. 197
Chief Justice John Marshall, for whom Marshall University is named

Many appeals are rejected because the justices agree with the decision made by the lower courts. Others are turned down because there are no important constitutional issues at stake. Usually, the Court does not accept a case unless it involves the Constitution in some way.

The Court meets in the Supreme Court Building in Washington, D.C. Sessions begin each year in October and last until June or July. In each case lawyers for both sides present *briefs*. A brief is a written statement that explains one side's arguments in a case. The lawyers also give oral arguments before the Court. Each lawyer is allowed one hour to speak. The justices ask many questions during the oral arguments.

The justices listen to arguments for about two weeks and then go into recess for two weeks. In recess they study briefs and think about the cases they have heard. On Fridays, the justices discuss cases and make decisions. A majority vote decides the outcome. Usually all nine justices vote on a case. However, at least six justices must vote for a decision to be reached. If there is a tie, the decision of the lower court stays in effect.

After the Supreme Court has reached a decision, a justice who favored the decision is asked to write the Court's *opinion*. The opinion gives the reasons for the Court's decision. Several opinions may be written if the vote was divided. One justice will write the *majority opinion*. It will explain why a majority of the justices voted as they did. Any justice who disagreed with the decision may write a *dissenting opinion*. Other justices who agreed with the decision might write a *concurring opinion*.

Checks on the Power of the Supreme Court. We have learned that the Supreme Court is very powerful. It can declare an act of government to be unconstitutional. Its decisions are final. However, there are ways to check the Supreme Court. We have a system of checks and balances. Both Congress and the president have ways to limit the power of the Supreme Court.

If the Supreme Court declares a law to be unconstitutional, Congress can sometimes change the law to get around the Court's objection. If that is not possible, Congress may propose a change in the Constitution. An amendment could permit an act the Court had turned down.

The Sixteenth Amendment was adopted for this purpose. In 1895 the Supreme Court ruled against an income tax law passed by

fig. 198
Recent Supreme Court hearings have dealt with the abortion issue

Congress. The Court said that the tax did not treat all citizens equally. This was because people with higher income would have paid higher taxes under the law. The Sixteenth Amendment permits an income tax. Congress proposed the amendment, and it was ratified by the states in 1913.

The president and the Senate may also influence the Supreme Court. When a justice dies or resigns, the president appoints a new person. Sometimes the president disagrees with recent decisions of the Court. He may appoint someone who thinks differently than the majority of justices. This might change future Court decisions. Sometimes this tactic doesn't work. New justices may not support the president's point of view in all cases.

The Senate also has a role in appointments. It has the right to reject a person appointed by the president. Senators may believe that he or she is unqualified for the Supreme Court. They might also disagree with the views of the appointee. They want the president to pick someone they can accept.

REVIEW OF SECTION THREE:
1. How many justices are on the Supreme Court?
2. What is the power of judicial review? How did the federal courts get this power?
3. What is a majority opinion?
4. How can Congress make a law constitutional if the Supreme Court declares it unconstitutional?

fig. 199
Reagan press conference to introduce William Bork as his nominee to be appointed to the Supreme Court. The appointment was later rejected by the Senate.

fig. 200, above
March to protest school segregation

fig. 201, left
Protest marcher during a 1960s civil rights march on Washington

SECTION FOUR: PROTECTING AND EXPANDING CONSTITUTIONAL RIGHTS

Not every part of the Constitution is completely clear in meaning. It is the role of the federal courts to interpret the meaning when a question comes up. Over the years interpretations of the Constitution have changed. Sometimes important new rights have been won by Americans because a federal court changed an earlier view.

Voting Rights. Voting rights are a good example of how the Supreme Court has given new constitutional rights to Americans. In our early history, only a minority of adults could vote. In most states a voter had to be male, white, over twenty-one years old, and a landowner. Amendments to the Constitution have given the *franchise* (right to vote) to the majority, but the Supreme Court has also made decisions that extended voting rights.

In 1966 the Supreme Court declared poll taxes to be illegal. A poll tax was a head tax required of all adult males that had to be paid in some states before a person could vote. This kept some poor people from voting. The Court also ruled that *literacy tests* (reading and writing tests) for voters are unconstitutional. These were used in some states to keep blacks and other minorities from voting. (Blacks often lacked equal access to schooling.)

In 1964 the Supreme Court ruled that one person's vote must be worth as much as anyone else's vote. This means that each district that elects Congressmen and state legislators must be equal in size. This has forced many states to change district lines to make sure that an equal number of voters live in all districts.

The West Virginia Flag Salute Case and the Supreme Court. In 1942 the West Virginia Board of Education passed a regulation requiring students to salute the American flag. While saluting the flag, the students were also required to recite the pledge of allegiance. Students who refused would be expelled from public school.

The Jehovah's Witnesses, a religious group, asked a federal district court to excuse their children from the rule. They said that their religious beliefs did not allow them to salute the flag. The decision was appealed to the United States Supreme Court. In West Virginia Board of Education v. Barnette, the Supreme Court agreed with the Jehovah's Witnesses. West Virginia schools cannot force students to salute the flag. The Court held that the state regulation violated the First Amendment, which guarantees all Americans freedom of religion.

The Rights of Accused Persons. The Supreme Court has also expanded the rights of people accused of crimes. The Fourteenth Amendment states that everyone must have equal protection under the law. The Court has made some major interpretations of this right.

The most famous case on the rights of the accused was *Miranda* v. *Arizona* in 1966. The Court ruled that an accused person must be told of his or her rights by the police. One has the right to have a lawyer present when being questioned by the police. If the accused cannot afford a lawyer, one must be provided. Suspects must be told by the police that they have the right to be silent. Anything suspects say may be used against them in court.

The *Miranda* decision has caused much controversy. Some say that these rights make it too hard to convict a criminal. Others believe that people need protection from any abuse of their rights by the police.

Civil Rights. The Supreme Court has issued other important decisions on civil rights. These often have helped minorities and women. The Court has ruled against many laws that *discriminate* against, or apply differently to, people because of their race, religion, or gender.

In the 1954 case of *Brown* v. *Topeka Board of Education,* the Supreme Court struck against racial discrimination. During the late 1800s and early 1900s many states passed *segregation laws.* Those laws required different races to use separate facilities such as school, hotels, and restaurants. In a case in 1896 the Supreme Court had set a "separate but equal" doctrine. It held that separate facilities for blacks were allowed if such facilities were equal to those of whites.

In 1954 the Court changed its interpretation. It ruled that separate public schools for black and white students are unconstitutional. Since then the Court has made all segregated public facilities illegal. Millions of Americans now have rights that were once denied to them.

REVIEW OF SECTION FOUR:
1. How have decisions of the Supreme Court strengthened voting rights?
2. Why was the Supreme Court decision in the *Miranda* case important to accused persons?
3. What was the "separate but equal" doctrine established by the Supreme Court in 1896?
4. What Supreme Court decision declared segregated public schools unconstitutional?

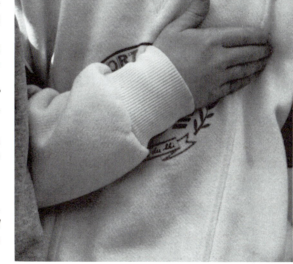

fig. 202

REFERENCES:
1. Close Up Foundation. *The Judiciary: Perspectives on Our Judicial System.* Arlington, VA: Close Up Foundation, 1987.
2. Constitutional Rights Foundation. *Criminal Justice in America.* Los Angeles: Constitutional Rights Foundation, 1983.
3. Lawson, Don. *Landmark Supreme Court Cases.* Hillside, NJ: Enslow Publishers, 1987.

Paying for the Federal Government

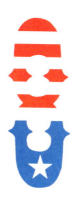

PREVIEW

The federal government has many duties and provides us with many programs. Most Americans want the government to serve them in hundreds of ways. However, the federal government cannot help us without spending large sums of money. In fact, the federal government spends over a trillion dollars each year. Deciding how to raise money for the government and how to spend it wisely is a major task. The president and the Congress make those hard decisions. All citizens are affected by each of their decisions. As we all help pay for government, we will now study public spending.

In Chapter Eight we will answer these questions:
1. What is the purpose of the federal budget?
2. How is the federal budget prepared and approved?
3. How does the federal government raise money?
4. What are the major expenses of the federal government?
5. Why is it difficult to balance the federal budget?

Pronounce and discuss the meanings of the following words found in this chapter. You may need to use a dictionary.

automatically	financial
benefits	grants
corporations	leasing
debt	profits
estimate	trillion

fig. 203, left and above
Pocahontas County Courthouse in Marlinton

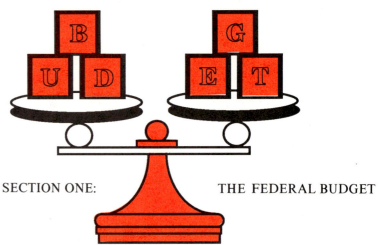

fig. 204
Balanced budget

fig. 205
*Have you ever closely examined the
elaborate and ornate artwork on
American money?*

SECTION ONE: THE FEDERAL BUDGET

The Purpose of the Federal Budget. A *budget* is a financial plan that shows how money will be raised and spent. It lists all the sources of *revenue,* or income, and shows how much revenue will come from each source. It also lists how money will be spent and shows how much each item will cost. People who prepare budgets try to balance them. A *balanced budget* is one in which the amount of revenue equals *expenditures* (money to be spent).

All businesses and many people work out a budget to help them plan. They want to spend their money wisely and not go too deeply into debt.

Governments also use budgets to guide their spending. Writing the budget of the federal government is quite difficult and takes a lot of time. There is never enough money to support every program people want. Important choices have to be made. Which programs will help the most people? Which should receive funds? How much money should each program cost? Where will the money come from? The president and the Congress make those hard decisions when they write and approve the federal budget.

Preparing the Federal Budget. Each year the president must propose a budget and send it to Congress to be approved. Many officials help the president with this task. Each executive department informs the president how much money it will need during the next year. Other agencies also send their requests for funds to the president. The president then turns to the *Office of Management and Budget* (OMB) for assistance.

The OMB is one of the agencies in the Executive Office of the President. It helps the president prepare his budget proposal. Specialists in the OMB estimate the amount of revenue the government will take in during the next year. They prepare complete reports for the president's advisers to read. After the federal budget has been approved, the OMB supervises spending. It must make sure that the budget is being followed when government money is spent.

The president, the cabinet, and other top advisers carefully study the many requests for money. They compare the requests with the OMB's revenue forecast. After much talk and debate, they decide which programs will get funds and how much they will receive. The OMB then writes the proposed budget the president will send to Congress. In its final form, the budget proposal is several hundred pages long. The president sends a message explaining the budget and asks Congress to approve it.

fig. 206
Which American leaders appear on these coins?

Approving the Federal Budget. Congress also plays a large role in the budget process. The Constitution gives Congress the power to raise and spend government funds. Therefore, the budget must be approved by Congress before it can go into effect.

After Congress has the president's proposal, it spends a few months going over the figures. Hearings on the budget are held by each house. Officials from executive departments, the OMB, and other agencies come to the hearings to answer questions. Reports from the Congressional Budget Office are studied. Finally, both the House and the Senate pass their own budget bills. The budgets passed by the two houses are usually different in some ways. They also differ with the president's plan most of the time.

The House and Senate bills go to a conference committee. After the committee has agreed, their compromise bill goes back to both houses for approval. The budget act is then sent to the president. In recent years the president has often disagreed with the budget passed by Congress. Sometimes several more months of work are needed before a final budget bill results. When the president approves the budget, it becomes law for one year.

REVIEW OF SECTION ONE:

1. What is a budget?
2. What is the purpose of the federal budget?
3. Who is responsible for preparing the proposed federal budget?
4. What is the role of Congress in the budget process?

SECTION TWO: SOURCES OF GOVERNMENT REVENUE

Taxation. Most of the money the federal government spends comes from taxes. A *tax* is a payment that people and businesses make to the government. We are required to pay taxes by the laws of the nation. There are several kinds of taxes paid to the federal government.

The chart in Section Two shows that the *personal income* tax produces over one-third of the government's revenue. It is a tax on the income individuals receive from wages, tips, rental property, and interest on bank accounts. The amount of tax a person must pay depends upon the size of his or her income. The more income a person has, the higher the tax.

fig. 207
National Computer Center in Martinsburg

The *corporation income* tax is paid by businesses known as corporations. The tax is based on the profits earned by the corporation and is higher for corporations with large profits than it is for those with small profits. About eleven cents of every dollar collected by the federal government comes from the corporation income tax.

Another major source of government revenue is the *social security* tax. Most workers and employers must pay this tax. The money supports the social security system. Social security provides workers with an income after they retire. It also pays for health care for the elderly and provides benefits for unemployed workers. Workers and their employers pay an equal amount into the fund.

Federal *excise* taxes are a smaller source of government revenue. Excise taxes are placed on certain goods and services. For example, when a person buys a tobacco product, he or she pays a tax that goes to the

federal government. Excise taxes are also paid on such items as alcoholic beverages, firearms, gasoline, and airline tickets.

Small amounts of federal money come from *estate* taxes and *gift* taxes. Estate taxes are placed on property when a person dies. The people who inherit the property must pay the estate tax only if the property is worth more than a certain amount. A gift tax must be paid by anyone who gives a valuable gift to someone. Gift taxes do not apply to husbands and wives.

The federal government raises some revenue by charging taxes on goods brought into the United States. These taxes are called *customs duties* or *tariffs*. Congress does not tax imports in order to raise money. Tariffs help to limit the number of imported goods. Many goods made in foreign nations are lower in price than similar American goods. Some people fear our businesses will be hurt and our workers will lose their jobs if too many goods are imported. The tariff raises the price of imports, making them cost as much or more than goods made in the United States.

Good Tax Principles. Nobody likes to pay taxes. People would rather use their money to buy things they need or want. Yet, taxes are needed to provide the public services we want. It is important to our nation that citizens are willing to pay their taxes. Therefore, our government tries to write tax laws that are based on several good principles.

Perhaps, the most important principle of American tax laws is that taxes should be fair. Usually, people are willing to pay if taxes are thought to be fair to everyone. Another good principle is that taxes should be based on the ability to pay. That is the idea behind the personal income tax. Taxes increase as one's ability to pay grows. Most Americans think that is fair.

A third good principle is that taxes should be based on benefits received. The people who gain the greatest benefit from a government program should pay something for that benefit. A good example is the excise tax on gasoline. The government builds many highways. Those who drive on those highways benefit from them. Therefore, drivers pay a tax on gasoline. The revenue from the tax is used to pay for the highways.

West Virginia and the National Computer Center

Did you know that the National Computer Center of the Internal Revenue Service (IRS) is located in Martinsburg, West Virginia? The IRS collects federal income taxes. It must check millions of tax returns to see if they are correct.

The National Computer Center was set up to help the IRS with that huge task. Data from employers, banks, and tax returns are fed into the computers in Martinsburg. These data allow the IRS to check the accuracy of tax returns very quickly.

When the National Computer Center was established in 1961, it had little equipment and only five employees. Today it has powerful computers and over seven hundred employees. In addition to checking tax returns, the National Computer Center develops and tests computer programs for the IRS. It also trains computer operators for all IRS offices across the nation.

A fourth principle of taxation used in the United States is that taxes should be broadly based. This means that all people should pay some taxes. Paying taxes gives people an interest in their government. It also helps us realize that government services are not free.

Other Revenue Sources. The federal government has several sources of revenue besides taxes. Court fines, the sale and leasing of public land, the sale of used equipment, and fees for government services produce money. The sale of timber from national forests and electricity produced by federal dams are other examples of this. However, all of these sources produce only a little more revenue than excise taxes.

The federal government also borrows large sums of money when revenues do not equal expenses. About 11 percent of its income is borrowed, primarily from large companies and banks. The government must repay these loans later. It must also pay *interest* on the loans. Interest is money a borrower must pay a lender for making a loan.

Other money is borrowed through the sale of bonds and Treasury Department certificates. The people who buy them get a promise that the federal government will repay them with interest. The government uses the money from the sale until it is time to repay.

fig. 208
Where the Federal Government Gets Its Money

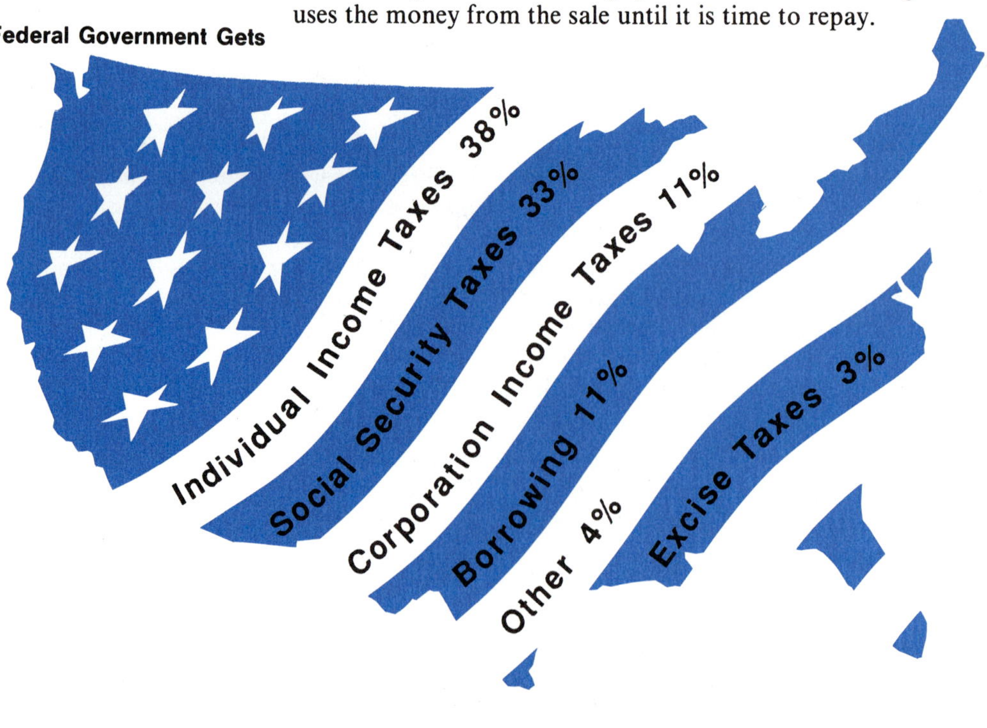

Individual Income Taxes 38%
Social Security Taxes 33%
Corporation Income Taxes 11%
Borrowing 11%
Other 4%
Excise Taxes 3%

Many years ago when most people could not read or write, officials used seals to stamp important documents. Sometimes the seal was engraved on a ring which the official wore. Melted wax was dripped onto documents and the face of the ring was pushed into the wax to make an impression of the seal. The seal served in place of a signature or to guarantee that signatures on a document were genuine. The ancient practice of using seals on some important documents such as treaties between nations is still used today.

The Great Seal of the United States was adopted by Congress in 1782. Since that time it has become another important American symbol. The Great Seal has two sides. One side is called the face and the other is called the reverse side. Both sides can be found on the back of one dollar bills.

On the face of the Great Seal is a bald eagle which is our national bird. The breast of the eagle is covered by a shield with 13 red and white stripes. The stripes and the 13 stars above the eagle's head represent the original states. In the eagle's right claw is an olive branch (the symbol of peace) with 13 leaves. This symbolizes the desire of the United States to live in peace with other nations. In the eagle's left claw are 13 arrows which are intended to show that the United States will defend itself if forced to do so. A ribbon held in the eagles's beak is inscribed with the Latin words E Pluribus Unum. The Latin phrase means "from many, one." It refers to the creation of one nation from many states.

The reverse side of the Great Seal shows a pyramid with 13 rows of stone which represent the original states. At the bottom of the pyramid is the date 1776 written in Roman numerals. Above the pyramid is an eye and the Latin phrase Annuit Coeptis, which means "He (God) favored our undertaking." Below the pyramid is another Latin phrase Novus Ordo Secolorum, which means "a new order of the ages."

fig. 209
The Great Seal of the United States

REVIEW OF SECTION TWO:

1. What is a tax?
2. What tax provides the largest share of federal government revenue?
3. What is the main purpose of customs duties or tariffs?
4. Explain two of the principles upon which federal taxes are based.
5. From whom does the federal government borrow money?
6. What items are there thirteen of on our Great Seal? What is the significance of this?

SECTION THREE: GOVERNMENT SPENDING

As we have seen, the federal budget shows sources of government revenues. It also lists how much money the government will spend on its programs. The chart in the text shows these expenditures for five basic types of programs. We will look at each of the areas shown on the chart to learn what kind of programs are included.

Payments for Individuals. The largest expense is direct benefit payments to individuals. Millions of Americans receive checks from the government. Most are sent by the Social Security Administration. Social security payments go to retired people, widows, children who have lost a parent, and many disabled people. The federal government also helps with payments to unemployed workers.

Several other agencies make payments to individuals. The Department of Veterans Affairs sends payments to many veterans who were permanently injured while they were in the armed forces. Retired government workers get pensions. Many needy people also receive help.

National Defense. The cost of defending the United States is also very high. In 1988 national defense costs were nearly three hundred billion dollars. Defense costs include the salaries of all the people in the armed forces. Much of the defense budget is spent on very

fig. 210
Federal Spending

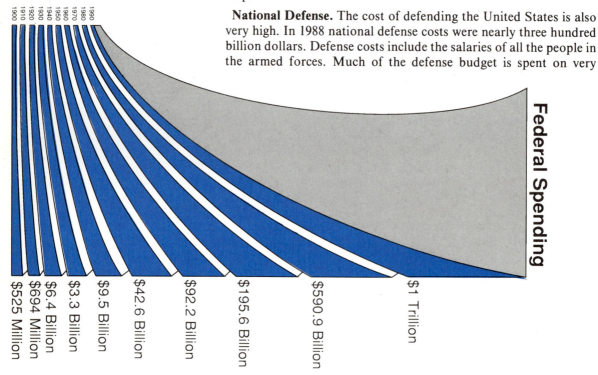

1900 1910 1920 1930 1940 1950 1960 1970 1980 1990

$525 Million
$694 Million
$6.4 Billion
$3.3 Billion
$9.5 Billion
$42.6 Billion
$92.2 Billion
$195.6 Billion
$590.9 Billion
$1 Trillion

Federal Spending

expensive weapons such as missiles, ships, tanks, and planes. A single fighter plane costs millions of dollars. An aircraft carrier costs hundreds of millions of dollars. A great deal of money is also spent on military bases in the United States and in some foreign nations.

Interest on the National Debt. Often the federal government does not take in enough money to support all of its programs. When that happens, the government borrows money to get the revenue it needs. The money owed by the government to lenders is known as the *national debt*. During this century the national debt has climbed to nearly three trillion dollars ($3,000,000,000,000).

When the government borrows money, it must pay interest to the people who loan the money. Each year the federal budget includes money to pay interest on the debt. As the national debt grows, the interest payments grow as well. In 1988 the government paid nearly two hundred billion dollars in interest. Interest payments took fourteen cents of every dollar spent by the government in that year.

Grants to State and Local Governments. The federal government grants some money to state and local governments. The money supports certain programs that state and local governments could not pay for alone. For example, West Virginia recently improved the West Virginia Turnpike by making it into a four-lane highway. This project cost more than four hundred million dollars. The federal government provided much of the money because the turnpike is part of the interstate highway system. It would have taken many years for West Virginia to complete the job without federal funds.

fig. 211
How the Federal Government Spends Its Money

(money represented in cents on the dollar)
(1988 estimate)

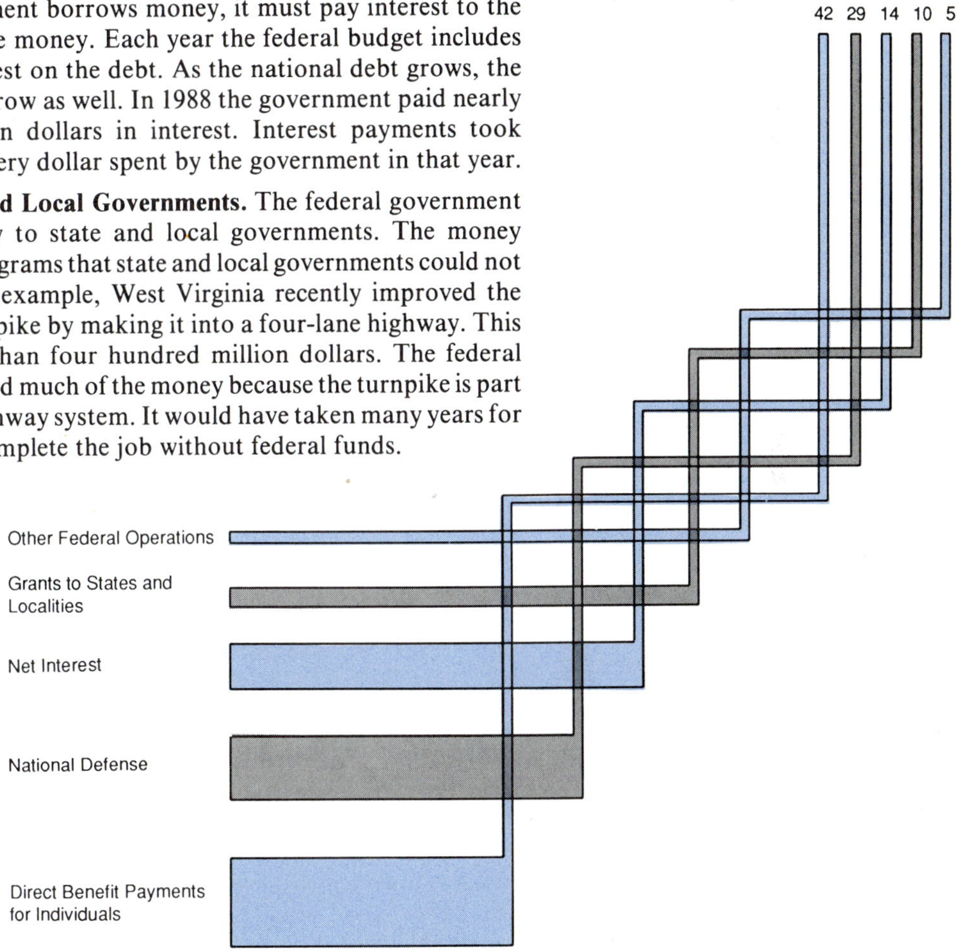

42 29 14 10 5

Other Federal Operations
Grants to States and Localities
Net Interest
National Defense
Direct Benefit Payments for Individuals

fig. 212
Annual Federal Deficits

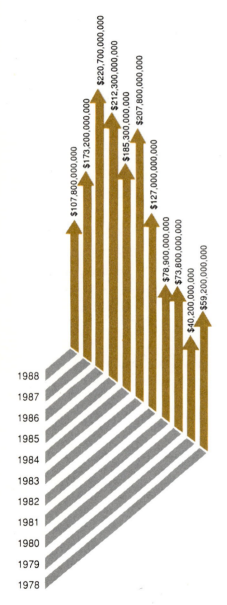

Federal grants also are used by state and local governments for such things as education and public libraries. New water and sewage systems, the preservation of historic sites, improvements in urban transit systems, and many other projects receive federal aid.

Other Federal Operations. In 1988 the federal government spent ninety-five cents of every dollar it collected on the four areas we have just described. That left only five cents from each dollar of revenue to cover the cost of all other federal programs. The salaries of over a million civilian employees of the government are paid from these funds. Other expenses include the operation of Congress, the courts, the executive branch, prisons, and national parks, forests, and recreation areas. New federal buildings, scientific research, aid to foreign nations, and hundreds of other programs also take these funds.

REVIEW OF SECTION THREE:
1. On which of the five major areas of the budget does the federal government spend the most money?
2. Why does national defense cost so much?
3. What is the national debt?
4. Why does the federal government grant money to state and local governments?

SECTION FOUR: THE DIFFICULT TASK OF BALANCING THE FEDERAL BUDGET

Most officials would like to have a balanced budget. Sometimes, however, that is impossible. For example, when we are involved in a war, the government has to spend huge sums of money. This also happens when the economy is weak and large numbers of people have no jobs. These crises lead to *deficit spending*. This means that the government spends more money than it collects. The budget is not balanced. When this happens, the government borrows money to cover its debts, and the national debt grows.

During most of our history, the federal government balanced the budget except during wars. However, since 1960 the federal budget has been balanced only once. That was in 1969. Every year the government borrows large amounts of money to cover the deficit. The chart in this section shows how the national debt has grown.

Many Americans believe it is unwise to allow the national debt to become so large. Most presidential and Congressional candidates promise to work for a balanced budget if elected. However, it seems to become harder every year to balance the federal budget. We will look at the major reasons for this.

Increased Costs. The cost of goods and services bought by the government increases every year. Military equipment, paper, building supplies, and medical care cost more than they did five years ago. The salaries of government workers go up every year or two. Government benefit payments increase most years. For example, social security payments are raised when the price of food and other goods increases. In addition, there are more elderly people today, because people now live longer. So the government must make social security payments to more people every year. In 1978 social security payments cost about 98 billion dollars. Ten years later the cost was 217 billion dollars.

The Growth of Government. Another reason for higher federal government expenses is that government has grown. New government programs require more employees, buildings, and supplies. Since 1965 five new executive departments have been formed: Housing and Urban Development, Transportation, Energy, Education, and Veterans Affairs. In 1989 those departments had over ninety thousand employees and spent billions of dollars. Some new executive agencies were also created during this time. Some of the programs that have been important in recent years, such as the space program, are very expensive.

Disagreement about Spending. Many Americans agree that government spending should be cut. However, we do not agree on which programs should be reduced. Elderly people oppose cuts in social security, and farmers are against cutting farm programs. Teachers and parents want more money for education. Workers, people in business, the needy, college students, veterans, and many other groups do not want to lose benefits. Many people feel that the government spends too much on defense. Others believe defense spending should be increased. In other words, most citizens favor less spending but only on programs that are not important to them.

The president and members of Congress are elected to office. They depend on the support of voters. They do not want to make large groups of voters angry by reducing programs the voters want. It is hard for political leaders to decide how to reduce government spending when many citizens oppose most cuts.

Disagreement about Taxation. Some people believe that federal taxes are too high. They argue that taxes must be reduced if our economy is to grow. They believe that if people have more money to

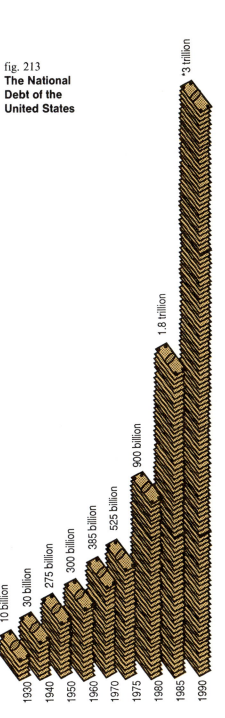

fig. 213
The National Debt of the United States

*3 trillion

1.8 trillion

900 billion

525 billion

385 billion

300 billion

275 billion

30 billion

10 billion

1930 1940 1950 1960 1970 1975 1980 1985 1990

spend, new business will result. This will lead to more jobs and a growing economy. During the administration of President Reagan federal taxes were lowered.

People who opposed the tax cuts believe that it has made balancing the budget more difficult. They argue that the cuts prevent government revenues from growing as fast as expenses. They would increase some taxes to help reduce the government's debts.

We have learned only a few of the reasons why it is hard to balance the federal budget. There are no easy answers to the problem. How can the cost of government be controlled when many Americans want and often need public services? Should taxes be raised or lowered even more? Is a balanced budget necessary? When we vote, we help make choices about spending and taxes.

REVIEW OF SECTION FOUR:
1. What is deficit spending?
2. Why has government spending increased so rapidly in recent years?
3. Why do Americans disagree about how to reduce government spending?
4. Why do some Americans feel that recent tax cuts were a mistake?

REFERENCES:
1. Davis, Bertha. *The National Debt*. New York: Watts, Franklin, Inc., 1987.
2. Junior Achievement, Inc. *Applied Economics*. Stamford, CT: Junior Achievement, Inc., 1985: pp. 143–59.
3. Mings, Turley. *The Study of Economics: Principles, Concepts and Applications*. Guilford, CT: The Duskin Publishing Group, 1987: pp. 373–95.

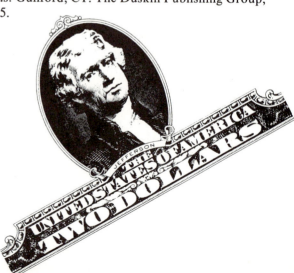

fig. 214
Did you know that not all the busts on American money are presidents?

The State of West Virginia and Its Constitution

PREVIEW

We have learned a great deal about the federal government of the United States. Now it is time to turn to the state government of West Virginia. Our federal system permits states to have certain rights and powers within their borders. The state governments are not all alike. However, when we learn about West Virginia, we will have a good idea about what most state governments do.

In this chapter we will learn how and why West Virginia became a state. Then we will read about our state constitution and the many amendments that have been added to it.

In Chapter Nine we will answer these questions:
1. Why was present-day West Virginia once a part of Virginia?
2. Why was there conflict between eastern and western Virginia?
3. How did the Civil War lead to the birth of West Virginia?
4. Why did West Virginia have two constitutions during its early history?
5. Why has our state constitution been amended so many times?

Pronounce and discuss the meanings of the following words found in this chapter. You may need to use a dictionary.

allies	invaded
bonuses	legalization
consecutively	plantations
decades	terrain
descended	uninterrupted

fig. 215, left page and above
Cabell County courthouse in Huntington

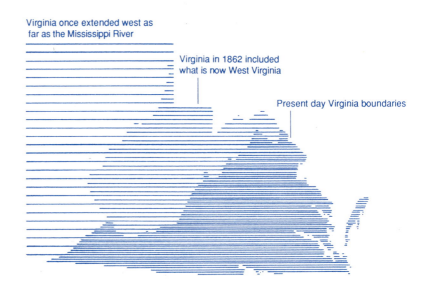

Virginia once extended west as far as the Mississippi River

Virginia in 1862 included what is now West Virginia

Present day Virginia boundaries

fig. 216
The state of Virginia in 1863 before West Virginia was formed

SECTION ONE: BEFORE STATEHOOD

The Colony of Virginia. West Virginia was a part of Virginia for over 250 years. English settlers founded the colony of Virginia in 1607. Under the charter of 1609, they claimed a large area that included present-day West Virginia. However, no settlers lived in western Virginia until about 1730.

Settling most of western Virginia was very difficult. The mountains and hills, all covered by heavy forests, made traveling slow and dangerous. There were no roads, and most streams were navigable for only short distances. The rough terrain also made it hard to find land that was good for farming.

Settlers faced dangerous enemies in the west. Several Indian tribes and France claimed the same land. Virginians fought hard for many years to win control of western Virginia. By 1763 the French were defeated. Though Indians were still a threat, more settlers moved into western Virginia and began to tame the wilderness.

When the Revolutionary War began in 1775, most western Virginians backed the cause of independence. Some fought in Washington's army, but many more stayed home to defend their settlements from England's Indian allies. There were many small but fierce battles between the Indians and western Virginians.

Western Virginia was a part of the colony of Virginia for 169 years. When the thirteen colonies declared their independence, they became states. For the next eighty-seven years western Virginia was part of the state of Virginia.

fig. 217, above
General Braddock's march

Conflict Develops between Eastern and Western Virginia. The eastern and western parts of Virginia were quite different from one another. The economy of much of eastern Virginia was based on raising tobacco. Tobacco was grown on large plantations. Thousands of black slaves did most of the work. In western Virginia, where the terrain was not suited for plantations, most people lived on small farms. They raised many kinds of crops as well as pigs, cattle, and sheep. There weren't many slaves in western Virginia.

Eastern and western Virginia differed in other ways. Most white people in the east were descended from English settlers. The people of western Virginia came from many backgrounds. Most were not English. The Episcopal church was large in the east, but most westerners were Baptists, Methodists, or Presbyterians. Eastern Virginia was much more developed than the west. For example, it had better roads and more schools than the west.

The many differences between eastern and western Virginia led to conflict. Western Virginians became upset about their poor means of transportation and lack of schools. They believed that western

Virginia was hurt by the lack of good roads, canals, railroads, and schools. They blamed their problems on Virginia's system of government.

The Constitutions of Virginia. Western Virginians did not like the Virginia *Constitution of 1776*. It gave the right to vote only to men who owned a certain amount of property. This kept many in the west from voting.

The constitution gave only a few seats in the legislature to the west. Each county had the same number of seats, regardless of size or population. Western Virginia had a few very large counties. This meant that most members of the legislature were from the east.

The governor was elected by the legislature and not the voters. He appointed the other state and county officials. The governor always came from the east, because most legislators were easterners.

Western Virginians complained strongly about the constitution, and years later a new one was written. However, they were also disappointed with the *Constitution of 1829–30*. It gave the west only a few more seats in the legislature. More men won the right to vote, but other changes favored by the west were not approved. Some westerners began to talk about separating from eastern Virginia.

Unrest in the west finally led to a third state constitution in 1851. This time many of the changes wanted by the west were adopted. Western seats in the legislature were greatly increased. All white males over twenty-one years of age could vote. Most state and county officials were to be elected. The west did not get everything it wanted, but most westerners were happy with the *Constitution of 1851*. Without the outbreak of the Civil War ten years later, the separation of Virginia would not have occurred.

fig. 218
Virginia state flag

REVIEW OF SECTION ONE:

1. Why was western Virginia settled much more slowly than eastern Virginia?
2. How did eastern and western Virginia differ?
3. What problems in western Virginia were blamed on Virginia's system of government?
4. Why were western Virginians unhappy with Virginia's first two constitutions?

fig. 219
"The Hercules of the Union" General Winfield Scott, is seen slaying the great dragon of secession in this political cartoon of 1861. It resides in the National Portrait Gallery in the Smithsonian.

SECTION TWO: WEST VIRGINIA BECOMES A STATE

Virginia Leaves the Union. In 1860 Abraham Lincoln was elected president of the United States. This upset Southern states so much that a terrible civil war was fought. For several decades, relations between the North and the South had grown worse. Arguments over slavery and tariffs drove the two sections further apart. Most Southerners had strongly opposed Lincoln. He supported Northern ideas and interests.

fig. 220
This "bleeder" was used during the Civil War to cut skin and let blood flow freely. This was thought to be a cleansing operation to prevent infection, but may have actually caused it.

fig. 221
Union soldiers

After Lincoln won the election, several Southern states decided to *secede,* or withdraw, from the United States. They formed a new nation called the Confederate States of America. President Lincoln and the United States government did not recognize Southern independence. War soon broke out between the two governments. The American Civil War lasted from 1861 to 1865. More than eight hundred thousand soldiers died in the fighting.

The Confederate States hoped that Virginia would join them. The Virginia legislature called for a special convention to discuss what Virginia would do. Delegates to the convention were elected from all parts of Virginia. On April 17, 1861, after weeks of debate, a majority voted in favor of secession. However, this decision had to be approved by the voters of Virginia in a special election.

Many western Virginians opposed secession. They wanted Virginia to stay in the Union. Most of the convention delegates from the west had voted against secession. Western Virginians feared that their section would be invaded by federal troops if Virginia joined the Confederacy. Few wanted to fight for slavery. There weren't many slave owners in western Virginia. In addition, the west did not want to lose its business ties with northern cities like Pittsburgh and Baltimore.

Western Virginians held meetings in Clarksburg and Wheeling to protest secession. They urged people to vote "no" in the coming election. However, voters in the east approved secession in large numbers. In late May Virginia joined the Confederate States.

Western Virginians Reorganize Virginia's Government. On June 11, 1861, men from thirty-four western counties met in Wheeling to decide what they should do about secession. Some delegates at this *Wheeling Convention* wanted a new state. The majority, however, decided to set up a new state government for Virginia. It would be loyal to the Union. They called it the *Reorganized Government of Virginia.* The delegates next chose a new governor and other state officials. They made Wheeling the state capital.

Leaders of the Reorganized Government claimed that the old government of Virginia was illegal, because it had left the Union. They said that only their government was legal. Unionists were a minority in Virginia, but the United States accepted the Reorganized Government of Virginia.

fig. 222
The Custom House, site of the 1861 Wheeling Convention

The Birth of West Virginia. In August 1861 the Wheeling Convention met again. Many delegates now favored splitting Virginia. They wanted to create a new state in the west. They couldn't do so earlier because of a clause in the Constitution of the United States. Article IV, Section 3, makes it very hard to create a new state out of another state. The older state must approve the new one. Delegates at the Wheeling Convention were sure that the Reorganized Government of Virginia would support this. They called for a special vote.

fig. 223
*Waitman Willey, an early senator
from Morgantown*

fig. 224

In October 1861, voters in thirty-five western counties approved the idea of forming a state in western Virginia. They also elected delegates to write a constitution for the new state.

The constitutional convention named our state West Virginia. The delegates decided what parts of Virginia would be put in the new state. They also drew up a form of government for West Virginia. Voters approved the constitution in April 1862.

The Reorganized Government of Virginia agreed to the split in May 1862. After a long debate, Congress and President Lincoln also approved. On June 20, 1863, West Virginia entered the Union as the thirty-fifth state.

The Constitution of 1863. West Virginia's *Constitution of 1863* was a big change from the Virginia constitution. The authors wanted their government to be similar to those of northern states. They wanted state government to be active and democratic.

The Constitution of 1863 established three branches of government. These were legislative, executive, and judicial. The constitution made all offices elective. It gave all white males the right to vote. The governor served only a two-year term but could be re-elected. The legislature met for forty-five days every year. The judiciary was made up of a Supreme Court of Appeals, circuit courts, and justice of the peace courts.

The most important change from the past was in local government. Virginia's system of county government was replaced by the *township system* used in New England. Each county was divided into townships. Local decisions were made by all voters who attended township meetings. This gave every voter the right to take part directly in public life.

The Constitution of 1863 also ended slavery in West Virginia. It required the legislature to set up a free public school system. Both of these provisions were favored by many West Virginians.

REVIEW OF SECTION TWO:
1. Why did many western Virginians oppose Virginia's secession from the Union?
2. What was the Reorganized Government of Virginia?
3. Why was it necessary to establish the Reorganized Government of Virginia before West Virginia could become a state?
4. Why did the authors of the Constitution of 1863 want West Virginia's government to be similar to the government of northern states?

NAMES	AGE	OCCUPATION	POST OFFICE
Gordon Battelle	47	Minister	Wheeling
John Boggs	48	Farmer	Mouth of Seneca
Richard Brooks	52	Farmer	Rock Cave
James Brown	42	Lawyer	Kanawha Court House
John Brown	35	Lawyer	Kingwood
William Brumfield	33	Farmer	Ceredo
Elbert Caldwell	52	Lawyer	Moundsville
Thomas Carskadon	24	Farmer	New Creek Station
Jason Cassady	40	Farmer	Fayette Court House
Henry Chapman	63	Physician	Spencer
Richard Cook	41	Farmer	Long Branch
Henry Dering	50	Merchant	Morgantown
John Dille	40	Lawyer	Kingwood
Abijah Dolly	44	Farmer	Greenland
David Gibson	32	Physician	Buckhannon
Samuel Griffith	32	Physician	West Columbia
Robert Hagar	51	Farmer	Boone Court House
Ephraim Hall	39	Lawyer	Fairmont
John Hall (President)	56	Farmer	Point Pleasant
Stephen Hansley	42	Lawyer	Marshall Court House
Thomas Harrison	37	Lawyer	Clarksburg
Hiram Haymond	55	Farmer	Palatine
James Hervey	41	Lawyer	Wellsburg
Johanis Hoback	26	Teacher	McDowell Court House
Joseph Hubbs	54	Farmer	St. Marys
Robert Irvine	47	Lawyer	Weston
Daniel Lamb	51	Cashier	Wheeling
Richard Lauck	49	Lawyer	New Martinsville
Edward Mahon	45	Farmer	Ravenswood
Andrew Mann	29	Farmer	Falling Springs
Jno. McCutcheon	51	Farmer	Summersville
Dudley Montague	61	Hotel Keeper	Red Hawk Shoals
Emmet O'Brien	42	Mechanic	Burnersville
Granville Parker	51	Lawyer	Guyandotte
Jason Parsons	49	Farmer	St. George
James Paxton	40	Merchant	Wheeling
David Pinnell	50	Physician	Buckhannon
Josiah Pomeroy	40	Minister	Fairview
John Powell	36	Minister	Buckhannon
Job Robinson	45	Farmer	Arnoldsburg
Andrew Ross	47	Teacher	West Liberty
Lewis Ruffner	64	Salt Manufacturer	Kanawha Salines
Edward Ryan	25	Minister	Gauley Bridge
George Sheets	38	Carpenter	Piedmont
Josiah Simmons	47	Farmer	Claysville
Harmon Sinsel	44	Carpenter	Prunytown
Benjamin Smith	63	Lawyer	Kanawha Court House
Abraham Soper	66	Lawyer	Sistersville
B. J. Stephenson	35	Farmer	Clay Court House
William Stevenson	40	Farmer	Parkersburg
Benjamin Stewart	52	Merchant	Newark
Gustavus Taylor	26	Lawyer	Braxton Court House
Moses Titchenell	56	Minister	Palatine
Thomas Trainer	42	Minister	Cameron
Peter Van Winkle	53	Lawyer	Parkersburg
William Walker	34	Lawyer	Oceana
William Warder	40	Farmer	Troy
Joseph Wheat	60	Farmer	Sir John's Run
Waitman Willey	50	Lawyer	Morgantown
Archibald Wilson	60	Farmer	Pennsboro
Ellery Hall (Secretary)	27	Lawyer	Fairmont
Sylvanus Hall (Assistant Secretary)	24	Clerk	Fairmont
James Orr (Sergeant-at- Arms)	33	Merchant	Wheeling
Henry Startzman (Doorkeeper)	38	Farmer	Kingwood

fig. 225
Representatives to the West Virginia constitutional convention

fig. 226
Does your town have any streets named after early founding fathers?

SECTION THREE: THE WEST VIRGINIA CONSTITUTION OF 1872

A New Constitution Is Adopted. Not all West Virginians were happy with the new state government. Many in the eastern and southern sections had supported Virginia during the Civil War. More than ten thousand West Virginians served in the Confederate army. For several years they were punished by our state. They were not allowed to vote, to hold office, to teach school, or to practice law.

After a few years most West Virginians thought that ex-Confederates had been punished enough. In 1871 an amendment was added to the constitution that allowed them to vote. In the next election, many former Confederates won public offices. These new officials did not like the Constitution of 1863. They wanted to replace it with one like Virginia's.

The legislature of 1871 passed an act calling for a constitutional convention. The voters of the state approved and elected seventy-eight delegates to write a new constitution. The delegates met in Charleston early in 1872. The voters approved their work in August. The *Constitution of 1872* has lasted to this day.

Changes Made by the Constitution of 1872. Those who wrote the Constitution of 1872 were *conservatives*. They wanted to go back to the system of government in Virginia. They wanted state government to be weak and not very active.

The Constitution of 1872 set up a weak and divided executive branch. The governor's term was lengthened to four years. However, a governor could not serve more than one term *consecutively* (in a row).

The governor shared executive power with several other officials. These included the secretary of state, attorney general, treasurer, auditor, and the superintendent of free schools. The governor could not propose the state budget or appoint state workers by himself. He shared these powers with the other executive officers. The division of executive power made it hard for the governor to bring about change.

The new constitution also made it difficult for the legislature to do much. The legislature met for only forty-five days every other year. Legislators had little time to pass laws that might lead to change.

The Constitution of 1872 removed several features of the state's first constitution. Its authors ended the township system of local government. They preferred the county system used in Virginia and other southern states.

fig. 227

Inauguration of Arthur Boreman, the first governor of West Virginia, as sketched by Joseph H. Diss Debar

The Bill of Rights. A major part of our state constitution is the Bill of Rights. We learned that the federal Bill of Rights is made up of the first ten amendments to the Constitution of the United States. They were added to the Constitution in 1791. The West Virginia Bill of Rights was not added after the constitution was written. It was included in the Constitution of 1872 as Article III.

The Constitution of 1872 gives all citizens of West Virginia a great many rights and freedoms. They include freedom to enjoy liberty and to own property. All people must be treated fairly by the courts and are guaranteed a trial by jury if accused of a serious crime. All are free from unreasonable searches of their homes and belongings by the police. No one can be forced to take an oath of political or religious loyalty in West Virginia. All persons have the freedom to worship or not to worship as they please. We may also assemble peaceably to state opinions or complaints. No laws may limit freedom of speech or freedom of the press.

The West Virginia Bill of Rights is quite long. A short version is found in this section. You will find that we have many other rights in addition to the ones mentioned.

REVIEW OF SECTION THREE:
1. What people were unhappy with the Constitution of 1863?
2. Why was a new state constitution written in 1872?
3. What important changes in state and local government were made by the Constitution of 1872?
4. Name five rights or freedoms included in the West Virginia Bill of Rights.

fig. 228
Pendleton County Confederate veterans: Ben, Ike, and George Hammer

THE WEST VIRGINIA

Article III of the Constitution of 1872 is entitled the Bill of Rights. The list below is a shortened version of the rights guaranteed to you in the state constitution.

1. All men are free and independent and have certain rights, namely: the enjoyment of life and liberty, the right to acquire property, and the right to pursue and obtain happiness and safety.

2. All power is vested in the people, and *magistrates* [public officials] are their trustees and servants.

3. Government is instituted for the common benefit, protection, and security of the people, nation, or community. When any government shall be found inadequate or contrary to these purposes, a majority of the community has a right to perform, alter, or abolish it.

4. The privilege of the *writ of habeas corpus* [an appeal for release from arrest if there is no incriminating evidence] shall not be suspended. No person shall be held for. . . (a) serious crime unless *indicted* [in-dīt'-ed] by a grand jury. No *bill of attainder* [a legislative act declaring a person guilty without trial], or ex post facto law [a law that applies to a time before the law was passed], or law impairing the obligation of a contract, shall be passed.

5. Excessive bail shall not be required, nor excessive fines imposed, nor cruel and unusual punishment inflicted. Penalties shall be proportional to the offense committed. No person shall be forced to leave the State for any offense committed within the State; nor shall any person in a criminal case be forced to witness against himself, or be twice put in *jeopardy* [jep'ar-dee—danger] for the same offense.

6. Unreasonable searches and seizures are prohibited. No *warrant* [authorization] may be issued except upon probable cause supported by an oath and a description of the place to be searched or the thing to be seized.

7. The freedom of speech and press are guaranteed. However, the legislature may restrain the publication and sale of obscene materials and provide for the punishment of *libel* [a statement that damages a person] and defamation of character.

8. In prosecutions and civil suits for libel the verdict shall be for the defendant if the jury decides that the matter charged as libelous is true, and was published with good motives, and for justifiable ends.

BILL OF RIGHTS

9. Private property shall not be taken or damaged without just compensation.

10. No person shall be deprived of life, liberty, or property, without due process of law, and the judgment of his peers.

11. No religious or political test oath shall be required as a *prerequisite* [requirement] or qualification to vote, serve as a juror, sue, plead, appeal, or pursue any profession of employment.

12. The military shall be subordinate to the civil power; and no citizen unless engaged in the military service of the State, shall be tried or punished by any military court for any offense. No soldier shall, in time of peace, be quartered in any house, without consent of the owner; nor in time of war, except in the manner prescribed by law.

13. In suits of law, where the value in controversy exceeds twenty dollars, the right of trial by jury, if requested by either party, shall be preserved; and in such suit in a court of limited jurisdiction a jury shall consist of six persons.

14. Trials of crimes, unless herein otherwise provided, shall be a jury of twelve men [and women], public, without unreasonable delay, and in the county where the alleged offense was committed, unless upon petition of the accused, and for good cause shown, it is removed to some other county. The accused shall be fully informed of the charges against him, and be confronted with the witnesses against him, and shall have the assistance of counsel, and a reasonable time to prepare for his defense, and a compulsory process for obtaining witnesses in his favor.

15. Religious freedom is guaranteed.

16. The right to assemble in a peaceable manner is guaranteed.

17. The courts of the State are open to all and justice shall be administered without sale, denial, or delay.

18. No conviction shall work corruption of blood or forfeiture of estate [no relative shall be damaged by a person's conviction].

19. No hereditary honors or privileges shall ever be granted by this State.

20. Free government and liberty can be preserved only by a firm adherence to justice, moderation, temperance, frugality, and virtue, and by a frequent recurrence to fundamental principles.

21. Regardless of sex all persons, who are otherwise qualified, shall be eligible to serve as petit jurors, as grand jurors, and as coroner's jurors.

SECTION FOUR: THE GROWTH AND DEVELOPMENT OF OUR STATE CONSTITUTION

Amending the Constitution. The authors of our state constitution were conservative, but they provided ways to bring about change. The Constitution of 1872 may be amended in two ways. An amendment may be proposed either by a constitutional convention or by the legislature. Amendments must be approved by the voters before taking effect.

The authors would have been surprised by the number of amendments approved since 1872. By the end of 1988, the constitution had been amended fifty-eight times. The Constitution of the United States has been amended only twenty-six times.

Why has our state constitution been amended so much? Mainly because conditions have changed a great deal. West Virginia became an industrial state after the constitution was written. The population grew fast, and so did the needs of the people. The need for better schools, roads, and other services caused many West Virginians to want an active government. For several decades after 1872 very few changes were made. During the twentieth century, however, the voters have approved many amendments.

fig. 229
Constitutions, like buildings, are amended as the needs change and the state grows. This amendment is near Huttonsville, WV.

fig. 230
Early inauguration day ceremony

The Amendments. Some amendments to the state constitution have made only minor changes. Others have had a big impact. Examples of minor amendments include changing the date of elections (1884) and legalizing bingo games (1980).

Among the important amendments are those that increased the number of days the legislature meets. The constitution required the legislature to meet for only forty-five days every other year. In 1872 that may have been enough time. However, in the twentieth century our legislature could not take care of its duties in a short session every two years. The length of legislative sessions has been increased several times. Today the legislature meets every year for at least a sixty-day session.

Constitutional amendments have also increased the power of the governor. In 1872 the constitution did not let the governor prepare the state's budget by himself. He had no more control over the budget than such officials as the secretary of state or the attorney general. With the *Modern Budget Amendment* of 1968 the governor gained more control. The governor is now the only executive official who prepares the budget for the legislature to consider.

Another important amendment for West Virginia's governors was passed in 1970. The *Governors Succession Amendment* made it possible for a governor to serve two uninterrupted four-year terms. Before this, a governor could not succeed himself in office. Very often

fig. 231
Memorial Arch, constructed for the state's semicentennial celebration in Wheeling, 1913.

governors could not achieve their goals in only four years. Even when a governor did a good job and was well liked by the people, he could not be re-elected when his term ended.

Several other amendments have produced big changes in West Virginia. Many roads and bridges have been built or improved by amendments passed in 1920, 1928, 1948, 1964, 1968, and 1972. Each of these "better roads" amendments let the state borrow large sums of money to build or repair highways and bridges. The *Tax Limitation Amendment* (1932) cut tax rates on property. As a result, West Virginia collects very little property tax compared to most states. Other amendments have increased funding for education and provided cash bonuses to military veterans.

West Virginia's constitution describes our system of state and local government. It helps protect our rights and freedoms. It also gives us a way to make changes. By using the amendment process, West Virginians have responded to new public needs.

REVIEW OF SECTION FOUR:

1. Who must approve proposed amendments to the state constitution?
2. Why has the state constitution been amended so often?
3. How have the sessions of West Virginia's legislature been affected by constitutional amendments?
4. Describe two constitutional amendments that increased the power of the governor.

REFERENCES:

1. Bice, David A. *A Panorama of West Virginia, II.* Marceline, MO: Walsworth Publishing Co., Inc., 1985: pp. 109–42.
2. Coffey, William E., Carolyn M. Karr, and Frank S. Riddel. *West Virginia Government.* Charleston, WV: Education Foundation, Inc., 1983: pp. 7–13.
3. Doherty, William T. *West Virginia Studies: Our Heritage.* Charleston, WV: Education Foundation, Inc., 1984: pp. 108–23 and 140–53.

fig. 232
*Centennial steam train in
Huntington*

fig. 233
*Centennial queen and princess,
1963*

The Political Process in West Virginia

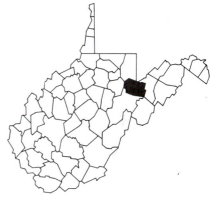

PREVIEW

We have learned that government in West Virginia has changed since the Constitution of 1872 was written. Our state government is better able to meet the needs of our people, thanks to the amendments that have been added. More citizens may participate in government, too. Citizens who are at least eighteen years old may vote and hold public office. They do not have to own property. They may be men or women, black or white. They may hold any political or religious view.

Most Americans agree that democracy is the best type of government. However, a democracy is strong only if people support it. They must know the issues, register, and vote. They may also join interest groups and hold public office.

In Chapter Ten we will answer the following questions:
1. How can West Virginians take part in the political process?
2. How do political parties and interest groups function in West Virginia?
3. How do we elect state and local officials in West Virginia?
4. How do West Virginians register and vote?

Pronounce and discuss the meanings of the following words found in this chapter. You may need to use a dictionary.

apathy	independents
Chamber of Commerce	polling place
computation	public relations
executive committee	publicize
file for office	rallies

fig. 234, left and above
Tucker County Courthouse in Parsons

fig. 235
*Governor's race campaign
memorabilia*

SECTION ONE: THE POLITICAL PARTIES OF WEST VIRGINIA

Our Two-Party System. As you have learned, the United States has a two-party system. The majority of voters belong to either the Republican or the Democratic parties. Most elected officials belong to one of the two major parties.

In West Virginia we also have a two-party system. The major parties play a big role in the political process. Most West Virginia voters register as Republicans or Democrats. There are not many independents in our state. That is because independents cannot vote for candidates of a political party in primary elections. In states where independent voters may vote in party primary elections, fewer voters register as Democrats or Republicans.

The Structure of West Virginia Political Parties. The political parties in West Virginia have been formed by the people of our state. Anyone may join a political party and take part in its work. Members choose party leaders in primary elections. In every county there is a Republican and a Democratic executive committee elected by party voters. There are also elected members of district executive committees and the state executive committees. County committees elect a chairman or chair. The state committee of each party also elects a chairman or chair.

West Virginia Political Parties at Work. The Republican and Democratic parties in West Virginia have the same goals as the national political parties. They want to win elections and influence government. Parties try to get good candidates to run for public office. They hold primary elections to nominate candidates. They adopt a platform at a state convention. They raise money for election campaigns. They set up campaign headquarters. They hold public rallies for their candidates. They work in many ways to help their nominees win office.

In election campaigns the parties recruit volunteers, including young people, to help out. Volunteers may hand out campaign materials, telephone party members, and help register voters. On election day party workers often take people who need transportation to a polling place.

The parties in West Virginia also have important public duties. For example, party executive committees appoint the people who conduct elections. These persons are called election commissioners.

If no candidate is nominated for an office in a primary election, party executive committee chairmen or chairs may name candidates for the general election. If an elected official dies or resigns from office, the executive committee of his or her party recommends up to three replacements to the governor, who then selects one.

The state political parties also work in the West Virginia legislature. In both the House of Delegates and the Senate, there are party organizations. Shortly before a new legislature meets, the party members of each house choose their leaders. The majority party selects the people who will be speaker of the House and president of the Senate.

REVIEW OF SECTION ONE:

1. Why are most voters in West Virginia Republicans or Democrats rather than independents?
2. What officials lead the major parties in West Virginia?
3. What are three public duties of the political parties in West Virginia?

fig. 236

Can you guess the party affiliation of this gubernatorial candidate?

SECTION TWO: POLITICAL INTEREST GROUPS IN WEST VIRGINIA

fig. 237
March 1989 began an eleven-month coal strike against the Pittston Coal Company with a sixty-mile march to the West Virginia Capitol by the miners and their families.

How Interest Groups Differ from Parties. The political parties of West Virginia have many thousands of members. We know that parties try to elect their members to office. They seek to win control of governments. Political parties also try to get laws passed that support the beliefs of their members.

In addition to joining political parties, many West Virginians take part in *political interest groups.* We read in Chapter Four that interest groups are sometimes called *pressure groups.* They try to influence what government does. They back candidates who agree with their aims. They use the media to *publicize* their cause. They pressure public officials to support them.

Interest groups are not as large as political parties. Some may have only a few active members. Others could have thousands of members in West Virginia but not as many members as the major political parties. Some interest groups in our state represent businesses or labor unions. Some want to protect the environment or help consumers. There are hundreds of interest groups concerned about public issues.

Unlike a political party, an interest group does not have many goals. It concentrates on a few concerns. It may be a *single-issue pressure group.* This means that it works on only one issue. Several years ago a small group of citizens in Lewis County, West Virginia, formed a group for one purpose. They tried to stop construction of the Stonewall Jackson Dam. They worked hard, but other people favored the dam, and the federal government has built it.

Types of Interest Groups in West Virginia. There are several hundred interest groups in West Virginia. Some of them are part of a national group. The National Rifle Association and Common Cause are two of these. Each has members in West Virginia. These members sometimes work to help their groups. They might hold public meetings in their communities. They might try to convince public officials to support their goals.

Many national interest groups have local chapters in West Virginia. These local groups have officers elected by members living in the state. For example, in America many teachers belong to the National Education Association. In West Virginia the members of the NEA also belong to the West Virginia Education Association. The WVEA elects its officers and employs lobbyists. Its members support the national aims of the NEA and also the state goals of the WVEA.

Other interest groups are entirely local. West Virginians sometimes unite on an issue that affects only the people in our state. The citizens of Lewis County who fought the Stonewall Jackson Dam were a local group. They were not part of a national organization.

Interest groups in West Virginia and other states are of several different types. One type includes business and government groups. Another type is a group of employees or professionals in the same line of work. A third kind is a "citizen interest group." It is made up of volunteers who agree on one or more public issues. They do not represent a business or a group of workers.

Two of our most important business groups are the West Virginia Chamber of Commerce and the West Virginia Coal Association. The Chamber of Commerce has members from businesses of all kinds. The West Virginia Coal Association includes representatives of the coal industry in our state. An interest group for governments is the West Virginia Municipal League. Officials from city governments belong to this group. They work for laws to benefit cities and towns.

fig. 238
An eleven day strike by schoolteachers was prompted in March, 1990 when election promises of a pay raise were denied, causing West Virginia teachers to remain in 49th place in the nation for salaries.

fig. 239
A special interest group that should concern students

fig. 240
*This souvenir shows who some of
your grandmothers might have
supported in the 1950s.*

fig. 241
Special Interest Group

There are several interest groups that support the welfare of workers. The largest is the West Virginia Federation of Labor. It is the state organization of the American Federation of Labor–Congress of Industrial Organizations (AFL–CIO), a national federation of many labor unions. Like certain business interest groups, the Federation helps candidates who will support their goals. The Federation also employs lobbyists to work in Charleston when the legislature meets.

The United Mine Workers of America (UMWA) is another important workers' interest group in West Virginia. The UMWA is a union that does not belong to the West Virginia Federation of Labor. Many of its objectives, however, are similar to those of other labor unions.

The citizen interest groups support many different causes. Some may support laws to protect animals. Others want to preserve the wilderness. The League of Women Voters of West Virginia, founded in 1943, is interested in good government. League members work without pay to register voters, organize candidates' debates, and encourage honest elections. Women founded the League, but today men may also join.

Some interest groups in our state have many members and much money. They can hire a staff and pay for lobbyists and expensive publicity. Others are small and depend on the work of unpaid volunteers. All of them are groups of West Virginia citizens who take part in the political process.

Lobbyists in West Virginia. Many of the political interest groups in our state hire lobbyists. Lobbyists work with government officials for the groups that hire them. They supply information. They try to persuade legislators to pass certain laws or to defeat others. They often help legislators write bills. They stay in contact with the executive branch, too. The executive branch enforces laws. Lobbyists may try to influence how a law will be enforced.

In a recent legislative session, more than two hundred lobbyists registered with the Senate Clerk. These lobbyists worked for interest groups or for corporations. Many of them represented more than one group or company. One lobbyist worked for seven.

What kind of people are lobbyists? They may be officers of a business or labor group. They may be members of a volunteer citizens' group. They may be lawyers who work on legal matters.

They may be employees of a company who work in public relations. Several lobbyists are former legislators. They are hired as lobbyists because they know members of the legislature and they know how the legislature works.

fig. 242
Getting in touch with the voters

REVIEW OF SECTION TWO:

1. What are some major differences between political parties and political interest groups?
2. Name an interest group that represents a business association, one that represents a workers' group, and one that represents citizen volunteers interested in a public issue.
3. What do lobbyists in West Virginia do?
4. What kind of West Virginians are lobbyists?

SECTION THREE: WEST VIRGINIA STATE AND LOCAL ELECTIONS

State Primary Elections. Political parties and interest groups provide us with two ways to take part in our democratic political process. However, elections offer citizens the most important way to participate. Therefore, all West Virginians should know how elections are organized and conducted in our state.

In a primary election, voters elect party nominees for political offices. Candidates for West Virginia's seats in Congress and all state and county offices are selected by the two major parties in the West Virginia primary election. This is done before a general election. In the general election, voters decide which party's candidates win the various offices.

fig. 243
Political rivalry

In West Virginia, primary elections take place several months before general elections. They are held in every even-numbered year on the second Tuesday of May.

The major political parties play a big role in West Virginia primary elections. Only members of the political party may vote for its candidates in the primary election. For this reason we call ours *closed primary elections.* They are closed to independents or to members of another party.

On primary election day in West Virginia, voters also elect candidates to some *nonpartisan* offices. This means that the candidates do not represent a political party. The most important nonpartisan office in many primary elections is member of the county school board. All registered voters, even independents, may vote in nonpartisan elections.

fig. 244
*Red, white, and blue in the breeze in
Gallipolis Ferry, WV*

Party officers are also elected in the primary election. These include members of county, district, and state executive committees. Only registered party members may vote in these races.

Thus, there are five elections on primary election day. Two are for choosing nominees of the major parties. A third is to elect nonpartisan candidates. The fourth and fifth are to elect officials of the Republican and Democratic parties.

Running for Elective Office. A candidate must *file* to run for election. This involves filling out a form and paying a fee. The fee is small for most offices. It is higher for statewide offices. The filing fee for the governor's race is $720. A candidate for a party's county executive committee pays only one dollar.

Candidates for all federal offices must file with the secretary of state. Candidates for any state office voted on by the people of more than one county must also file with the secretary of state. This includes candidates for state executive offices and the Supreme Court of Appeals and most of the people running for the state legislature.

Candidates for all county offices are required to file with the circuit clerk of the county. Candidates for the state legislature who will be selected by the people of only one county also file with the circuit clerk.

West Virginia's municipalities (cities and towns) have elected governments, too. Candidates for muncipal offices file with the municipal clerk.

A candidate for a federal, state, county, or party office must file at least ninety-three days before the primary election. This gives election officials time to prepare the ballot. Time limits on filing for municipal office differ from city to city.

State General Elections. General elections are held in West Virginia and all other states on the Tuesday following the first Monday of November of every even-numbered year. In the general election, all registered voters may vote for any candidate in each race. An independent may vote for a Democrat, a Republican, or an independent. Democrats and Republicans have the same choice.

Some people vote for a "*straight ticket.*" This means that they vote for all of the Democrats or all of the Republicans on the general election ballot. However, most voters vote for at least some candidates of both major parties.

As soon as the polls close on election day, election officers begin reporting the returns. Candidates gather at the county clerk's office or at campaign headquarters to wait for news. Many voters are also anxious to learn who won. Before midnight most of the votes are counted and the winners are declared.

Other Elections in West Virginia. We have some other elections in West Virginia besides the state primary and general elections. Municipalities often conduct separate elections for their officials. In these elections, residents of a town or city vote for members of city council and sometimes the mayor.

There are also statewide special elections. When an amendment to the constitution of West Virginia is proposed, the people must vote on it. Sometimes amendments are voted on in special elections rather than the general election.

fig. 245

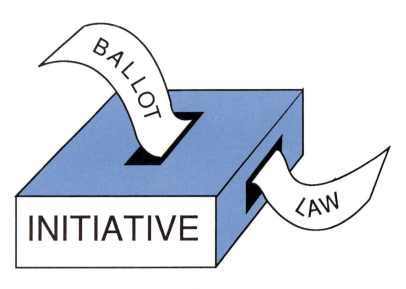

fig. 246

Initiative, Referendum, and Recall. In some states voters have an opportunity to do much more than elect state and local officials. Around 1900 the people of several states amended their constitutions so voters would have more power. They wanted to play a more direct part in passing or rejecting laws. They also wanted to be able to remove from office elected officials who did not carry out their duties properly. Today, the voters of a sizeable number of states have these powers which are known as *initiative, referendum,* and *recall.* West Virginia's constitution, however, does not provide for initiative or recall and requires the use of the referendum only in special cases.

Let us look at each of these three powers in more detail. The *initiative* is a process which allows voters to initiate, or propose, amendments to their state constitutions or new laws. Seventeen states permit voters to initiate constitutional amendments while 21 allow them to propose laws. In order for voters to initiate an amendment or law a certain number of them must sign a petition that describes the proposal. The number of required signatures varies from state to state.

In some states laws proposed by the voters are then sent to the legislature. The legislature may approve the law. However, if the legislature rejects the proposal, the people have an opportunity to vote on it in the next election. They can pass the law despite the legislature's opposition. Proposed amendments to state constitutions are always voted on by the people.

Most states that have the initiative do not send proposed laws to the legislature. They go directly to the voters for approval or rejection.

In almost every state, including West Virginia, certain acts of the legislature or local governments must be approved by the voters before they can go into effect. An election in which the people vote on these acts is called a *referendum*. In West Virginia, for example constitutional amendments proposed by the legislature and property tax increases proposed by local governments must have the approval of the voters. The voters of some states, however, have even more opportunities to use the referendum.

fig. 247

In 24 states voters may require that any act of the legislature be submitted to a popular vote. In other words, this type of referendum gives voters a chance to veto any bill passed by the legislature. A referendum on a legislative act is also brought about by a petition signed by a certain number of voters. The referendum is usually part of a general election.

Another power of voters in a few states is *recall*. Recall is a process by which voters can remove an elected official from office. Voters have this power in only 14 states. Once again the first step is to prepare a petition which must be signed by a certain number of voters. If enough signatures are obtained, a special election is then held. The voters decide whether or not the official in question should be removed from office.

Some people in West Virginia feel that the voters of our state should have the power to use the initiative, referendum, and recall. They argue that better laws and more responsible public officials would be the result. Other people disagree. They believe that it is the responsibility of our elected legislators to make our laws and to remove public officials who do a poor job.

REVIEW OF SECTION THREE:

1. When are primary and general elections held in West Virginia? In what years during the rest of this century will these elections be held?
2. What is the difference between a primary election and a general election?
3. What is a nonpartisan office?
4. Who may run for political office in West Virginia?
5. What powers do the initiative, referendum, and recall give to voters?

SECTION FOUR: VOTING IN WEST VIRGINIA

The Importance of Voting. Americans love their country and their state. We enjoy many rights and freedom in our democracy. Of course, a democracy is strong only if the people support it and take part in its public life. One basic duty of every citizen is to register and vote. If we don't vote, others will decide things for us.

In the United States, too many people don't take part in elections. In most presidential elections only a little more than half of all citizens old enough to vote cast a ballot. Young Americans between the ages of eighteen and thirty vote in even smaller numbers. In many other democratic countries voter turnout is higher. In France and Spain, for example, more than 80 percent of all adults vote. The figures on voter turnout refer to the percentage of adult citizens who vote—not to the percentage of registered voters who cast a ballot.

There are many reasons for voter apathy in the United States. Some voters believe that their vote won't make a difference. Others don't learn about the issues or the candidates. Some believe that it doesn't matter who wins. For some, it is too much trouble to register.

The nonvoters are wrong. Voting does make a difference. Elections are sometimes decided by only a few votes. Citizens who don't vote give up their chance to take part in making important decisions. They are failing to carry out an important duty of all citizens in a democracy.

fig. 248
Television has become the new way of getting candidates' messages out to large numbers of voters.

fig. 249
The county clerk registers voters.

fig. 250
A voter's registration card must be presented at the polls when going to vote.

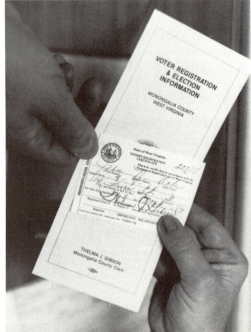

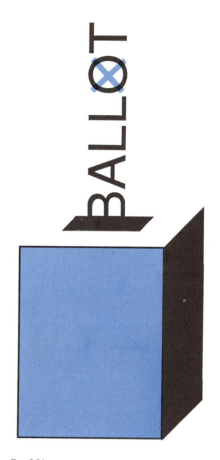

Registering to Vote. Some people don't vote because they don't bother to register. In 1988 almost one in three adults in West Virginia were not registered. Therefore, they could not vote.

Registration is needed to keep elections honest. One has to register at least four weeks before a primary or general election. Only citizens can vote. They must vote in the *precinct* (voting district) where they live. This is a way to make sure that only state residents vote in our elections. It also prevents people from voting at more than one polling place.

Once we register, we may vote. There are two reasons why we might have to register again. First, we must register again if we move to a new address. Second, if we don't vote in at least one primary or general election during a four-year period, our names are removed from the register.

Potential voters register at the county courthouse in the office of the county clerk. There one fills out a form with his or her name and address. The clerk assigns each voter to a precinct where the voter lives. The voter gets a registration card with the precinct number written on it.

The law has been changed in recent years to make registration easier. Now a voter may register by mail. During election campaigns, volunteers set up tables at many public places where people may register.

fig. 251
In West Virginia, most voters mark a paper ballot in the privacy of a voting booth.

fig. 252
Ballots are folded and put in a ballot box to be counted by poll workers after the polls close.

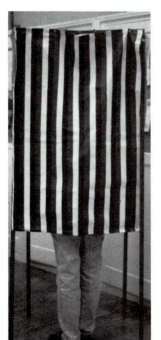

POLLING PLACE

POLLS OPEN 6:30 A. M. - CLOSE 7:30 P. M.

Precinct No. 4   District

How to Vote. On election day in West Virginia, the polling places in every precinct open at 6:30 A.M. Registered voters may cast a ballot at any time during the day. At 7:30 P.M. the polls close.

Voters can prepare to vote several days before the election. An official ballot is printed in newspapers that shows the names and parties of all candidates. The political parties also give out sample ballots for voters to study.

On election day a voter goes to the polling place in his or her precinct. This is usually set up in a school, a church, or a community center. The voter gives his name and address to an election commissioner at a table. The voter signs a slip of paper and is given a ballot.

In large counties voting is done by a simple machine in a small voting booth. It is called the "punch card machine." A card is inserted into a slot. The voter punches holes in the card beside the names of candidates. With each punch the vote is recorded electronically. This machine is accurate. It allows for very rapid computation of votes at the end of the day.

A few counties use larger "lever machines." On these machines voters turn a lever beside the names of candidates they choose. Most of the smaller counties of West Virginia use paper ballots. Voters mark an "x" beside the names of candidates. Paper ballots must be counted by hand, but this is not too difficult in a small county. In the 1988 election, twenty-nine counties used paper ballots. Twenty-two used punch card machines, and four used lever machines.

If a voter will be away from home on election day, it is possible to vote by *absentee ballot*. To do so, a voter applies for an absentee ballot from the clerk of the circuit court in his or her county. The ballot is marked and sealed in an envelope. It will be opened and counted at the end of election day.

fig. 253
Party symbols

REVIEW OF SECTION FOUR:

1. Why is it important to vote in a democracy?
2. How does one register to vote in West Virginia?
3. Where does a registered voter vote on election day?
4. How can a voter cast a ballot if he or she will be away from home on election day?

REFERENCES:

1. Coffey, William E., Carolyn M. Karr, and Frank S. Riddel. *West Virginia Government.* Charleston, WV: Education Foundation, Inc., 1983: pp. 14–24.
2. Davis, Claude J., et al. *West Virginia State and Local Government.* Morgantown, WV: Bureau for Government Research, 1963: pp. 59–78.
3. Hechler, Ken. *Running for Office, 1988.* Charleston, WV: Office of the Secretary of State, 1987.
4. Lambert, Oscar D. *West Virginia and Its Government.* Boston: D.C. Heath and Co., 1951: pp. 187–208.

fig. 254
A sample ballot is published in local newspapers before each election.

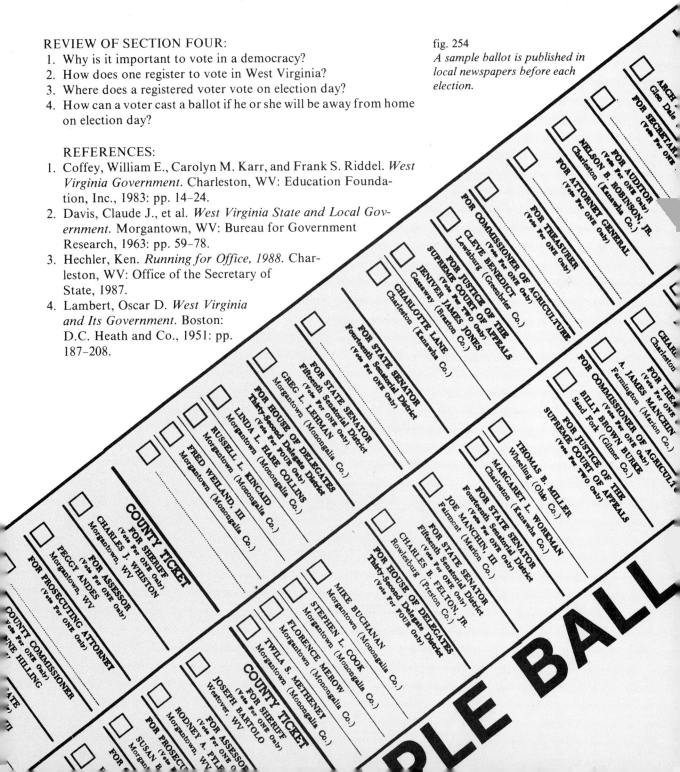

The West Virginia Legislature

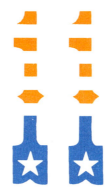

PREVIEW

In Chapter Three we learned about our federal system of government. We learned that the Constitution of the United States divides power between the federal government and the state governments. Many of the laws that affect us are federal laws. Many of the services we have come from the federal government. However, we also live under state laws, and we receive many services from our state government.

State governments are generally organized in the same way as our federal government. There are three branches of government, each with separate powers and duties. We will begin our study of West Virginia's government by looking at the state legislature.

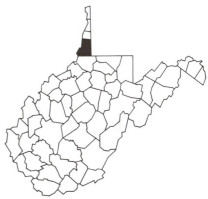

In Chapter Eleven we will answer these questions:
1. How many members are there in the House of Delegates and in the Senate?
2. What determines the number of members each district has in the House of Delegates and in the Senate?
3. Who are the leaders of the two houses? How are they selected?
4. What qualifications must be met by delegates and senators?
5. Who are the people who serve in the legislature?
6. What are the functions of the legislature?
7. How does a bill become a law in West Virginia?

Pronounce and discuss the meanings of the following words found in this chapter. You may need to use a dictionary.

appointee	controversial
architect	data
chambers	ineligible
chandelier	podiums
compensation	turnovers

fig. 255, left and above
Marshall County Courthouse in Moundsville

fig. 256
The United States and West Virginia both have a bicameral (or two-house) legislature.

SECTION ONE: THE STRUCTURE OF THE WEST VIRGINIA LEGISLATURE

The federal legislature, Congress, is *bicameral.* It has two houses: the Senate and the House of Representatives. Forty-nine states also have bicameral legislatures. Only Nebraska has a unicameral, or single house, legislature. In West Virginia, the bicameral legislature consists of the *House of Delegates* and the *Senate.*

The House of Delegates. The size of state legislatures varies a great deal. State senates vary from seventeen to sixty-seven members. The lower houses in state legislatures, such as our House of Delegates, range from thirty-five to four hundred members. The West Virginia Constitution of 1872 set up a House of Delegates with sixty-five members. As the state grew, more delegates were added. In 1964 the legislature passed a law fixing the number in the House at one hundred.

West Virginia has forty *delegate districts.* Each district elects at least one member of the House of Delegates. Some districts have several delegates. The number elected by each depends on the district's

fig. 257

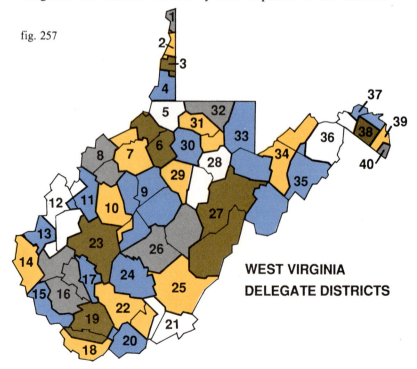

WEST VIRGINIA DELEGATE DISTRICTS

population. Look at a map for the data on delegate districts. Notice that the districts containing West Virginia's largest cities have the most delegates.

The legislature uses population figures from the United States census to decide how many delegates each district will have. Every ten years it must look at the census figures and see that each district receives a fair number of delegates.

The Senate. The West Virginia Senate is much smaller than the House of Delegates. In 1872 the Senate had only twenty-four members. The 1964 law that set the number of delegates at one hundred also determined the number of senators to be thirty-four.

West Virginia is divided into seventeen *senatorial districts*. Each elects two senators. Look at a map for the data on senatorial districts. Districts vary greatly in size. Some are made up of several counties and are very large. Others contain only one county and part of a second county. Kanawha County makes up two senatorial districts by itself. This occurs because each district must have about the same number of people. Senatorial districts may have to be redrawn each time the United States census is taken.

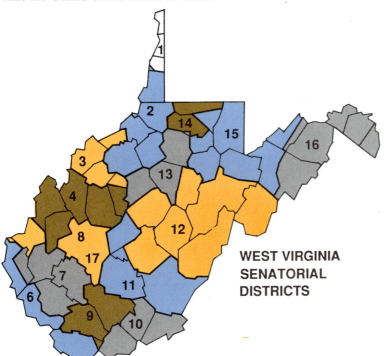

WEST VIRGINIA SENATORIAL DISTRICTS

fig. 258

fig. 259
West Virginia Legislature

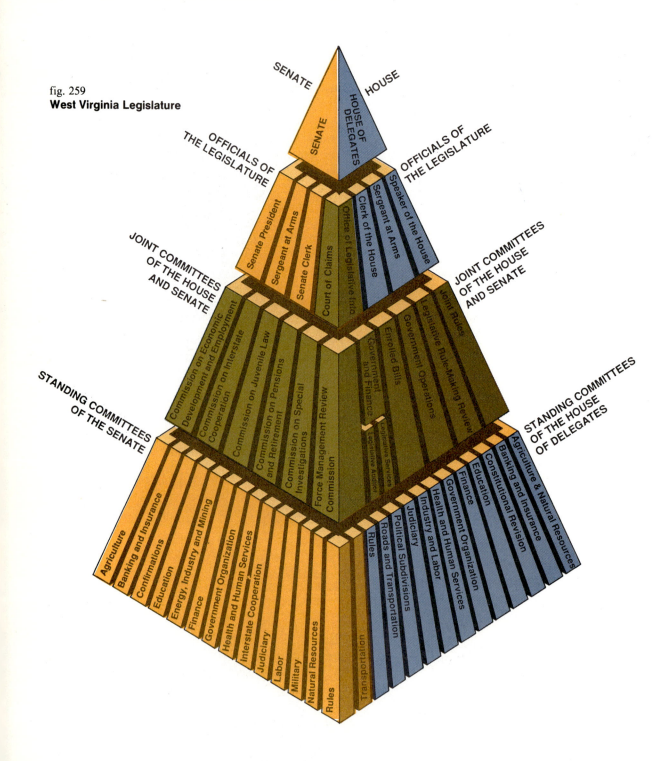

Legislative Officers. Our state legislature is organized much like Congress. Each house of the legislature has a presiding officer. There are majority and minority leaders, party whips, and a clerk.

Most important are the presiding officers—the *speaker of the House of Delegates* and the *president of the Senate.* They are elected on the first day of the legislative session in odd-numbered years by each house. The majority party in each house actually selects its presiding officers during the party caucus before the session begins. Both the speaker and the president serve for two years.

The minority party selects its leaders and whips during its party caucus. However, the presiding officers appoint the majority party's leaders and whips.

The presiding officers of the House and Senate have the power to appoint members of committees. They also choose committee chairmen. They decide which committee will consider a bill. The presiding officers also lead the sessions of the two houses. This gives them the power to decide how a bill will be handled. They can help pass bills they favor and defeat those they oppose.

fig. 260
Do you suppose the detail on the outside of this government building is indicative of activity on the inside?

Legislative Committees. Like Congress, the state legislature does most of its work in committees. Many bills are introduced in every session of the legislature. A member cannot study all bills. The House and the Senate use committees to consider bills. Each house has several *standing committees,* listed on the chart in this section. Each standing committee is responsible for a special subject. Bills introduced are sent to the proper standing committee. For example, a bill to change the courts would go to the Judiciary Committee. That committee would recommend what to do with it.

Like Congress, the state legislature has other types of committees. *Select committees* are sometimes formed to deal with special problems. Their members are appointed by the speaker of the House or the president of the Senate. These committees recommend how the legislature should deal with the problems. When they complete their work, they are disbanded.

The legislature also has *joint committees* with members from both houses. They deal with matters on which both houses must work together. The joint committees are also shown on the chart.

Conference committees are appointed by the speaker and the president when the two houses pass different versions of the same bill. Each house has members on a conference committee. The committee must agree on the same version before a bill can be sent to the governor.

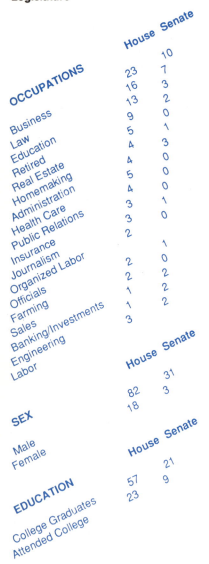

fig. 261
Profile of the West Virginia Legislature

REVIEW OF SECTION ONE:

1. How many members are there in the House of Delegates and in the Senate?
2. What is a delegate district and a senatorial district?
3. What determines the number of delegates or senators elected in each district?
4. Who are the presiding officers of the two houses, and how are they selected?
5. What are the functions of the following types of legislative committees: standing committees, select committees, joint committees, and conference committees?

SECTION TWO: OTHER FACTS ABOUT THE LEGISLATURE

Terms. State senators serve four-year terms. Their terms are fixed so that half of the Senate is elected every two years. Delegates are elected only for two-year terms. Therefore, the entire House of Delegates is chosen every two years in the general election. There is no limit on the number of terms a legislator may serve.

Qualifications. The qualifications for a legislator are set by the state constitution. Legislators must be citizens who are eligible to vote. They must have lived in their districts for at least a year before their election. Senators must be at least twenty-five years of age. Delegates may be elected at age eighteen. If a person holds another public office or a state job, he or she may not serve in the legislature. A person convicted of a serious crime is also ineligible.

Salaries. The salaries of legislators in most states have been quite low until recently. For many years most Americans felt it was a civic duty and an honor to serve as a legislator. They did not believe legislators should receive much pay. Today, however, legislators in many large states work full time. In states such as California and New York the legislature meets most of the year. Those states pay their legislators well. In West Virginia legislators are paid a salary and substantial fringe benefits for their service.

In most small states like West Virginia, legislators are still paid small salaries. Our legislators spend only part of their time on public business. Most have other jobs when the legislature is not in session. In 1988 senators and delegates in West Virginia were paid $6,500.00 per year plus expenses. They receive more for a special session.

The legislature sets the salary of its members. However, the salary may not exceed the recommendation of the *Citizens Legislative Compensation Commission.* This is a commission made up of seven citizens appointed by the governor.

Makeup of the Legislature. Who are the people who serve in the West Virginia legislature? They come from many occupations. People in business, lawyers, and educators are the most numerous. It is difficult to serve in the legislature, because most people are not able to leave their jobs for part of the year. That explains why many legislators are self-employed.

Legislators are usually well educated. More than half of the members of the 1988 legislature were college graduates. The majority of members were between thirty and fifty years of age. More and more women are serving in the West Virginia legislature. In the 1988 session there were three women in the Senate and eighteen in the House.

Most legislators are members of Protestant churches, and most were born in small towns in West Virginia. There is a rapid turnover in membership in the legislature. In other words, much of the membership changes from session to session. Most delegates serve no more than three terms, and most senators serve only two terms.

Sessions. *Regular sessions* of the legislature begin in January of each year. In West Virginia a regular session lasts only sixty days. In many states they are longer. In a few states, such as Kentucky, the legislature meets only every other year.

The legislature's work is supposed to be finished during the regular session. When that is not possible, it may be necessary to extend the regular session. The governor may extend the session if the state budget is not ready. If the governor calls for an *extended session,* only work on the budget can be done. This has happened several times.

The legislature can also extend the regular session if two-thirds of its members vote to do so. When this happens, the legislature can take up any matter. The legislature rarely votes to extend the session.

The governor may also call the legislature into session at any time if there is a serious problem. This is known as a *special session.* The governor must call a special session if three-fifths of the members make a request in writing. Governors sometimes do call for special sessions, but the legislature rarely does.

AGE DISTRIBUTION

	House	Senate
18-29 years	1	
30-39 years	18	0
40-49 years	39	6
50-59 years	14	10
60 years and up	21	11
Age Unknown	7	3
		4

TERMS SERVED

	House	Senate
One	21	10
Two	25	16
Three	30	4
Four	5	1
Five	10	3
More than Five	9	0

RELIGIOUS PREFERENCE

	House	Senate
Protestant	73	25
Catholic	14	4
Jewish	0	1
None Given	13	4

REVIEW OF SECTION TWO:

1. How long are the terms of senators and delegates?
2. What qualifications must be met by senators and delegates?
3. How are legislative salaries set?
4. What kinds of people are elected to the legislature?
5. How do the following types of legislative sessions differ: regular sessions, extended sessions, and special sessions?

SECTION THREE: FUNCTIONS OF THE LEGISLATURE

Legislative Functions. The chief function of the legislature is to make the state's laws. This is not an easy task. Many of the issues are controversial. For example, should the state execute some criminals? Should public employees have the right to strike? Should the tax on soft drinks be raised?

fig. 262
House chambers

When the legislature deals with such questions, it must consider who will be affected by a new law. Different groups have different views about what laws should be passed. Businesses that sell soft drinks will oppose raising the "pop" tax. Many people do not think that state workers should be allowed to strike. Teachers often favor a tax increase. This would provide more money for their salaries and school improvements. If more money is needed for schools, roads, and other services, who should be taxed?

Conflicting views on public issues make passing laws difficult. Legislators have their own views, but they must try to please the voters. Dozens of pressure groups work to influence them. Usually, many compromises must be made before a law is passed. The public is often unaware of the compromises made in the legislature. Without them, few laws would be made.

Each year the West Virginia legislature passes about two hundred laws. They cover many topics. Some raise or lower taxes. Others provide money for roads, schools, and state parks. Other laws may deal with public health, education, regulation of business, or the sale of liquor. Our state laws affect us every day.

Nonlegislative Functions. In addition to making the state's laws, the legislature has some other major functions. It may propose amendments to the state constitution. It approves many appointments made by the governor. It may remove an official from office. Legislators also try to help the voters.

Proposing Amendments. The West Virginia Constitution can be amended in two ways. The legislature must start the amendment process in both cases. First, a majority of each house may vote to form a constitutional convention. The convention would be elected to consider changes. Its work would be subject to a vote of the people.

Second, the legislature may put an amendment on the ballot. This requires a vote by two-thirds of the members in each house. The voters then must approve or reject the amendment. All fifty-eight amendments to the Constitution of 1872 have been made by the second method.

Approving Appointments. Many of the governor's appointments to the executive branch must be approved. This is the job of the Senate. A majority vote is required to approve an appointee. If the Senate votes "no," the governor must choose someone else for the job.

Where the Legislature Meets. The West Virginia legislature meets in the capital city of the state. Charleston has been the state capital since 1885. Before then the capital was moved several times between Wheeling and Charleston. Charleston was made the permanent capital after citizens of the state voted to put it there.

The building in which the legislature meets is the West Virginia Capitol. It is one of the most beautiful capitol buildings in the United States. It was designed by Cass Gilbert, a famous architect who also designed the United States Supreme Court Building. Work on the capitol began in 1924 and was completed in 1932.

The legislative chambers are the showpieces of the capitol. The House chamber is at the east end and the Senate chamber at the west end. Massive marble columns mark the entrances of the two chambers, which are separated by a large rotunda. A chandelier with ten thousand pieces of crystal hangs from the skylight of each chamber. The desks of the legislators and the podiums of the presiding officers are made of West Virginia black walnut. The walls are made of marble, and the floors are covered with red carpets.

Impeachment and Trial. The legislature may impeach and try any state official for committing crimes or failing to do his or her job. The House of Delegates must impeach, or bring charges against, the official. If a majority of the House votes for impeachment, the accused must resign from office or stand trial in the Senate. The Senate hears the evidence and decides whether the accused is innocent or guilty. A two-thirds vote in the Senate is needed for conviction. A convicted official is removed from office.

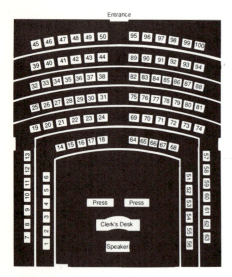

fig. 263
House chambers

fig. 264
Senate chambers

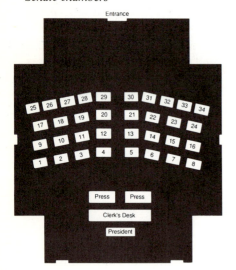

Helping Constituents. Legislators also work for their *constituents,* the people they represent. Many West Virginians rely on their legislators for help. For example, people may want the State Department of Transportation to repair a road or a bridge that they use. They may seek help from a delegate or senator who represents them. Legislators also receive many letters and phone calls from their constituents. Some complain about laws. Others try to influence how a legislator will vote. Constituents are voters, so legislators must try to help them if it is possible.

REVIEW OF SECTION THREE:
1. Why is it difficult for the legislature to pass laws?
2. What are the nonlegislative functions of the legislature?
3. What are the two methods of amending the state constitution?
4. How can state officials be removed from office?

SECTION FOUR:
HOW BILLS BECOME LAWS

Though the legislature has important nonlegislative functions, its major duty is lawmaking. Proposed laws come from many sources. Legislators, the governor, legislative committees, special interest groups, and citizens may suggest new state laws. More than fifteen hundred bills are introduced during each term of the legislature. Only a small number of those bills will become laws. Being able to have a bill passed is difficult. Most bills are killed during the process.

We will look at the process of making bills into laws. The process in West Virginia is similar to the way in which Congress works on federal laws.

HOUSE ACTION ON A BILL

Introducing a Bill. Bills may be introduced in either house. Sometimes the same bill is introduced in both the House and Senate. Usually, a bill begins in only one house. If it passes there, it is sent on to the other.

Before it is introduced, a bill must be drafted into written form. This may be done by a legislator. After a bill has been drafted, it must be introduced by a member of the House. The clerk will give the bill a number such as HB2000. The bill is also given a title. On the next day, the clerk will read the titles of all new bills. As the clerk reads the titles, the speaker assigns them to a standing committee. If, for example, HB2000 is about taxes, it will be sent to the Finance Committee.

Committee Action. Committee members discuss the bill. The committee may hold public hearings. Members of the committee want to hear from people who support or oppose the bill. After studying the bill, the committee must make a decision. It may kill the bill, approve it, amend it, or write a new bill. Most bills approved by committees are amended in some way. Many are changed completely. If the committee approves the bill, it goes back to the whole House.

Action in the House. Most bills sent back to the house by committees are placed on the calendar. The calendar lists bills in the order in which the House will take them up. The bill is then ready for its *first reading* before the House. The clerk simply reads the bill by number and title. The bill is then printed, and every member of the House receives a copy to read and study. The bill is now ready for its *second reading*.

fig. 265

The second reading of a bill is very important. At this stage delegates may offer amendments. Usually, the whole bill is not read aloud by the clerk. However, if two or more members of the House demand it, the entire bill must be read aloud.

Delegates who dislike the bill might offer amendments. Each amendment must be voted on. If a majority of delegates favor an amendment, the bill will be changed. Sometimes, the amendments change a bill completely. This device is often used to "kill" a bill that is opposed by several delegates.

License plates often show your representatives in legislature.

After all proposed amendments have been approved or rejected, the delegates vote again. They decide whether or not the bill should go to its third reading.

The *third reading* of the bill is much like the first two. Unless two or more delegates object, the clerk reads aloud only the number and title. Delegates are now asked to vote on the bill. If a majority votes against the bill, it dies. If a majority supports the bill, it is signed by the clerk and speaker and sent to the Senate.

Senate Action on a Bill. When the bill is received by the Senate, it will be handled much as it was in the House. It will be introduced, given a number and title, and assigned to a standing committee. If the committee approves, it goes back to the full Senate. It will go through three readings. It may be amended before the Senate votes on it. If the bill passes, it is signed by the clerk and the president of the Senate.

Next, three things could happen to the bill. If the Senate passed the House version of the bill, it will be sent to the governor. However, the

fig. 266

HOW A BILL BECOMES A LAW IN WEST VIRGINIA

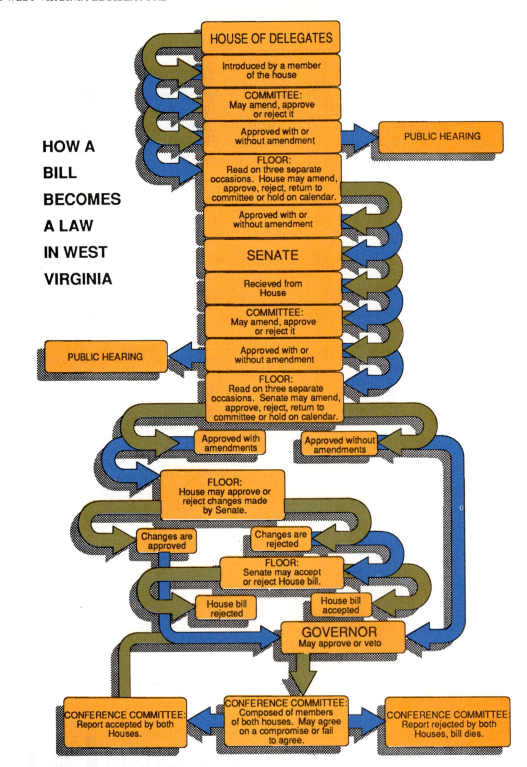

Senate bill will often differ from the House version. When that occurs, the Senate may ask the House to accept its version of the bill. If the House agrees, the bill can be sent to the governor. If the House refuses the Senate bill, a conference committee must work out an agreement.

The Conference Committee. Conference committees are usually made up of three members from each house. The speaker of the House and the president of the Senate each appoint three. The conference committee will work on the bill until a compromise is reached. The compromise bill is then returned to the two houses for approval. It is usually approved.

Action by the Governor. The governor has five days to act on a bill. He may sign the bill into law, veto it, or allow it to become law without his signature. If the governor vetoes the bill, he must explain his reasons. The legislature can override the governor's veto by a majority vote in each house. However, not many bills are passed over the governor's veto.

As we have seen, the process of making laws is slow and difficult. That might keep some good proposals from becoming law. However, it also stops hastily considered and unwise bills. The process also gives citizens a chance to state their views and to influence the laws of our state.

REVIEW OF SECTION FOUR:
1. Where do ideas for new state laws come from?
2. Trace the steps by which a bill becomes a law in West Virginia.
3. Why are conference committees often necessary?
4. What choices does the governor have when he receives a bill that has been passed by the legislature?

REFERENCES:
1. Coffey, William E., Carolyn M. Karr, and Frank S. Riddel. *West Virginia Government.* Charleston, WV: Education Foundation, Inc., 1983: pp. 25–35.
2. Kopp, Donald L., and Eleanor Ringel. *Manual of the Senate and House of Delegates.* Charleston, WV: The West Virginia House of Delegates, 1987.
3. Office of Legislative Information. *The West Virginia Legislature.* Charleston, WV: Office of Legislative Information, 1988.
4. Senate of West Virginia. *The West Virginia Capitol: A Commemorative History.* Charleston, WV: Senate of West Virginia, 1982.

The Governor and the Executive Branch of West Virginia

PREVIEW

After the state legislature makes laws for West Virginia, the executive branch must carry them out. Because of this duty, the executive branch is larger than the legislative branch. It contains more than 150 agencies or departments. It employs thousands of people. It spends most of the state budget. It must enforce thousands of state laws and provide services that West Virginians want from their state government. In this chapter we will study the executive branch of West Virginia's state government.

In Chapter Twelve we will answer these questions:
1. How does West Virginia's executive branch differ from the federal executive branch?
2. Who are the six most important state executive officials?
3. What qualifications must be met by West Virginia's elected executive officials? What are their terms of office?
4. What are the powers and duties of the governor of West Virginia?
5. What are the powers and duties of the other elected executive officials?
6. What are the responsibilities of the administrative and regulatory bodies in the executive branch?

Pronounce and discuss the meanings of the following words found in this chapter. You may need to use a dictionary.

administrative	custodian	utilities
application	dependable	
auditing	implement	
boards	invest	
commissions	pesticides	

fig. 267, above and left
Monongalia County Courthouse in Morgantown

SECTION ONE: THE STRUCTURE OF THE EXECUTIVE BRANCH

The Division of Executive Power. The executive branch of any government has one main task. It implements, or carries out, the laws made by the legislative branch. This is the job of our federal government's executive branch. The same task belongs to the executive branch of our state government. However, West Virginia's executive branch differs from the federal executive branch in one important way.

Where the Governor Lives. The house in which the governor lives is sometimes called the governor's mansion. However, its official name is the West Virginia Executive Mansion. The mansion sits on the capitol grounds and overlooks the Kanawha River. The governor can leave the mansion and be in his office in the capitol in just a few minutes.

The Executive Mansion was built in 1924 and 1925, and has been remodeled on several occasions since then. Work on the mansion and the capitol began about the same time. The three-story mansion is built of brick and has a slate roof. In front is a high porch supported by four large columns. On both sides are one-story porches with balconies on top.

The front door opens into a large reception hall with a black and white marble floor. Twin staircases lead from the hall to the second floor. The main floor also contains a living room, ballroom, state dining room, sitting room, and library. There are eight bedrooms, four baths, and a family room on the second floor. The third floor has two more bedrooms. The mansion is surrounded by enclosed gardens.

The president of the United States is the nation's chief executive. He is very powerful and controls the executive branch. He may appoint and dismiss all workers in the executive departments. Therefore, department heads do as the president wishes.

In West Virginia the governor is the chief executive. Like the president, the governor has many powers. However, he does not have as much control as the president because the five most important executive department heads in West Virginia are elected. The governor does not appoint them, and he cannot fire them.

The secretary of state, auditor, treasurer, commissioner of agriculture, and attorney general direct the major departments of our state government. They may not even be members of the governor's political party. It is difficult for the governor to operate the executive branch as he would like if these officials oppose him politically or philosophically.

The Board of Public Works. Sometimes all of the elected executive officers, plus the state superintendent of schools, hold meetings. This group is called the *Board of Public Works.* Some years ago the board made many decisions, but today this is no longer true. The Board of Public Works now has only one important duty. It determines the value of property owned by utility companies in West Virginia. They decide how much the property is worth for tax purposes.

In addition to the governor and the five elected department heads, the executive branch has many other agencies. We will discuss those in Section Four.

Qualifications and Election. It is not hard to qualify for an elected office in the executive branch. The five department heads are required to be state citizens. The attorney general must be at least twenty-five years old. The governor must be at least thirty years old. He or she must also have lived in West Virginia for at least five years just before election. Many people could meet these legal qualifications, but it is not easy to win an executive office.

To be elected, all candidates must be well known throughout the state. They must have the support of a major political party. Successful candidates must also appeal to a large number of voters and have the money to pay for a campaign.

The governor and the five department heads are elected by the voters of West Virginia. They are chosen in the general election every four years on the Tuesday after the first Monday in November. To have a good chance of being elected, the candidates must win the nomination of a major political party. There are usually several people in both parties who run for these offices. The state primary election is held on the second Tuesday in May so each party may select its candidates.

fig. 268
Governor's mansion

fig. 269
Governor Gaston Caperton

fig. 270
Governor Arch Moore held two successive terms and was later re-elected to a third term.

Terms of Office. All of the elected executive officials, including the governor, serve four-year terms. For many years the governor could not succeed himself. This meant that he could not serve a second consecutive term of office. However, in 1970 the state constitution was amended to allow a governor to serve two consecutive terms. There is no limit on the number of terms the other elected executive officials may serve.

Filling Vacancies. No governor of West Virginia has ever died in office or been removed by the legislature. Only one governor has resigned. Yet, the office could become vacant. If this happened, how would the office be filled?

The state constitution says that a new election must be held if the governor has not been in office three years. If the governor has served at least three years, the president of the Senate would complete the governor's term. Vacancies that occur in any of the other elected executive offices are filled by appointments made by the governor.

Salaries. The salaries of all elected executive officials are set by the legislature. The legislature cannot change those salaries during a term. In 1987 the governor's salary was $72,000 per year. In addition, the governor is provided with a residence, several cars, an airplane, and a helicopter. The salaries of the other elected officials vary. In 1988 they ranged from $43,200 to $50,400 per year.

REVIEW OF SECTION ONE:
1. Why does the governor of West Virginia have little control over some important officials in the executive branch?
2. What qualifications must be met by the elected officials in the state executive branch?
3. What is the term of office of elected executive officials?
4. How are vacancies in the executive branch filled?
5. What is the governor's salary? How are executive salaries determined?

SECTION TWO: THE POWERS AND DUTIES
OF THE GOVERNOR

The governor of West Virginia shares power with five other officials. Even so, the governor is the most important person in the executive branch. We will look at the major powers and duties of the governor so that you will understand the importance of this office.

Chief Executive. The state constitution makes the governor the chief executive officer of West Virginia. He must see that laws passed by the legislature are implemented and enforced, a large task that the governor cannot do alone. The five elected department heads must help the governor carry out state laws. However, many other departments and agencies have been organized to work with the governor.

The governor appoints and dismisses the heads of these departments with the approval of the Senate. The power to appoint and remove is important to the governor. He is responsible for how well the executive branch works. Therefore, he must have dependable people in executive positions.

Another of the governor's duties is to prepare the state budget. Until 1968 the Board of Public Works prepared the budget. The *Modern Budget Amendment* of 1968 gave the governor alone this power. The governor must also see that state money is spent properly.

Legislative Powers. The governor has certain ways to influence the state legislature. The constitution requires him to inform the legislature of conditions in West Virginia and to suggest new laws. The governor does this at the start of each session of the legislature. He delivers the *State of the State Address* to a joint meeting of the House of Delegates and the Senate. In his speech he explains why certain laws should be passed. He also describes the budget that he must submit. Sometimes he asks for higher or lower taxes.

fig. 271, far left
Governor Caperton delivering the State of the State Address

fig. 272
The governor addressing a special interest group

The governor may send messages to the legislature at any time during its session. He often does this when he wants the legislature to work on a particular need or problem.

The governor also has the power to extend regular sessions of the legislature. He can call special sessions to deal with needs or problems. The governor often talks to legislative leaders. He may try to persuade them to support or oppose certain bills.

The governor's most important legislative power is the veto, which stops a bill passed by the legislature from becoming a law. The legislature can override a veto, but this doesn't happen often.

Judicial Powers. The governor has several judicial powers. For example, he may *remit* fines. When a person is convicted of a crime, the court may fine him or her. The governor may reduce or remove the fine if he chooses.

The governor may also grant *reprieves* and *pardons*. A reprieve delays carrying out a court sentence. It gives a convicted person time to appeal the case or to gather new evidence. A pardon frees a person convicted or accused of a crime.

Commander in Chief. The governor is commander in chief of the state militia, the West Virginia National Guard, and appoints its highest officers. He commands the militia in an emergency. For example, when bad floods have hit parts of the state, governors have sent the militia to give help.

Other Powers and Duties. In addition to his other powers and duties, the governor serves on many state boards and commissions. The governor is also the official representative of our state. Therefore, he must perform many ceremonies and appear throughout the state. He also attends many national meetings with other governors or federal officials.

Most governors hold several press conferences each year. At these meetings with reporters the governor states his views on public issues.

fig. 273
National Guard, the state militia

The governor's words are reported to the public by the mass media. He also meets with leaders of his party and may help his party's candidates in election campaigns.

REVIEW OF SECTION TWO:
1. What are the governor's chief executive powers and duties?
2. How does the governor influence the legislature?
3. What judicial powers does the governor have?
4. For what reasons does the governor sometimes use the state militia?

SECTION THREE: THE OTHER ELECTED EXECUTIVE OFFICERS

There are five elected officials in the executive branch in addition to the governor. They direct five important departments of our state government. Each has powers granted by the constitution and state law. Each must enforce certain state laws. As they are elected rather than appointed, the governor has little control over them.

The Secretary of State. The secretary of state is the chief record keeper of West Virginia. He or she is in charge of the state seal, which is placed on all documents issued by the state. All state laws, executive records, and regulations are filed in this office. The secretary also publishes state laws and collects some fees.

fig. 274
Ken Hechler, Secretary of State

The secretary of state is our chief election official. All candidates for state offices must submit an application to the secretary. The secretary sees that voters are properly registered. Sometimes employees of the secretary check lists of voters in county courthouses. They do this to find out if all the people on the list are eligible to vote. The names of voters who have died or moved from the county must be removed from the list. The secretary's staff also observes some polling places to see that elections are fair. After an election the secretary publishes the official results.

fig. 275

The Auditor. The auditor is the official bookkeeper of the state. He or she reviews bills sent to the state. If the bills are correct, the auditor notifies the state treasurer that the bills should be paid. The auditor also keeps track of income and expenditures.

One of the biggest tasks is auditing, or examining, the accounts of all county and state officials who collect money. For example, the sheriff of each county collects taxes. The auditor must check the accounts of all sheriffs to see that they are correct.

The auditor also collects some taxes and fees and keeps records of land that has been sold for taxes. If a landowner does not pay the taxes owed on his or her property, the state may sell the land. This does not happen often, but when it does the auditor must record the sale.

Each year at the end of June, the auditor must give the governor a report on the condition of the state's finances. The report shows the source of all state income of the past year and how it was spent. The report also states how much money is left in the treasury.

The Treasurer. The treasurer is the custodian, or keeper, of state funds. All money collected by state agencies goes through the treasurer's office. There funds are recorded and deposited in banks around the state. When the treasurer receives a bill approved by the auditor, he or she pays it.

The treasurer also keeps a record of items the legislature has voted to fund. He or she then keeps track of the money being spent on each item. If the legislature decides to spend $100,000,000 on roads in a year, the treasurer must see that no more than that is spent.

Another duty is to invest money collected by the state so that it will earn interest. He or she must decide where to invest funds so that the state will earn as much interest as possible.

The Commissioner of Agriculture. The commissioner of agriculture heads a department that helps the state's farmers. The Department of Agriculture sends useful information to farmers about such problems as fighting insects and diseases that harm plants and animals. The department also sets up markets around the state where farmers can sell their products.

The Department of Agriculture helps protect the health of the public. It enforces rules on the safe use of fertilizers and pesticides. It also regulates the handling of farm products to make sure that sanitary procedures are followed.

fig. 276
Tent caterpillars are one of the more destructive pests in West Virginia and one which the Commissioner of Agriculture must attempt to control.

The Attorney General. The attorney general is the chief law enforcement officer of the state. It is the attorney general's duty to give legal advice to all state officials. He or she also acts as the state's lawyer in court cases involving the state government. The attorney general is often an important political figure in West Virginia. Several men who have held the office later became governor.

Should Executive Officials Be Elected? Some people think that West Virginia's executive officials should be appointed by the governor rather than elected. They argue that the offices of auditor, treasurer, and attorney general require people with special training. It is possible for anyone to be elected to these offices regardless of education and experience. Some also think that the governor could manage the state better if all executive officials were responsible to him.

fig. 277
In 1989, voters were asked to decide whether or not to keep three executive positions. In the same year the treasurer was nearly impeached when he admitted he didn't fully understand the reports in his department and allowed 270 million dollars to be lost from the treasury through poor investments.

Partly cloudy with highs in the upper 50s. Chance of rain increases tonight with lows near 40. Details on Page 2A.

PARTLY CLOUDY

Valley ed
Charlest

the Charleston Gazette

The State Newspaper — Our 117th Year

Thursday
March 23, 1989

Impeachment charges approved 19-6

By Patty Vandergrift
STAFF WRITER

The House Judiciary Committee approved on a vote of 19-6 Wednesday more than a dozen impeachment charges against Treasurer A. James Manchin for his handling of the state investment fund.

The vote was technically a preliminary one, but a clear indication that the committee will recommend impeachment to the full House.

Judiciary Chairman John Hatcher, D-Fa... the committee will vote again on fo... impeachment, which will be based... approved Wednesday.

If the full House votes to impeach... Senate would conduct a trial, probab... ...ted of the charges, Manchin woul...

The committee charges Manchin with "maladministration, neglect of duty, high crimes and misdemeanors and incompetence," the impeachment grounds listed in the state constitution.

The specific charges allege Manchin failed to properly supervise the operation of the Consol... vestment Fund that was man... failed to recognize... delegat...

The committee also voted to consider a possi... public reprimand or censure against... Gainer for allegedly failing... member of the... seen...

WVU slows Terrapins Page 1-C

One Pa

torial, "Ge...
...norance
...D-Wyom...
...timon...
...he F...
...s o...

Dominion POST
Morgantown, West Virginia

...te voters defeat amendmen... Statewide tally c...

...the amendments.
The second amendment would have given the governor greater authority over the state primary and secondary education system. The third would have given state...

More on Page 1-B, 1-D

...duties under the governor's con... "The people of West Virginia have sent a great victory at the polls today," said Secretary of State Ken Hechler, an opponent of...

— Continued on 2A

Reque...

B

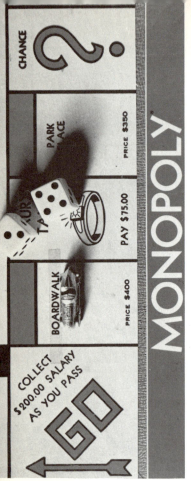

fig. 278
State regulatory bodies help avoid monopolies (exclusive ownership of a service or supply). You know the principle from this popular Parker Brothers game.

fig. 279
Before laws against monopolies, they were seen as a big problem, as this old political cartoon illustrates.

REVIEW OF SECTION THREE:

1. Identify the executive officials described below:
   a. the chief record keeper and election official of West Virginia
   b. the official bookkeeper of West Virginia
   c. the custodian of state funds
   d. one who helps farmers and protects public health
   e. the chief law enforcement officer of West Virginia

2. Why do some people believe that the elected department heads of the executive branch should be appointed?

SECTION FOUR: ADMINISTRATIVE AND REGULATORY BODIES

We have learned about the governor and five other elected officials in the executive branch of our state government. In addition to these, there are many more officials who work in many offices. Look at the chart of the executive branch found in the text. As you can see, some executive agencies are called departments, while others are called boards, commissions, or authorities.

These executive agencies can be divided into two types, either *administrative* or *regulatory* bodies. Administrative bodies manage set tasks. For example, the Department of Transportation manages the state highway system.

Regulatory bodies are formed by the legislature to enforce certain state laws. They control certain businesses and professions. The

Public Service Commission is a good example. It regulates companies that provide water, gas, electricity, and public transportation in West Virginia. Other examples are the Real Estate Commission and the Hearing-Aid Dealers Board.

Some executive agencies are very small. Their members may serve only part-time and receive no salary. For example, the Women's Commission, which works on the status of women, has only seventeen members, none of whom receives a salary. There are only two paid employees in the Women's Commission.

Other agencies have hundreds of full-time employees. Both the Department of Transportation and the Department of Commerce, Labor and Environmental Resources are very large. The heads of large agencies are appointed by the governor and approved by the Senate.

Through the years, West Virginia's executive branch has grown very large. By the 1980s, there were more than one hundred executive agencies and thousands of state employees. In addition, there were dozens of boards and commissions made up of people who served part-time and were not paid for their services.

In 1988 Gaston Caperton was elected governor. He believed the executive branch had grown too large to work well and was too expensive for the state. He asked the legislature to reorganize the executive branch. In 1989 the legislature passed a law creating seven new executive departments. The seven departments took over the duties of 104 executive agencies.

The people in charge of the new departments are known as secretaries and are appointed by the governor. The secretaries faced a difficult task. They were expected to run their huge departments effectively and provide necessary services to West Virginians. However, one of the reasons their departments were created was to cut the cost of government. So the secretaries were expected to reduce the number of people working in their departments and find ways to provide services more cheaply.

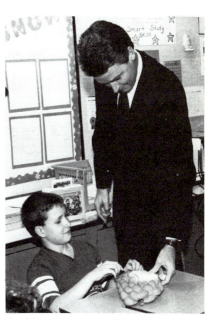

fig. 280
The governor listens to you, too

fig. 281

THE WEST VIRGINIA EXECUTIVE BRANCH

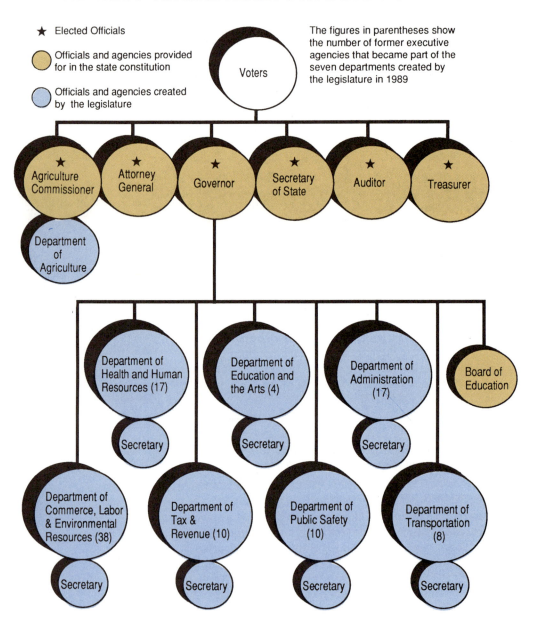

★ Elected Officials

Officials and agencies provided for in the state constitution

Officials and agencies created by the legislature

Voters

The figures in parentheses show the number of former executive agencies that became part of the seven departments created by the legislature in 1989

★ Agriculture Commissioner

★ Attorney General

★ Governor

★ Secretary of State

★ Auditor

★ Treasurer

Department of Agriculture

Department of Health and Human Resources (17)

Department of Education and the Arts (4)

Department of Administration (17)

Board of Education

Secretary

Secretary

Secretary

Department of Commerce, Labor & Environmental Resources (38)

Department of Tax & Revenue (10)

Department of Public Safety (10)

Department of Transportation (8)

Secretary

Secretary

Secretary

Secretary

NOTE: A complete list of executive agencies and a description of their duties can be found in the West Virginia Blue Book.

fig. 282
The Governor's limousine can be easily recognized by the license plate.

Look at the chart of the executive branch. The executive branch is so large the chart shows only the most important agencies. Many boards and commissions have been omitted. You have read about the duties of the six elected officials of the executive branch. Now we will describe the responsibilities of the other executive agencies shown on the chart.

The Department of Administration. The Department of Administration has several important tasks. It helps the governor prepare the budget by providing him with information about the state's finances. After the budget has been passed by the legislature, this department sees that state agencies follow the spending plan outlined in the budget. Most of the supplies and equipment used by state agencies are purchased by the Department of Administration. It is also in charge of the health insurance and retirement funds for all state employees.

fig. 283
Among other wildlife, the Department of Labor/Commerce and Environmental is concerned with the striped skunk.

The Department of Commerce, Labor and Environmental Resources. This department was created to help West Virginia's economy. It promotes products from our state in other parts of the United States and in foreign countries and tries to attract new industries to West Virginia. It also advertises West Virginia's many tourist attractions and manages the state's parks. The department is also responsible for protecting and developing the state's natural resources and wildlife. Other important concerns of this department include assisting and protecting workers and consumers and supervising banks and loan companies.

The Department of Education and the Arts. All of West Virginia's colleges and universities are under the control of this department. It is also responsible for assisting the state's libraries and its educational radio and television stations. The department also helps preserve the history and culture of West Virginia and supports the arts.

fig. 284
The Department of Human Resources assists West Virginia citizens with handicapped spaces. Along with innovations such as this scooter, these help persons who have trouble walking to maintain normal lifestyles.

fig. 285
The state lottery is run by the Department of Tax and Revenue.

The Department of Health and Human Resources. This department provides assistance to many West Virginians. It has programs to help veterans, the unemployed, injured workers, the handicapped, the elderly, and many others in need. It is also responsible for protecting and improving the health of West Virginians and controlling the cost of health care.

The Department of Public Safety. Both the West Virginia State Police and National Guard are part of this department. The department enforces criminal and traffic laws, promotes highway safety, and deals with some emergencies. It also runs the prison system and is in charge of the probation and parole of criminals.

The Department of Tax and Revenue. All taxes owed to the state government are collected by this department. It also supervises the sale of alcoholic beverages, manages the state lottery, regulates insurance companies, and invests state funds.

The Department of Transportation. The Department of Transportation is responsible for the construction and repair of all roads in West Virginia except city streets. The state's airports are under the supervision of this department. It also registers motor vehicles and licenses drivers.

The State Board of Education. The board makes rules and regulations for all of the state's elementary and secondary schools, including the training of teachers, the length of the school year, and graduation requirements. The board also hires the state superintendent of schools. The superintendent is responsible for seeing that the decisions of the board are carried out.

REVIEW OF SECTION FOUR:

1. What is the difference between an executive administrative body and a regulatory body?
2. Give examples of an administrative body and a regulatory body.
3. Name the seven executive departments.

REFERENCES:

1. Coffey, William E., Carolyn M. Karr, and Frank S. Riddel. *West Virginia Government*. Charleston, WV: Education Foundation, Inc., 1983: pp. 36–47.
2. Davis, Claude J., et al. *West Virginia State and Local Government*. Morgantown, WV: Bureau for Government Research, 1963: pp. 122–65.
3. Lambert, Oscar D. *West Virginia and Its Government*. Boston: D.C. Heath and Co., 1951: pp. 240–57.

fig. 286
The Department of Commerce oversees West Virginia's parks and recreation areas, which have attracted even Vice President Quayle and his family.

The West Virginia Judiciary

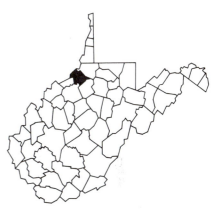

PREVIEW

The third branch of our West Virginia state government is the judicial branch. In many ways it works much like the judiciary of the federal government. Federal courts apply and interpret the Constitution of the United States and the laws passed by Congress. Our state courts apply and interpret the Constitution of West Virginia and the laws passed by the state legislature.

The system of justice is a very important part of our democracy. A true democracy must give all citizens equal justice under the law. Most legal cases in the United States are handled by state courts. Therefore, state judicial systems like that in West Virginia are important to all.

In Chapter Thirteen we will answer these questions:
1. What are the functions of West Virginia's courts?
2. What jurisdiction do the courts of West Virginia have?
3. How are the judges of West Virginia courts selected?
4. What are the powers and duties of the Supreme Court of Appeals, circuit courts, and magistrate courts?

Pronounce and discuss the meanings of the following words found in this chapter. You may need to use a dictionary.

critics	proceedings
dismiss	restrictions
justify	supervised
licensed	unified
preliminary	verdict

fig. 287, left and above
Tyler County Courthouse in Middlebourne

SECTION ONE: THE JUDICIAL SYSTEM OF WEST VIRGINIA

The Judicial Reform Amendment. The judicial branch of our state government was set up by the Constitution of 1872. Many changes have occurred in West Virginia since then. However, the judicial system did not change much for many years. Several attempts at change were made, but they all failed. At last, in 1974 the voters approved an amendment to the constitution that reformed the judicial system.

The Judicial Reform Amendment of 1974 established a *unified court system* for West Virginia. The system has three levels. These are the Supreme Court of Appeals, thirty-one circuit courts, and many magistrate courts. It is called a unified system because all state courts are supervised by the Supreme Court of Appeals.

Functions of the State Courts. The state court system has several major tasks. One is to protect the rights given us by the state constitution. We learned that the West Virginia Constitution has a bill of rights. The federal courts protect the rights guaranteed by the United States Constitution. Our state courts see that the rights contained in our state constitution are protected by both state and local governments.

Another responsibility of the court system is to act as a check on the legislative and executive branches of state government. The Supreme Court of Appeals may decide whether or not acts of the legislative and executive branches are constitutional.

State courts also decide the guilt or innocence of people accused of breaking the criminal laws of West Virginia. The courts then set the punishment for lawbreakers. As we have read, criminal laws define crimes such as murder or robbery. The federal government passes some criminal laws, but most are passed by state governments.

A final function of state courts is to hear and decide civil cases. Civil cases involve disputes. Some are between two or more people. Others are between individuals and a *state* or *local government*.

The Jurisdiction of State Courts. The term *jurisdiction* refers to the type of cases a court is allowed to hear and decide. The courts of West Virginia have jurisdiction in cases that involve a state law or the state constitution. The Supreme Court of Appeals and the circuit courts have both *original* and *appellate jurisdiction* in such cases. Magistrate courts have only original jurisdiction. Original jurisdiction means that a case begins in that court. For example, circuit courts have

fig. 288

Some organizations have found ways of enforcing regulations beyond state controls.

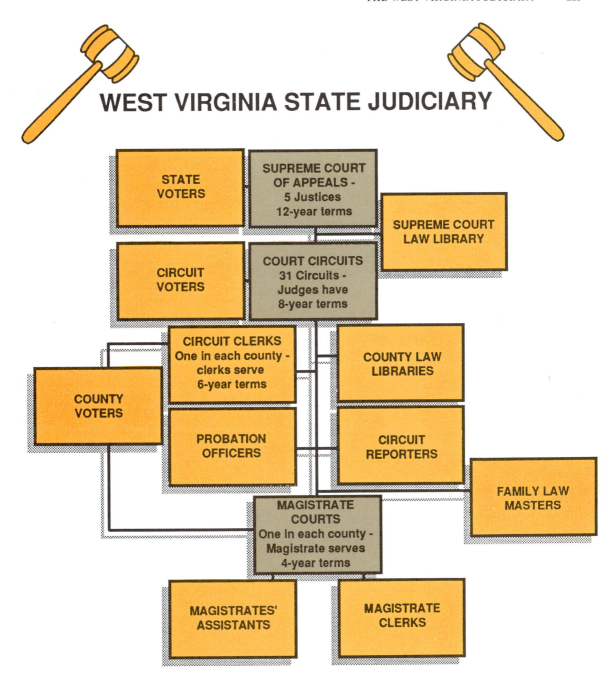

WEST VIRGINIA STATE JUDICIARY

STATE VOTERS

**SUPREME COURT OF APPEALS -
5 Justices
12-year terms**

SUPREME COURT LAW LIBRARY

CIRCUIT VOTERS

**COURT CIRCUITS
31 Circuits -
Judges have
8-year terms**

**CIRCUIT CLERKS
One in each county -
clerks serve
6-year terms**

COUNTY LAW LIBRARIES

COUNTY VOTERS

PROBATION OFFICERS

CIRCUIT REPORTERS

FAMILY LAW MASTERS

**MAGISTRATE COURTS
One in each county -
Magistrate serves
4-year terms**

MAGISTRATES' ASSISTANTS

MAGISTRATE CLERKS

* Family law masters are appointed by the governor, but are employees of the judicial branch. There are 21family law masters in the state. Each one serves from one to four counties. They are responsible for dealing with legal problems that affect families such as divorce, adoption and child support payments.

fig. 289

fig. 290
Swearing in a witness

original jurisdiction in all murder cases. Murder cases cannot be tried in the Supreme Court of Appeals or in a magistrate court.

When a court has appellate jurisdiction, it may review cases appealed to it from a lower court. Decisions of a magistrate court may be appealed to a circuit court and subsequently to the Supreme Court of Appeals. Decisions of a circuit court may be appealed to the Supreme Court of Appeals.

Appeals may be made to a higher court only on the grounds that an error was made by the lower court. The higher court does not hold a new trial. No juries or witnesses are called. The higher court's only function is to review the original trial to see if any legal errors were made.

If no legal errors were made, the verdict of the lower court will stand. If a mistake was made, the higher court will overrule the decision of the lower court. It will either dismiss the case or order a new trial.

State Judges. There is one big difference between our state judges and federal judges. Federal judges are appointed by the president. Our state judges are elected by the voters on a *partisan* basis. This means that they run for office as members of a political party. In some states judges are elected on a *nonpartisan* basis.

Many experts oppose electing judges. They say that judges should be chosen on the basis of their ability and experience. They shouldn't be chosen because of their popularity. Critics say that most voters have no way to judge the abilities of candidates for the judicial branch.

REVIEW OF SECTION ONE:
1. What courts make up the West Virginia judicial system?
2. Why is the judicial system in West Virginia called a unified court system?
3. What are the four major functions of the state court system?
4. In what types of cases do state courts have jurisdiction?
5. Which state courts have appellate jurisdiction?
6. How are state judges selected? Why do some people oppose the method of selecting judges in West Virginia?

SECTION TWO: THE SUPREME COURT OF APPEALS

Supreme Court Justices. The highest court in West Virginia is the *Supreme Court of Appeals.* It has five judges known as *justices.* They are elected by the voters of the state for twelve-year terms. Justices must be residents of West Virginia at the time of their election. They must also have been licensed to practice law for at least ten years. There are no restrictions on the number of times a justice may be elected.

Each year the justices choose one of their members to be the chief justice of the court. The salary of justices is set by the legislature. In 1988, the salary was $72,000 per year.

Justices of the Supreme Court can be removed from office by the legislature. The House of Delegates may impeach justices for incompetence, gross immorality, and neglect of duty. The Senate must then try the justice. If the justice is found guilty, he or she can be removed from the court.

If a justice leaves office before the end of a term, the governor appoints a replacement. The replacement serves until the next general election.

Supreme Court Terms. The Supreme Court of Appeals holds two regular terms each year, meeting in Charleston to hear cases during January and September. Each term lasts as long as necessary to handle its cases. Special terms of the court may be held at other times and places if the court decides to do so.

fig. 291
Members of the West Virginia Supreme Court of Appeals

Powers and Duties of the Supreme Court of Appeals. The Supreme Court of Appeals has both original and appellate jurisdiction. However, only a few special types of cases begin in the Supreme Court of Appeals. Almost all of its cases are appeals.

Many cases are appealed to the court every year from circuit courts and magistrate courts. The decisions of the Supreme Court of Appeals are final in most instances. Sometimes a decision of the Supreme Court of Appeals may be appealed to the United States Supreme Court. This may be done if a case involves the federal constitution or a conflict between a federal law and a state law. State laws must never conflict with federal laws or violate the Constitution of the United States.

The Supreme Court of Appeals also has the power of judicial review. It can decide whether or not actions of the legislative and executive branches are constitutional. State laws or the decisions of a state official must not violate the state constitution. The court may also overrule the acts of local governments in West Virginia.

Since adoption of the Judicial Reform Amendment in 1974, West Virginia has had a unified court system. Now the Supreme Court of Appeals must supervise all of the state's lower courts. The rules and procedures that the courts follow are made by the Supreme Court of Appeals.

Where the Supreme Court of Appeals Meets

The chamber of the West Virginia Supreme Court of Appeals is on the third floor of the capitol. Columns of white marble surround the room. The steps leading up to the justices' platform are made of green marble. Above the chamber is a skylight made of stained glass. The sides of the skylight are decorated with bronze carvings of the "Book of Law" and the "Scales and Balance" of justice.

Along the top of the chamber walls are quotations from two famous Americans. "THE TRUE FOUNDATION OF REPUBLICAN GOVERNMENT IS THE EQUAL RIGHT OF EVERY CITIZEN IN HIS PERSON AND PROPERTY AND IN THEIR MANAGEMENT," Thomas Jefferson. "FIRMNESS IN THE RIGHT AS GOD GIVES US TO SEE THE RIGHT," Abraham Lincoln.

REVIEW OF SECTION TWO:

1. How many justices are on the Supreme Court of Appeals?
2. How are justices of the Supreme Court of Appeals selected? How long are their terms of office?
3. How can justices of the Supreme Court of Appeals be removed?
4. Are decisions of the Supreme Court of Appeals always final? Explain your answer.
5. How can the Supreme Court of Appeals check the power of the legislative and executive branches of our state government?

SECTION THREE: THE CIRCUIT COURTS

Circuit Judges. The map in this chapter shows that West Virginia has thirty-one *judicial circuits.* Each circuit contains from one to four counties. Every circuit has a *circuit court.* Each court has at least one judge elected by the voters living in the circuit.

Circuits with a large population elect several judges. In 1988 there were sixty circuit judges. The Thirteenth Circuit is the largest circuit and has seven judges. It is located in Kanawha County, which is our most populous county. When there are two or more judges in a circuit, one is the chief judge. The Supreme Court of Appeals divides the work among judges.

Circuit judges are elected for eight-year terms. There is no limit on the number of terms each may serve. A circuit judge must reside in West Virginia. He or she must also have been licensed to practice law at least five years before being elected. The salary of circuit judges is set by the legislature. In 1988, circuit judges were paid $65,000 a year.

Circuit judges can be removed from office by the legislature for doing a poor job or for committing a crime. If a vacancy occurs in the office of a circuit judge, the governor appoints a replacement. The replacement serves until the next general election is held.

Circuit Court Terms. Circuit courts meet for three terms of court each year. The Supreme Court of Appeals sets the dates when each circuit court will be in session. Circuit courts are in session three times in each of the counties within the circuit. Court is held in the courthouse of each county. For example, the Fifth Judicial Circuit is made up of Jackson, Roane, and Calhoun counties. There is only one judge in that circuit. He holds court three times a year in Ripley, Spencer, and Grantsville, the county seats.

fig. 292
Interior detail of the West Virginia Supreme Courtroom

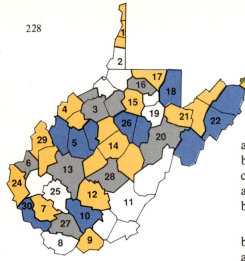

fig. 293
West Virginia State Judiciary

Jurisdiction of the Circuit Court. Circuit courts have both original and appellate jurisdiction. Civil cases may begin in a circuit court or be appealed to it from a magistrate court. The amount involved in a civil case must be more than one hundred dollars if it is to be heard by a circuit court. If the amount is less than one hundred dollars, it must be handled by a magistrate court.

Circuit courts also try criminal cases. All *felony* cases must be tried by a circuit court. Felonies are serious crimes such as murder and armed robbery that can result in long prison sentences and sometimes large fines.

Misdemeanor cases begin in the circuit court or are appealed to it from a magistrate court. Misdemeanors are less serious crimes, such as reckless driving and trespassing. They may result in fines or short jail sentences.

How Criminal Trials Work. In criminal cases the charges against the accused are first heard by a grand jury. In West Virginia grand juries are made up of sixteen people from the county where the crime occurred. The grand jury decides if there is enough evidence to justify a trial. At least twelve jurors must think that there is enough evidence for a trial. If they do, the accused will be tried in a circuit court.

fig. 294

JUDICIAL CIRCUITS   (number of circuit judges)

(4) 1st Circuit:	Brooke, Hancock, Ohio		(2) 16th Circuit:	Marion
(2) 2nd Circuit:	Marshall, Tyler, Wetzel		(2) 17th Circuit:	Monongalia
(1) 3rd Circuit:	Doddridge, Pleasants, Ritchie		(1) 18th Circuit:	Preston
			(1) 19th Circuit:	Barbour, Taylor
(3) 4th Circuit:	Wirt, Wood		(1) 20th Circuit:	Randolph
(1) 5th Circuit:	Calhoun, Jackson, Roane		(2) 21st Circuit:	Grant, Mineral, Tucker
(4) 6th Circuit:	Cabell		(1) 22nd Circuit:	Hampshire, Hardy, Pendleton
(2) 7th Circuit:	Logan			
(2) 8th Circuit:	McDowell		(1) 23rd Circuit:	Berkeley, Jefferson, Morgan
(2) 9th Circuit:	Mercer			
(3) 10th Circuit:	Raleigh		(1) 24th Circuit:	Wayne
(2) 11th Circuit:	Greenbrier, Monroe, Pocahontas, Summers		(2) 25th Circuit:	Boone, Lincoln
			(1) 26th Circuit:	Lewis, Upshur
(2) 12th Circuit:	Fayette		(1) 27th Circuit:	Wyoming
(7) 13th Circuit:	Kanawha		(1) 28th Circuit:	Nicholas
(2) 14th Circuit:	Braxton, Clay, Gilmer, Webster		(2) 29th Circuit:	Mason, Putnam
			(1) 30th Circuit:	Mingo
(2) 15th Circuit:	Harrison		(1) 31st Circuit:	Berkeley, Jefferson, Morgan

A *petit jury,* or trial jury, is then selected. The petit jury is made up of twelve county citizens. It must decide on the guilt or innocence of the defendant. The jurors hear witnesses and the arguments of the prosecutor and the defense attorney. After receiving instructions from the circuit judge, the jurors go to a separate room to discuss the case. The jury must reach a *unanimous verdict.* That means that all of them must agree.

If the jurors all agree that the accused is guilty, the judge hands down a sentence. If the verdict is "not guilty," the accused is freed. If the jury cannot reach a verdict, the accused can be tried again. People convicted by a circuit court can appeal the decision to the Supreme Court of Appeals.

REVIEW OF SECTION THREE:
1. West Virginia has how many judicial circuits?
2. How are circuit judges chosen? How long are their terms of office?
3. Where are circuit court sessions held?
4. What kinds of cases are heard by circuit courts?
5. How do grand juries and petit juries differ?

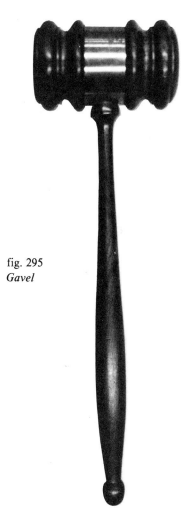

fig. 295
Gavel

fig. 296
Judge Larry Starcher

fig. 297
Sergeant at Arms guards the jury while it deliberates on a case.

SECTION FOUR: THE MAGISTRATE AND MUNICIPAL COURTS

Magistrates. Each county in West Virginia has a *magistrate court* in the courthouse or annex. The judges in these courts are called *magistrates.* The number of magistrates in each court depends on the size of the county's population. The smallest number a county may have is two. The most it may have is ten. There are thirty-one counties that have only two magistrates; only Kanawha County has ten.

In 1988 there were 155 magistrates in West Virginia. The judge or chief judge of the circuit court divides the work among them. The judge may also appoint a chief magistrate for a county.

Magistrates are elected by the voters of the county for a term of four years. There is no limit on the number of times each may serve. The qualifications for magistrates are not difficult. They do not have to be lawyers. A magistrate must be at least twenty-one years of age and have a high school education. Magistrates must reside in the county in which they serve. They must not have a criminal conviction.

Before a magistrate can take office, he or she is enrolled in a training course, which teaches magistrates what they need to know about laws and legal proceedings. While in office they must attend other training courses set up for them by the Supreme Court of Appeals.

A magistrate may be removed from office by the circuit court for several reasons. These include violating court rules or being convicted of a crime. They can also be removed for doing poor work. If a vacancy occurs in the office of magistrate, the circuit judge appoints a replacement. The replacement serves until the next general election.

The salaries of magistrates are set by the legislature. The salaries depend on the size of the population each magistrate serves. In 1988 magistrates in small counties earned $20,625 per year. Those serving large counties earned $27,000.

Jurisdiction of Magistrate Courts. Magistrate courts have only original jurisdiction. No case can be appealed to a magistrate court. They may hear both civil and criminal cases of a minor nature. For example, magistrates may hear and decide civil cases if the amount involved in the dispute is not more than two thousand dollars. They may also try misdemeanor cases and can hold *preliminary hearings* in felony cases.

When a policeman arrests a suspect in a felony, the accused may be brought before a magistrate for a preliminary hearing. After hearing the evidence, the magistrate decides whether the case should be turned over to the grand jury. That is all a magistrate can do in a felony case. He or she cannot try, convict, or sentence a person accused of a felony.

Magistrates handle minor legal tasks such as giving oaths. They also have the authority to issue *search warrants* and *arrest warrants* to the police. A search warrant lets the police search property. An arrest warrant permits the police to arrest a suspect. Magistrates may issue warrants only if there is some evidence linking the property or the suspect to a crime.

Municipal Courts. Any city, town, or village in West Virginia that has a government is called a *municipality*. We will study municipalities in Chapter Fifteen. However, we will mention them briefly now, because they also have courts.

The courts that try violators of city, town, or village laws are called *municipal courts*. Municipal courts in cities like Charleston and Huntington and in some larger towns have a municipal judge. The mayor is often the judge in smaller towns and villages. Many cases handled by municipal courts involve traffic violations.

fig. 298
Circuit courtroom

fig. 299
Magistrate giving oaths to a new class of state troopers

REVIEW OF SECTION FOUR:

1. How is the number of magistrates in each county determined?
2. How are magistrates selected? How long is their term of office?
3. What qualifications must a magistrate meet?
4. What types of cases are brought before a magistrate court?
5. What is the purpose of municipal courts?

REFERENCES:

1. Coffey, William E., Carolyn M. Karr, and Frank S. Riddel. *West Virginia Government*. Charleston, WV: Education Foundation, Inc., 1983: pp. 49–59.
2. Davis, Claude J., et al. *West Virginia State and Local Government*. Morgantown, WV: Bureau for Government Research, 1963: pp. 225–44.
3. Lambert, Oscar D. *West Virginia and Its Government*. Boston: D.C. Heath and Co., 1951: pp. 258–82.

Paying for Our State Government

PREVIEW

Like the federal government, our state government provides many programs and services. It spends more than three billion dollars each year. Raising that money and deciding the best way to spend it is not simple. The governor and the legislature make those hard decisions. The citizens of West Virginia also have a role. They pay for government. They elect the people who represent them at the state capitol. In this chapter we will learn how the state budget is made. We will see how the state raises revenues and where it spends the money.

In Chapter Fourteen we will answer these questions:
1. How is the state budget prepared and approved?
2. How does the state government raise revenues?
3. What are the major expenses of our state government?
4. Why were there so many difficulties with the state budget during the 1980s?

Pronounce and discuss the meanings of the following words found in this chapter. You may need to use a dictionary.

beverages	franchise
billion	lottery
consumer	maintenance
declined	severance
fees	tuition

fig. 300
Jefferson County Courthouse in Charles Town

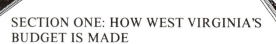

234

A budget is a financial plan. It shows how money is to be raised and how it will be spent. Every level of government—federal, state, county, and municipal—uses a budget to guide its spending.

No government has enough money to pay for all of the services people need or want. Therefore, all governments must decide which programs to support and how much money each program will receive.

Next, decisions must be made about how the funds will be raised. At the state level those decisions belong to the governor and the legislature. Together they must work out a budget. The budget is a plan for collecting and spending state funds during each year.

The Governor and the Budget. Every year the governor proposes a budget for West Virginia. He or she presents it to the legislature for approval. The governor does not prepare the budget alone. He receives requests for funds from all state agencies. Each agency must show how the money would be spent.

fig. 301
Governor Caperton delivering the budget proposal to the speaker of the House and president of the Senate after the State of the State Address

The Department of Administration gives the governor a lot of help with the budget. It is a large department with many duties. It works on budget planning, and it checks spending by all state departments. The Department of Tax and Revenue and the state treasurer also give the governor information needed for the budget.

One of the governor's tasks is to estimate the amount of revenue the state will collect in the coming year. This is very important, because the governor's estimate determines how much the state can spend. Unlike the federal government, our state cannot spend more money than it collects. The state constitution forbids deficit spending.

The governor's power to estimate revenue gives him control of the total amount of money in the budget. The legislature may change the amount of money the governor wants to spend on certain programs. The legislature can also decide to spend less money than the governor wants to spend. However, it cannot increase the total revenue in the budget.

After the governor has studied data from all state agencies, he puts the budget together. The proposal must list every program to be

funded and how much money would go to each program. The budget must also list all sources of revenue, showing how much money will come from each source.

The proposed spending in the governor's budget cannot be greater than the revenue estimate. Sometimes the governor will ask the legislature to raise taxes. This is necessary if the governor wants to spend more money than the state will collect without new taxes.

The governor presents the budget proposal to the speaker of the House and the president of the Senate. He does this in the State of the State Address to the legislature. Part of the address explains the proposed budget.

The Legislature and the Budget. The next step in the budget-making process takes place in the legislature. It is the legislature, not the governor, that has the power to raise taxes and spend money. The legislature must approve the budget before it goes into effect.

After the legislature has the governor's proposal, it begins to review the figures. The finance committees of the two houses do much of the work on the budget. They conduct public hearings. State officials and interested citizens come to the hearings to answer questions about the budget. After the finance committees recommend a budget, each house passes a budget bill. The House and Senate bills usually differ in some ways. They often differ with the governor's proposal, too.

Both houses of the legislature must pass the same budget bill. When the budget bills of the two houses differ, they go to a conference committee. The conference committee will agree on a compromise. Both houses must approve the compromise bill. The legislature must complete the budget during a regular session or the governor will have to extend the session.

Final Action on the Budget. The budget bill of the legislature goes to the governor. If the governor approves the bill, it becomes law. The governor may also veto the bill. When that happens, the legislature may override the governor's veto. More often, the legislature will make some changes in the budget so that the governor will sign it into law.

REVIEW OF SECTION ONE:
1. Who submits a proposed state budget to the legislature?
2. Why is the governor's estimate of state revenue so important?
3. What is the role of the legislature in budget-making?
4. What happens if the legislature has not passed a budget bill by the end of a regular session?

SECTION TWO: SOURCES OF STATE REVENUE

Taxation. Our state government spends over three billion dollars each year. Most of that money comes from taxes. Individuals and businesses must pay several different kinds of taxes to the state government. These taxes were established by laws of the legislature.

The chart in the text shows how the state raised its revenue in 1988. It shows that the *personal income tax* produces much of the state's revenue. It is a tax on the income individuals earn from wages, tips, rental property, and interest. Income taxes must be paid both to the federal government and to the government of West Virginia. The amount of tax a person pays depends on the size of his or her income. The more a person earns, the higher the rate of tax.

West Virginia also has a *corporation income tax*, which must be paid by certain businesses. It is a tax on the profits earned by those businesses. The larger the profits, the more one pays to the state.

Another major source of state money is the *consumer sales tax*. We all know about it, because consumers must pay a 6 percent sales tax on most of the goods and services they buy. For example, when you purchase a pair of jeans, you pay the sales tax. The sales tax is also placed on some services such as auto repairs.

Excise taxes are also an important source of state revenue. Excise taxes are similar to the sales tax. They are placed on certain goods such as gasoline, cigarettes, and soft drinks. They are ultimately paid by consumers. Excise taxes are higher than the sales tax. The state excise tax on gasoline is 15.5 cents a gallon. On a package of cigarettes it is 17 cents.

There are several smaller taxes in West Virginia. Businesses must pay a *franchise tax* in order to do business in the state. Companies that mine coal, cut timber, pump oil and natural gas, or quarry limestone and sandstone are charged a *severance tax*. Some people who inherit property in West Virginia that is worth more than $600,000 may have to pay an *estate tax*.

Other Sources of Revenue. Besides taxes, the state government also receives revenue from a few other sources. Fees provide money. Toll fees are collected from drivers using the West Virginia Turnpike. There are fees for license plates and driver's licenses. Profits from the sale of lottery tickets and alcoholic beverages amount to several million dollars each year. Other revenue comes from tuition paid by students who attend state colleges and universities.

fig. 302
The State Dollar: Where It Came From

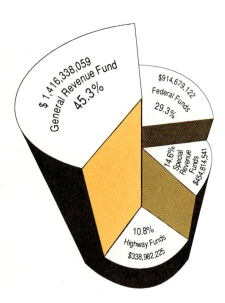

$1,416,338,059
General Revenue Fund
45.3%

$914,679,122
Federal Funds
29.3%

14.6%
Special
Revenue
Funds
$454,814,541

10.8%
Highway Funds
$338,982,225

The federal government grants West Virginia funds for highways, libraries, water and sewage systems, and educational and social welfare programs. West Virginia also earns millions of dollars each year in interest on state money that is invested.

Sometimes the state government borrows large sums of money. The state borrows money by selling bonds. People who buy the bonds are promised that our government will repay them in several years. They will also receive an interest payment from the state. The state is able to use the money from bond sales for several years before it has to be repaid. The state can use the borrowed money to pay for major projects such as building highways or schools.

REVIEW OF SECTION TWO:
1. What tax produces the largest share of state revenue?
2. What is the difference between the consumer sales tax and excise taxes?
3. Name two sources of state revenue besides taxes.

fig. 303
How the State Raised Revenues

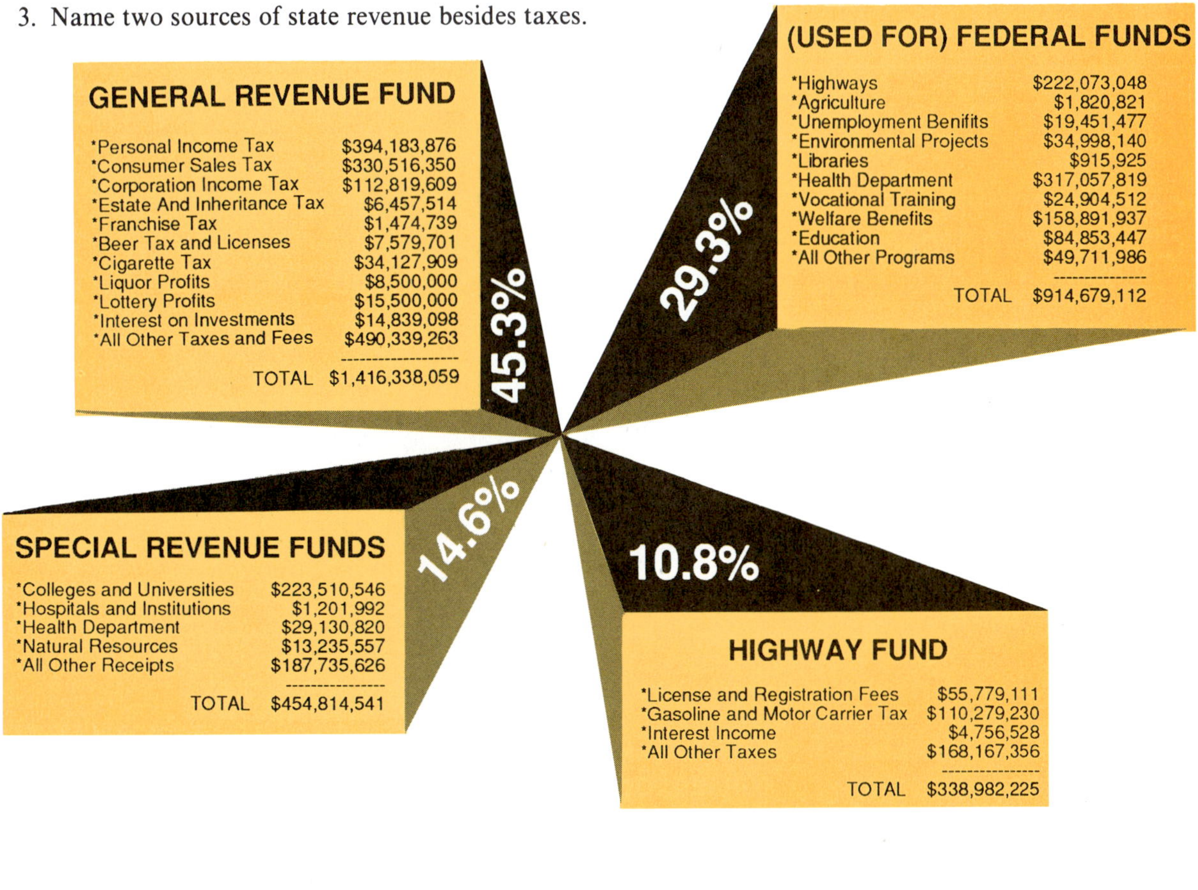

GENERAL REVENUE FUND

*Personal Income Tax	$394,183,876
*Consumer Sales Tax	$330,516,350
*Corporation Income Tax	$112,819,609
*Estate And Inheritance Tax	$6,457,514
*Franchise Tax	$1,474,739
*Beer Tax and Licenses	$7,579,701
*Cigarette Tax	$34,127,909
*Liquor Profits	$8,500,000
*Lottery Profits	$15,500,000
*Interest on Investments	$14,839,098
*All Other Taxes and Fees	$490,339,263
TOTAL	$1,416,338,059

45.3%

29.3%

(USED FOR) FEDERAL FUNDS

*Highways	$222,073,048
*Agriculture	$1,820,821
*Unemployment Benifits	$19,451,477
*Environmental Projects	$34,998,140
*Libraries	$915,925
*Health Department	$317,057,819
*Vocational Training	$24,904,512
*Welfare Benefits	$158,891,937
*Education	$84,853,447
*All Other Programs	$49,711,986
TOTAL	$914,679,112

14.6%

10.8%

SPECIAL REVENUE FUNDS

*Colleges and Universities	$223,510,546
*Hospitals and Institutions	$1,201,992
*Health Department	$29,130,820
*Natural Resources	$13,235,557
*All Other Receipts	$187,735,626
TOTAL	$454,814,541

HIGHWAY FUND

*License and Registration Fees	$55,779,111
*Gasoline and Motor Carrier Tax	$110,279,230
*Interest Income	$4,756,528
*All Other Taxes	$168,167,356
TOTAL	$338,982,225

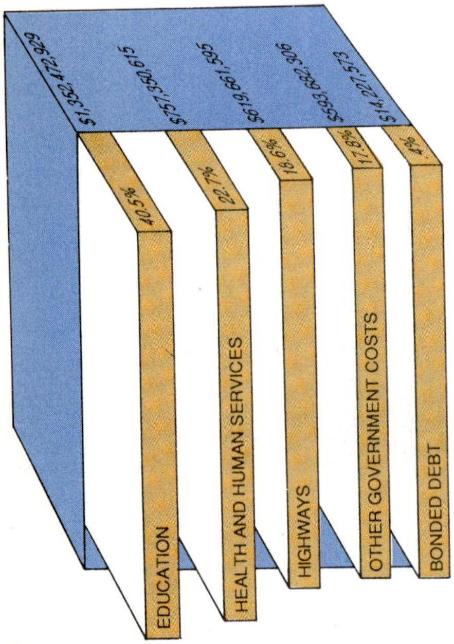

fig. 304
The State Dollar: Where it Went (1988)

fig. 305
State Dollar: Where It Goes

Source: State Auditor's Office, *Analysis of Receipts and Expenditures, 1988*

SECTION THREE: STATE GOVERNMENT SPENDING

The state spends money for many programs and services. We cannot describe all of them. The charts in this section show these expenditures in a simple way. All state programs are grouped in one of the five sections shown on the charts. We will look at each of the five in order to learn what kinds of programs they include.

Education. More than 40 percent of West Virginia's revenues are spent on education. Most of the funds go to counties for support of elementary and secondary schools. Some of the money goes to state colleges and universities. It takes considerable money to pay for

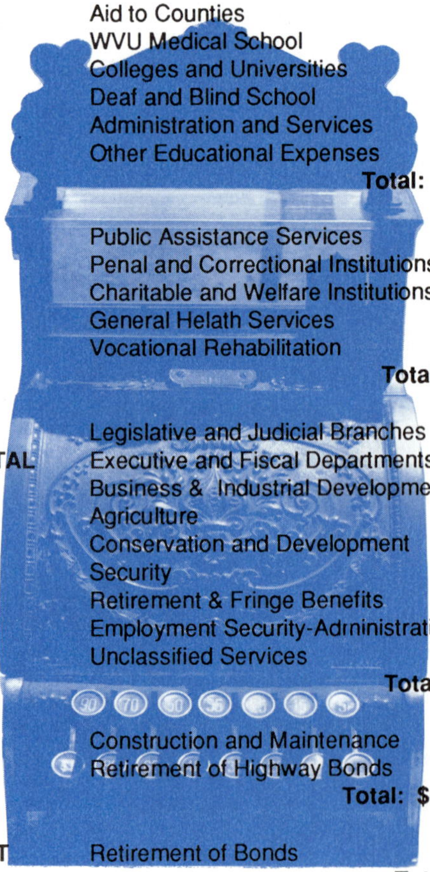

EDUCATION	Aid to Counties	$705,935,642
	WVU Medical School	9,597,175
	Colleges and Universities	460,356,186
	Deaf and Blind School	5,845,279
	Administration and Services	24,215,553
	Other Educational Expenses	146,523,094
	Total: $1,352,472,924	
HEALTH AND WELFARE	Public Assistance Services	$491,834,033
	Penal and Correctional Institutions	23,299,783
	Charitable and Welfare Institutions	54,680
	General Helath Services	207,417,777
	Vocational Rehabilitation	34,744,342
	Total: $757,350,615	
OTHER GOVERNMENTAL COSTS	Legislative and Judicial Branches	$32,724,588
	Executive and Fiscal Departments	222,136,259
	Business & Industrial Development	97,362,337
	Agriculture	13,153,531
	Conservation and Development	88,781,826
	Security	34,216,001
	Retirement & Fringe Benefits	76,472,190
	Employment Security-Administration	22,070,101
	Unclassified Services	6,765,473
	Total: $593,682,306	
HIGHWAYS	Construction and Maintenance	$537,827,973
	Retirement of Highway Bonds	81,833,662
	Total: $619,661,595	
BONDED DEBT	Retirement of Bonds	$14,227,573
	Total: $14,227,573	
GRAND TOTAL OF ALL EXPENDITURES		**$3,337,395,018**

buildings, buses, supplies, equipment, and maintenance. Even more money is needed to pay the salaries of thousands of teachers, administrators, secretaries, cooks, drivers, and other workers.

Highways. The cost of building, maintaining, and repairing highways is also very high. About 18 percent of the state's budget is spent on highways. Highways are costly, because of West Virginia's rugged terrain and its climate. It costs much more to build roads and bridges when the land is hilly than when it is flat or rolling. Cold winters in our state also damage our highways. Each spring and summer the Department of Transportation spends millions of dollars repairing the damage from the previous winter.

Some of the money in the highway budget is used to pay off bonds that have been sold to build highways. Every year some of those bonds must be paid with interest.

fig. 306
Symbol for the West Virginia Commission on Aging

Health and Human Services. West Virginia has many programs to support health care, to help people in need, and to punish lawbreakers. The state spends nearly 23 percent of its revenue on these programs. Some of the more costly services are direct payments to needy people and medical treatment for the elderly and the poor. The state also operates mental hospitals and prisons.

Other Governmental Costs. There are many other state government costs. Part of the budget is spent to operate the legislature and the court system. There are other departments in the executive branch, too. Thousands of state workers must be paid. Buildings must be maintained. Supplies and equipment are needed. The state also owns and operates many state forests and parks. These other costs take about 18 percent of the state's revenues.

Bond Debt. We know that the state government sometimes borrows money for big projects by selling bonds. Each year about 0.5 percent of the state's revenue is used to pay off some of those bonds and to pay interest owed on others. This does not include payments on highway bonds. At the end of 1988, West Virginia owed more than nine hundred million dollars to the people who have bought state bonds.

REVIEW OF SECTION THREE:
1. On which of the five sections in the budget does West Virginia spend the most?
2. Why is the cost of building and repairing highways so high in West Virginia?
3. What is meant by bond debt?
4. Why does West Virginia have a bond debt?

fig. 307
**The Growing Cost
of Education in
West Virginia**

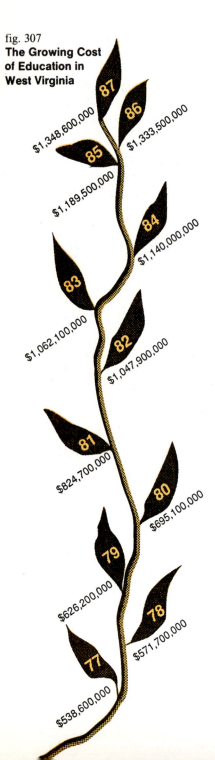

87 $1,348,600,000
86 $1,333,500,000
85 $1,189,500,000
84 $1,140,000,000
83 $1,062,100,000
82 $1,047,900,000
81 $824,700,000
80 $695,100,000
79 $626,200,000
78 $571,700,000
77 $538,600,000

SECTION FOUR: PROBLEMS WITH WEST VIRGINIA'S BUDGET

In Chapter Eight we learned about how hard it is to balance the federal budget. In most years the federal government's expenditures are higher than its revenues. Therefore, the national debt grows each year.

Our state government has different problems with its budget. It cannot spend more money than it expects to receive. The major problem of our state government during the past ten years has been a shortage of revenues. This has made it hard to pay for all of the state programs.

To balance the budget some taxes have been raised. Several programs have ended or been reduced. Very few new programs have been started. We will look at some of the reasons for West Virginia's budget problems.

Smaller Revenues. For several reasons West Virginia's economy was not strong during the 1980s. Many businesses closed or moved to other states. Many workers lost their jobs. Our coal industry continues to produce a lot of coal. However, more of the work is done by machines and fewer miners are needed. The price of coal has also declined.

Fewer taxes were collected by the state as the economy fell. This meant that there was less money to spend on state programs and services.

Increased Costs. At the same time that revenues fell, the cost of the government rose. Salaries of state workers were higher. Goods and services cost more in the 1980s than in the past. Total state spending for education in West Virginia in 1975 was less than five hundred million dollars. Ten years later the state spent over one billion dollars annually on education. The same increases occurred in many other sectors of state spending.

Disagreements about Taxation and Spending. Faced with smaller revenues and larger costs, our state leaders did not have many choices. They could raise taxes, cut programs, or do both. It was not easy to choose the taxes to raise or the programs to cut.

Some legislators thought that business taxes were too high in West Virginia. They wanted to lower these taxes so that new businesses would come to our state. Others opposed raising the income tax or the sales tax when so many people were out of work. In addition, there were arguments about the planned increase in the property tax.

It was also hard to agree on how to reduce spending. Although people agreed that cuts should be made, they disagreed about what programs should get less. Students, parents, and educators opposed cuts for education. The elderly, the handicapped, and farmers wanted to keep the programs that helped them. Everyone wanted their highways and bridges to be maintained.

The governor and the legislature must make hard choices about taxation and spending. However, they are responsible to the voters. They do not want to make decisions that will anger many voters. It is never easy to prepare and pass the state budget. Even when the state's economy is strong, compromises have to be made before the budget is passed. When the state has economic problems, decisions on taxes and spending are harder to make.

Disagreements about taxes and spending were frequent in the 1980s. The legislature had to meet in special session several times to complete work on the budget. The governor sometimes vetoed budgets passed by the legislature. Many citizens were unhappy with the budgets, because taxes were raised and programs reduced.

There are no easy answers to the state's budget problems. If the economy improves, it will be easier for the government to provide programs and services.

fig. 308
Progress and budgets are complex problems. When needed roads are built, sometimes the new traffic routes cause businesses to close.

REVIEW OF SECTION FOUR:

1. Why did the state revenue not grow during the 1980s?
2. Why have government costs gone up in recent years?
3. Why do West Virginians disagree about raising taxes and reducing government spending?

REFERENCES:

1. Coffey, William E., Carolyn M. Karr, and Frank S. Riddel. *West Virginia Government*. Charleston, WV: Education Foundation, Inc., 1983: pp. 60–67.
2. State Auditor, *Analysis of Receipts and Expenditures*. Charleston, WV: State Auditor's Office, 1988.
3. *West Virginia Blue Book*. Charleston, WV: Jarrett Printing Co., 1987.

County and Municipal Government in West Virginia

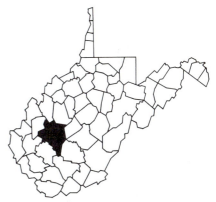

PREVIEW

Our federal and state governments meet many of our needs. However, they cannot solve every local problem. They cannot supply every service in our counties and towns. For that reason we have local governments. County and municipal governments meet local needs that are not taken care of by the federal or state governments. These local governments are close to each of us. We have more contact with them than with the federal and state governments.

In Chapter Fifteen we will answer these questions:
1. How many counties are there in West Virginia and how were they formed?
2. What are the functions of county and municipal governments in West Virginia?
3. How are West Virginia's county and municipal governments organized?
4. What are the major problems of county and municipal governments in West Virginia?

Pronounce and discuss the meanings of the following words found in this chapter. You may need to use a dictionary.

abuse	policymakers
commission	professional
communities	residents
efficient	suburbs
minerals	units

fig. 309, left and above
Kanawha County Courthouse in Charleston

fig. 310
**West Virginia Counties and
County Seats**

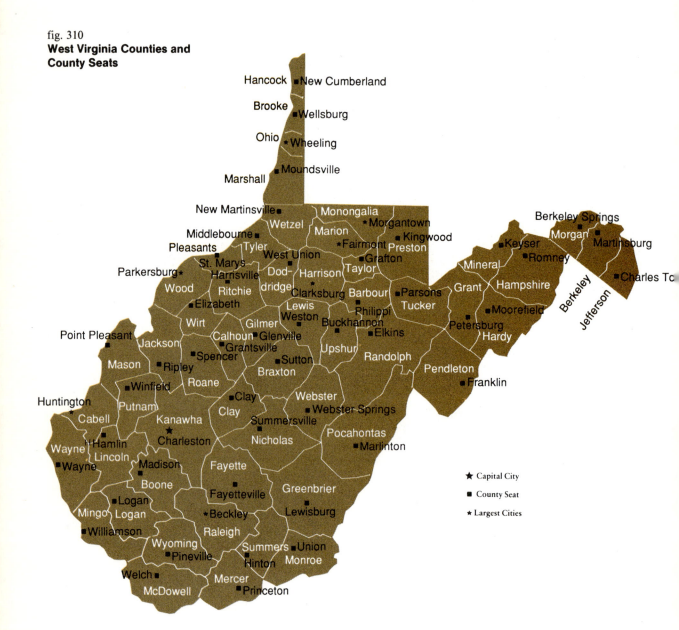

SECTION ONE: THE COUNTIES AND MUNICIPALITIES OF WEST VIRGINIA

West Virginia's Fifty-five Counties. Forty-nine states in our country are divided into units called *counties.* Louisiana is the only state that does not have counties. Its comparable units are called *parishes.*

West Virginia has fifty-five counties. Each county has a town or city that is called the *county seat.* The county seat has a *county courthouse,* which serves as the headquarters for county government. Our counties are quite different from one another in size and population. The largest in size is Randolph County, which contains 1,046 square miles. Little Hancock County has only 88.5 square miles. Kanawha County has the largest population. In 1980, 230,000 people lived there. The population of Wirt County was only 4,992.

Most of the counties of West Virginia were formed from older, much larger counties. In 1776 very few people lived in what is now West Virginia. There were only four counties in western Virginia: Berkeley, Hampshire, Monongalia, and Ohio. The large counties eventually were split to form new, smaller counties. When West Virginia became a state in 1863, it had fifty counties. Since then, Grant, Mineral, Lincoln, Summers, and Mingo counties have been formed.

How can new counties be formed in West Virginia? The state constitution requires that a new county be at least four hundred square miles in size and have at least six thousand people. A majority of the voters living in the area that will become the new county must vote in favor of its formation.

It is unlikely that any new counties will be formed in our state. Most people feel they would not gain anything if an existing county was divided into two counties. It would be difficult to persuade voters to support such a division.

Some people think West Virginia has too many counties. They feel that some of the smaller counties should be joined together to form larger ones. They argue that larger counties could afford to provide their citizens with better services. The state constitution does not allow counties to join together. In 1989 the legislature approved an amendment to the constitution that would permit two or more counties to become a single county. However, the voters of the state did not approve the amendment.

fig. 311
One service counties provide is the sheriff's patrols.

fig. 312
The Mountaineer Balloon Festival in Monongalia County has become a spectacular event attracting many out-of-state visitors.

fig. 313
The Buckwheat Festival in Preston County involves youth participation in exhibits and shows.

The Functions of Counties. Counties in West Virginia are closely controlled by the state government. Their governments can do only what is required or permitted by the constitution and the laws of the state.

The functions of West Virginia counties have changed over the years. Before 1933, counties built and repaired most roads. Today the state does this. Counties once gave aid to the poor. Today the state and federal governments do more to help the needy. At one time counties controlled the public schools. In 1933 the state government increased its control over the public schools. It also began paying much of the cost of education.

While counties have lost some powers, the state legislature has let them take on some new functions. In 1949, a new state law allowed counties to establish water and sewage systems. Two years later they were allowed to provide fire protection.

The state constitution requires some things of counties. Counties must keep certain records, enforce state laws, hold elections, and collect property taxes. They also must provide for public schools.

Today many counties provide services in addition to those required by the state. All counties have public health workers. Some counties operate hospitals, health clinics, ambulance service, youth centers, and public libraries. Some have animal shelters, 4-H camps, and parks.

Municipal Corporations. All West Virginians live under at least three governments: federal, state, and county. About one-half live in a city or town that also has a *municipal government.*

Why do people want to live under a fourth government? The main reason is that they want more public services. Think of all that people expect from their communities. They want police and fire protection, street lighting, street repairs, garbage and sewage disposal, and clean water. Some municipalities also have public libraries, parks, playgrounds, and swimming pools. Some provide public buses, health services, and housing.

The legislature has passed rules for forming a municipality, or *municipal corporation.* After a community has become a municipal corporation, it may organize a municipal government. Some small communities in West Virginia are unincorporated. They are not municipal corporations. They do not have a municipal government.

fig. 314
Have you ever noticed the wealth of organizations that each incorporated city presents at its city limits?

fig. 315, *Ravenswood fire department*

fig. 316

In West Virginia, a municipal corporation must be at least a quarter of a square mile in size. It also must have at least one hundred people. Thirty percent of the property owners must file a petition with the county commission asking for an election on incorporation. If a majority of the voters favor incorporation, the county commission will make the community a municipality.

A municipality may draw up a *municipal charter* that describes how it will be governed. Residents then elect a government that may pass *municipal ordinances* (laws) and carry out other functions. Municipal governments are not controlled as much as county governments. However, they can do only what the county commission allows them to do. Municipal governments may put a tax on dogs, but they may not levy an income tax.

REVIEW OF SECTION ONE:
1. How were the counties of West Virginia formed?
2. Who decides what functions county governments are required or permitted to perform?
3. How have the functions of counties changed over the years?
4. What services do municipal governments provide?
5. Who determines the powers of municipalities in West Virginia?

SECTION TWO: THE ORGANIZATION OF COUNTY GOVERNMENTS

The County Commission. The most important government body in West Virginia counties is the *county commission*. The county commission has both legislative and executive duties. Within the limits of state law, it sets the property tax rate of a county. It prepares county budgets and supervises spending. It administers county officials such as the sheriff. The commission also decides how many public services the county will offer.

In 1880, an amendment to the state constitution fixed the size of county commissions. All counties have three county commissioners except Jefferson County, which has five commissioners, and Preston County, which has eight.

The Judicial Reform Amendment of 1974 allows the voters of a county to ask for a change in the size of their county commission. The state legislature must approve each change.

Commissioners are elected to terms of six years. They must meet at least four times a year, but all meet more often. The salaries of county commissioners are set by the legislature. They differ according to the size of the county.

Other Elected County Officials. In addition to county commissioners, there are other elected county officials. These include the *clerk of the county commission,* who is also called the county clerk, and the *clerk of the circuit court.* Their major duty is keeping certain public records. Both are elected to six-year terms.

The county clerk keeps all records of the county commission and other county offices. He or she also keeps records of births, deaths, marriages, divorces, and certain licenses. The county clerk is also in charge of voter registration. No one can vote who has not registered with the county clerk.

The clerk of the circuit court is often called the circuit clerk. The circuit clerk keeps all records of circuit court actions in his or her county. The circuit clerk also issues absentee ballots to voters who cannot go to the polls on election day. All candidates for county offices and most candidates for the state legislature must file in the circuit clerk's office.

The *assessor* is another elected county official. He or she serves a term of four years. The assessor sets the value of property so it can be taxed. The assessor fixes the value of both *real property* and *personal property.* Real property includes land, minerals, and buildings. Personal property refers to such things as cars and trucks, trailers, and boats.

fig. 317
This handsome taxable property is in Ravenswood, West Virginia.

fig. 318
Deeds to property are kept in county offices in huge record books, as are birth, death, and marriage records.

fig. 319
This wonderful ironwork is on the jail entrance in Middlebourne, WV. It is one of the last jailhouses that has the sheriff's house attached to the facility. In the early days, this convenience allowed the sheriff's wife to cook meals for the inmates.

The county *sheriff* is also elected to a four-year term. The state constitution limits a sheriff to two consecutive terms. Sheriffs are the only county officials upon whom such a restriction has been placed.

The sheriff does two very different jobs. One is to enforce the law as a police officer. He or she may arrest lawbreakers and hold them for trial. The sheriff is in charge of the county jail and the care of prisoners. The sheriff also delivers legal papers from the circuit court. The sheriff hires deputies to assist with the police work.

The sheriff's second task is to serve as county treasurer. He or she collects all property taxes paid in the county. The sheriff controls the money until it is spent by county agencies.

Another county law enforcement official is the *prosecuting attorney*. The prosecuting attorney is the chief legal officer of the county. He or she is elected to a four-year term. The prosecuting attorney prosecutes people accused of committing crimes. He or she brings charges against the accused in the circuit court and presents evidence about the crime to the grand jury. If the grand jury indicts the accused, then a trial must be held. During the trial the prosecuting attorney presents the evidence against the accused person to the petit jury.

fig. 320

The County School System. An important duty of government is providing public education. The West Virginia Board of Education has a great deal of control over our public schools. However, the counties also have a large role in education.

Each county in West Virginia has a public school system. It is supervised by the *county board of education.* The board of education is made up of five members who are elected to four-year terms. Members are elected during the primary election. School board elections are nonpartisan, that is, candidates do not run as members of a political party.

The county board of education has several duties. It approves the budget of the school system. The board hires the *county superintendent of schools.* It also approves the hiring of school principals, teachers, and other workers. The state board decides what subjects will be taught and how teachers will be trained. It prepares a list of textbooks that can be used in the state's schools. The county board selects textbooks for its schools from the list approved by the state board. It also decides where schools will be built and when schools must be closed.

The county school board can decide how to spend money. However, it cannot decide how much money the school system will have. About half of the money for schools comes from local property taxes. The property tax is levied by the county commission, not by the board of education. The rest of the money comes from the state and federal governments.

fig. 321
Monongalia County passed the school bond issue in this election which allowed renovation of grade schools. But then, who could turn these guys down?

REVIEW OF SECTION TWO:
1. Which county officials have both legislative and executive duties?
2. Describe two duties of county commissions.
3. Describe one duty of each of these county officials: the county clerk, circuit clerk, assessor, sheriff, and prosecuting attorney.
4. What elected officials supervise the county school system?
5. From where does funding for the public schools come?

fig. 321

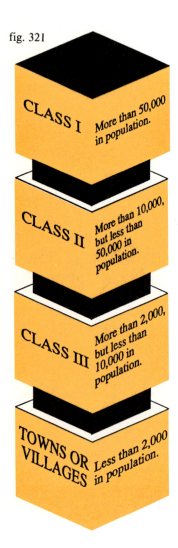

SECTION THREE: FORMS OF MUNICIPAL GOVERNMENT

West Virginia municipalities are divided into groups based on their populations. Those with two thousand or fewer people are "towns" or "villages." Those with more than two thousand are "cities." *Class I* cities have more than fifty thousand people. Class II cities have more than ten thousand but less than fifty thousand. *Class III* cities have populations of more than two thousand but less than ten thousand.

Towns and villages in West Virginia use the mayor-council form of government. Cities may choose one of four types of municipal government. These are the mayor-council form, the strong-mayor form, the commission form, and the council-manager form.

fig. 322   **MAYOR-COUNCIL FORM OF MUNICIPAL GOVERNMENT**

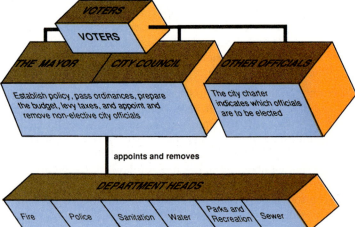

The Mayor-Council Form. The *mayor-council form* is the oldest type of municipal government in the United States. A majority of municipalities in West Virginia must use this form because they are towns or villages. Many of the state's cities have also chosen the mayor-council form.

Under the mayor-council form, the mayor and members of the council are elected by the voters. Other officials may be elected or appointed by the council. The size of the council varies widely in West Virginia. Small municipalities usually have four or five council members. Larger cities may have ten or more.

Other municipal officials include the recorder or clerk, chief of police, city attorney, water superintendent, fire chief, and street superintendent. Small municipalities might not have all of these officials. Larger cities may have other officials in addition to these. Some have a health officer, a building inspector, and a recreation director. Some cities also have commissions to deal with concerns such as parks, housing, zoning, or human rights.

Under the mayor-council form, the council is stronger than the mayor. The mayor is the formal head of the city and presides at council meetings. In small municipalities the mayor might serve as judge of the municipal court. However, the mayor has only one vote on issues before the council. The mayor cannot veto acts of the council. The whole council appoints and removes officials, sets the budget, and makes policy. This type of government is often called the *weak-mayor form*.

Those who like the weak-mayor-council form say that is is very democratic. All policymakers are elected. No one person has too much power. Critics of this form say that under a weak-mayor form it is hard to know who is in charge.

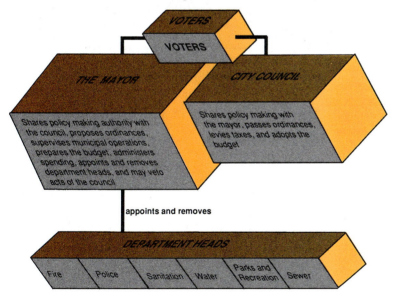

fig. 323
**THE STRONG-MAYOR FORM
OF MUNICIPAL GOVERNMENT**

The Strong-Mayor Form. The *strong-mayor form* of municipal government also provides for an elected mayor and city council. However, the mayor has greater power. He or she shares policymaking with the council but can veto acts of the council. The mayor also prepares the budget and oversees spending. He or she supervises city operations and hires department heads. Several of West Virginia's larger cities, such as Charleston, Huntington and Parkersburg, use this form of government. The strong-mayor form makes it easy to know who is responsible. The mayor is in charge. A strong mayor can get things done quickly.

Critics point out that it is easy for a strong mayor to abuse power. A mayor might give city jobs to his friends even if they are not qualified. If the mayor and council do not get along, city government won't work very well. The council might refuse to pass the ordinances and the budget proposed by the mayor, while the mayor could veto acts of the council.

fig. 324

**THE COMMISSION FORM
OF MUNICIPAL GOVERNMENT**

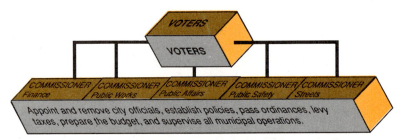

fig. 325
This is a sidewalk grating. What artifacts in your town are marked by its name?

The Commission Form. The *commission* form is quite different from the two forms of municipal government discussed above. Under the commission form voters elect the heads of specific municipal departments. These heads are called commissioners. In West Virginia there must be either three or five commissioners. Each commissioner heads a department such as finance, public works, public safety, or streets.

Together, the commissioners make up the *city commission*. They select one member to serve as mayor. The mayor has no more power than the other members. He or she is the formal head of the city. Other workers are hired by the commission or by each department head. The city commission passes ordinances and makes city policies. A few West Virginia cities including Keyser, Petersburg, and Romney have the commission form of government.

Some people like the commission form because it is easy to understand and more democratic than the other forms. No one person can have too much power under this form. Critics say that is is a weak form of government, under which it is hard to assign responsibility for town policy.

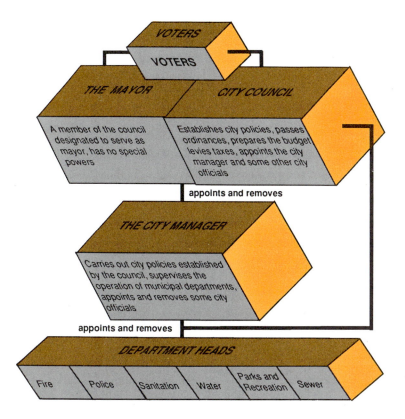

fig. 326
**THE COUNCIL-MANAGER FORM
OF MUNICIPAL GOVERNMENT**

The Council-Manager Form. The *council-manager* form of municipal government has both an elected council and an appointed *city manager*. This type of government usually has a mayor, too. The mayor is one of the council members who presides at meetings and performs ceremonies. He or she has no more power than the other members of the council.

The council passes city policies and ordinances. It prepares and adopts the budget and levies taxes. The city manager carries out city policies and supervises departments. The city manager is appointed by the council and can be removed at any time. In most states the city manager appoints department heads and other city workers. In West Virginia, however, the city council usually appoints some workers.

The council-manager form is the most popular type of government in American cities. Some West Virginia cities with this form of

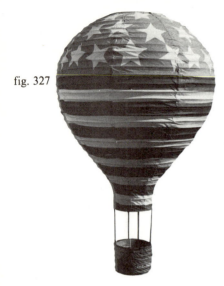

fig. 327

government are Bluefield, Clarksburg, Fairmont, Grafton, Morgantown, Moundsville, Oak Hill, Philippi, Princeton, St. Marys, Weirton, and Wheeling.

Those who favor the council-manager form say that it is simple to understand. The city manager is in charge of most tasks. Critics say that this form of government is not democratic, because the city manager is not elected. This form is not efficient when there are conflicts between the council and the city manager. Conflicts often lead to the firing of city managers.

REVIEW OF SECTION THREE:
1. What form of government must be used by towns and villages in West Virginia?
2. What is the major difference between the mayor-council and the strong-mayor forms of municipal governments?
3. How does a city commission differ from a city council?
4. Why do some people feel the council-manager form of government is not democratic?

fig. 328

Some city ordinances affect your age group by prohibiting skateboarding in the downtown area. Does your town have an ordinance like this?

SECTION FOUR: PROBLEMS OF LOCAL GOVERNMENTS IN WEST VIRGINIA

The Shortage of Revenue. County and municipal governments have many duties and functions. The public demand for more local services has grown fast. These services cost a great deal of money to do well. The greatest problem faced by most West Virginia counties and municipalities is a shortage of money. Their revenues are growing too slowly to meet local needs.

What is the cause of revenue shortage? County governments receive almost all of their revenue from property taxes. However, West Virginia has a very low property tax compared to most other states. County governments cannot raise property taxes beyond a certain point established by the state constitution.

Our counties are not permitted to levy other types of taxes, nor can they impose a sales tax or an income tax. For these reasons county governments have a hard time raising more revenue.

West Virginia's municipal governments have the same problems. There are several causes for this. First, the federal government has cut back the money it gives to cities. During the 1970s, the federal government gave a lot of money to municipal governments. This was called *revenue sharing*. Cities expanded their services, because they had federal funds to pay for them. However, revenue sharing was reduced in the 1980s.

A second cause of the problem is a lack of financial help from the state. Most state governments provide some support to cities. That is not true in West Virginia. In 1949 the Supreme Court of Appeals banned state aid to towns and cities.

A third cause of the shortage is the state government's control of the power to tax. The state government does not allow our municipalities to levy many taxes. They may levy a property tax, a gross sales tax, an amusement tax, and a dog tax. They may also tax businesses and liquor sold in state stores. Only the property tax and the gross sales tax produce much revenue, and the state government strictly limits the size of those taxes. Until the limits are raised or the state lets cities impose new taxes, municipal revenues will be low.

fig. 329
City services at your service!

fig. 330
*Some of our towns and small cities
begin to lose family run businesses in
competition with national chains.*

A final cause of the shortage is that people and businesses have moved out of many cities. Many people have gone to the suburbs. They no longer pay municipal property taxes. Many new businesses in West Virginia are located in suburban shopping centers outside a city. Some older businesses have also relocated. When this happens, cities lose taxes.

Because of their financial problems, municipalities in West Virginia must rely on service fees. Cities levy fees for garbage collection, sewage disposal, and police and fire protection. They may charge fees for paving streets and sidewalks, and for the use of other services.

Other Problems of County Government. In addition to a shortage of revenue, our counties face other problems. The state constitution requires that all counties have the same form of government. Each county must have almost the same number of elected officials. The problem is that the counties are very different. Their needs are not the same. The county commissions of Kanawha County and Wirt County are the same size, yet Kanawha County is much larger than Wirt County. Some people think that a three-person commission cannot do a good job in a large county.

Another problem is that some county officials are elected to positions that require special training. These officials may not have that training. The sheriff may have no training for police work or handling financial accounts. The assessor may know little about setting property values.

Local government in West Virginia is not very efficient. Money is wasted because cities and counties often provide the same services. These include fire and police protection, recreation, and garbage collection. To deal with these problems, several reforms of local government could be made, such as:

1. Giving counties and municipalities more freedom to raise revenues.
2. Amending the state constitution to let counties create the form of government best suited for them.
3. Appointing certain officials, such as the assessor and the sheriff. Professional training should be required for these positions.
4. Allowing counties and cities to join together to provide public services. This is done in many states.

In 1989 the legislature approved a constitutional amendment that would allow counties to choose from among three different forms of county government. The amendment also would have permitted county and municipal governments to join and form a single local government. However, the amendment was not approved by the state's voters.

REVIEW OF SECTION FOUR:
1. Why do county governments in West Virginia have so little revenue?
2. Explain two of the reasons why West Virginia municipalities have so little revenue.
3. Besides a shortage of revenue, what other problems face West Virginia counties?
4. What reforms have been recommended to improve local government?

REFERENCES:
1. Coffey, William E., Carolyn M. Karr, and Frank S. Riddel. *West Virginia Government.* Charleston, WV: Education Foundation, Inc., 1983: pp. 68–87.
2. Davis, Claude J., et al. *West Virginia State and Local Government.* Morgantown, WV: Bureau for Government Research, 1963: pp. 426–68.
3. Lambert, Oscar D. *West Virginia and Its Government.* Boston: D.C. Heath and Co., 1951: pp. 283–302.

fig. 331
Very personal property

fig. 332
The city of Sistersville offers the last ferry service across the Ohio River.

The Federal System at Work in West Virginia

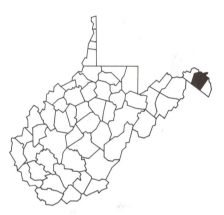

PREVIEW

We have read about the four levels of government in the United States. We have seen that the federal, state, county, and municipal governments affect our lives in many ways. We have seen how each level of government is organized. We know something about how each works. We will end our study of American government by showing how the four levels of government work together to better meet our needs.

In this chapter we will answer the following questions:
1. What are some advantages of a federal system of government?
2. Why have there been conflicts between federal and state officials over who has the power to deal with certain issues and problems?
3. When and why did the federal and state governments become more cooperative?
4. What is meant by cooperative federalism?
5. In what ways does the federal government assist West Virginia?

Pronounce and discuss the meanings of the following words found in this chapter. You may need to use a dictionary.

categorical	engineer
competition	Great Depression
competitive	pension
cooperative	relief programs
corps	vocational

fig. 333, left and above
Berkeley County Courthouse in Martinsburg

SECTION ONE: THE AMERICAN FEDERAL SYSTEM

Reviewing the Meaning of Federalism. We know that the authors of our Constitution wanted to form a strong and effective national government. However, they did not want state governments to be too weak. They solved this problem with a federal system of government.

Under our federal system, political power is divided between the national and state governments. The Constitution gives the federal government the right to make and enforce laws that affect the whole nation. The states may control matters that affect people within their own borders. Some powers are shared by both levels of government.

The federal system includes only the national and state governments. However, each state also shares power with local governments. State constitutions provide for counties and municipalities. These local governments are given some rights by the states.

The Advantages of Federalism. At times in our nation's history there have been problems with the federal system. However, most of the time it has worked well. The federal system of government has some advantages over other systems.

The United States is a very large nation. The geography differs. It has several distinct regions. Americans come from many backgrounds. Their way of life is not the same everywhere.

figs. 334, 335

An Eskimo yoyo from Alaska works on similar principles of tension as the more common yoyo, but it balances the force of two balls against each other as they swing in opposite paths. The difference between this yoyo and the Duncan yoyo, known in most of the U.S., demonstrates some of the special differences among citizens of our country.

The needs and problems of one region or group are never the same as others. For example, the problems faced by coal-mining towns in West Virginia differ from those of Eskimo villages in Alaska. It would be very hard for federal officials to know the needs and problems of all the people. It would be even harder for them to take care of all those needs and problems.

The federal government can take care of needs important to all of us such as national defense. State and local officials know the special needs and problems in their states better than do federal officials. The federal system lets state and local governments decide what is best for their communities.

fig. 336
Four levels of government

Another advantage of the federal system is the cooperation among the four levels of government. The federal government cooperates with state and local governments. It helps them pay for some of their programs. It also helps them plan for the future by giving them support and data. Information from the Census Bureau is very useful to state and local governments. The U.S. Army and Air Force provide training and equipment for National Guard units in each state.

State and local governments also help the federal government. For example, state and local police often capture criminals who are wanted for breaking federal laws. The president and members of Congress are chosen in elections held by state and local governments.

Cooperation among the four levels of government in the United States is important. When the different levels of government cooperate, they do a better job for the American people. The federal system makes this cooperation possible.

REVIEW OF SECTION ONE:
1. Why did the authors of the Constitution create a federal system of government for the United States?
2. What is meant by a federal system of government?
3. What are some advantages of a federal system of government?

SECTION TWO: FROM COMPETITION TO COOPERATIVE FEDERALISM

The Period of Competitive Federalism. The national and state governments have always cooperated in some important ways. However, for a long time there was also a great deal of competition between the two levels of government.

The Constitution gives the federal government many powers and reserves some powers for the states. The Constitution does not clearly state which level of government may make decisions in every case that might come up.

For example, the authors of the Constitution could not know that the United States would someday be a great industrial nation. Therefore, they did not say which level of government has the power to pass laws dealing with industry. As industry grew and problems arose, federal and state officials argued about who had the power to regulate industries. There were many such disputes over other issues, too.

fig. 337
Civil War mural in the President's Cottage at White Sulphur Springs

The Supreme Court of the United States has settled many of the disputes between the federal and state governments. Sometimes the justices decided a case in favor of the federal government. At other times they sided with the states. The Supreme Court became the referee in the fight for power between the two levels of government.

At one time the struggle between the federal government and the Southern states grew very intense. In 1861 eleven Southern states left the Union and formed a new nation called the Confederate States of America. These states believed that the federal government was too powerful. They opposed interference in their affairs.

The national government did not accept the split in our country. The American Civil War (1861–1865) was fought as a result of this dispute. The defeat of the South made it clear that the federal government would remain more powerful than state governments.

Even after the Civil War there were still conflicts. New problems developed between the federal and state governments. The Supreme Court continued to settle disputes. The long period of competition did not end until the 1930s.

Competition Gives Way to Cooperation. The states and the federal government began to cooperate more during the *Great Depression*. In 1929 the United States began to have major economic problems, which lasted through the 1930s. Millions of Americans were out of work, and many banks and other businesses closed. Large numbers of people were quite poor. This terrible event was known as the Great Depression.

When the Great Depression began, state and local governments tried to help the needy. However, they didn't have enough money to help all those in need. The federal government began spending large sums for relief programs in all of the states. It also started new federal programs to help the economy. State and federal officials became allies in the struggle to solve economic and social problems.

Since the Great Depression, cooperation among governments has grown. This has been good for the American people, for government is now better able to deal with problems and meet new needs.

REVIEW OF SECTION TWO:
1. Why have the federal and state governments argued over who has the right to deal with certain issues and problems?
2. What body has the power to settle conflicts between the federal government and state governments?
3. Why did eleven Southern states leave the union in 1861? How was this problem settled?
4. Why did the Great Depression lead to more cooperation between the federal and state governments?

fig. 338
The Great Depression caused many people to be evicted from houses when they could not pay rent.

SECTION THREE: COOPERATIVE FEDERALISM IN WEST VIRGINIA

Federal Aid to State and Local Governments. The different levels of government in the United States help each other in many ways. One important way the federal government helps state and local governments is by sharing its revenue with them. For example, it sells timber from national forests and charges rent to companies that build power plants on federal land. Income from these sources is shared with state governments. Much more money is given to state and local government through the *federal grant-in-aid* program.

fig. 339

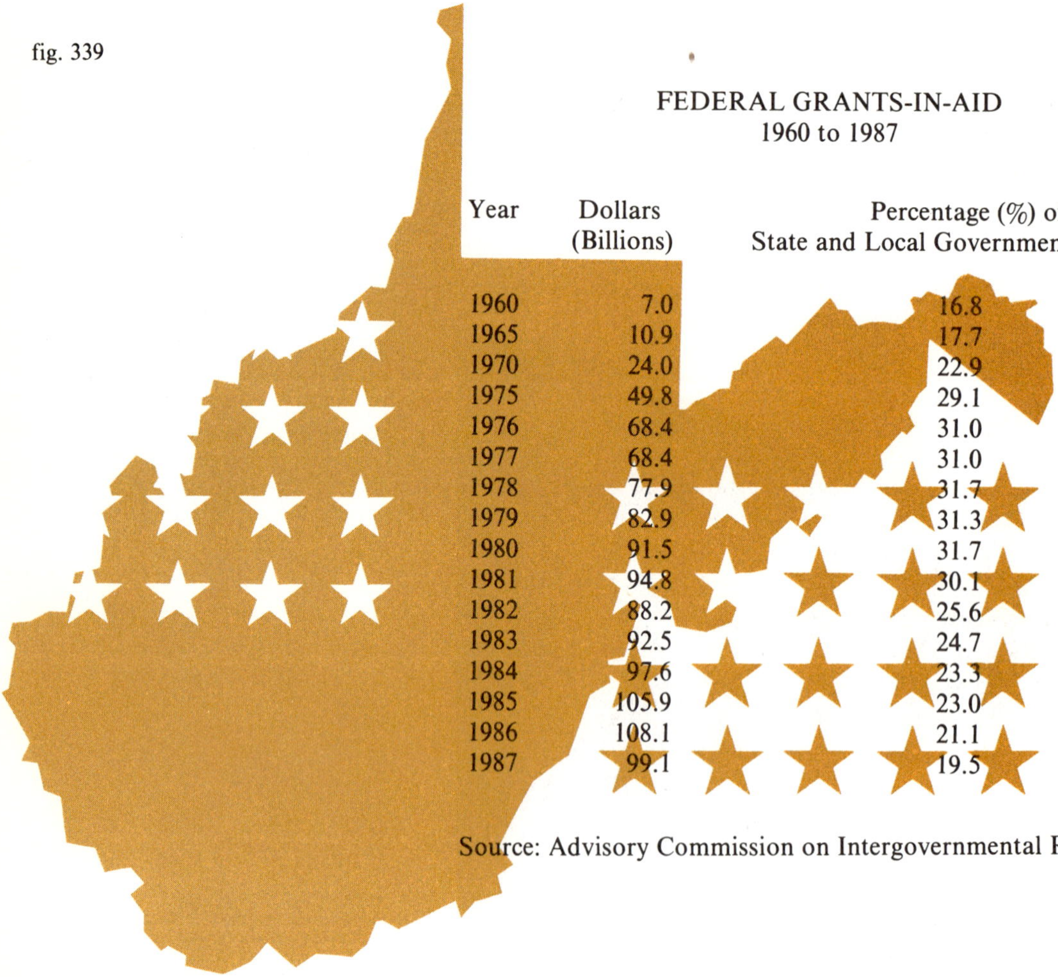

FEDERAL GRANTS-IN-AID
1960 to 1987

Year	Dollars (Billions)	Percentage (%) of State and Local Government Revenues
1960	7.0	16.8
1965	10.9	17.7
1970	24.0	22.9
1975	49.8	29.1
1976	68.4	31.0
1977	68.4	31.0
1978	77.9	31.7
1979	82.9	31.3
1980	91.5	31.7
1981	94.8	30.1
1982	88.2	25.6
1983	92.5	24.7
1984	97.6	23.3
1985	105.9	23.0
1986	108.1	21.1
1987	99.1	19.5

Source: Advisory Commission on Intergovernmental Relations

Federal Grants-in-Aid. Huge sums of federal money are granted to state and local governments every year. The chart in the text shows how much state and local governments received from 1960 through 1987. It also shows the portion of state and local revenues that came from federal grants. Without these large federal grants, state and local governments could not afford many of the programs they now provide.

Types of Federal Grants-in-Aid. There are three types of federal grants-in-aid. First, there are *categorical grants.* These are grants Congress makes for specific purposes, such as building highways or sewage systems. There are more than four hundred programs that are funded by categorical grants.

A state government must agree to do certain things in order to receive a categorical grant. It must follow federal rules on how to spend the grant money and carry out the project. It must pay for part of the cost of the project. State officials often complain about the many rules they must follow when they have a categorical grant.

A second type of federal grant-in-aid is a *project grant,* which is harder to obtain than a categorical grant. State and local governments compete for project grants. They must submit plans for the projects they wish to carry out. The plans must state why the project is needed, whom it will help, and how much it will cost. Federal officials decide which projects should receive grants. Programs to fight drug abuse or provide help for handicapped people are examples of projects the federal government often supports.

The third type of federal grant-in-aid is a *block grant.* They are grants for broad purposes such as improving schools or health care. This type of grant is easier to obtain than the other types of grants. There are also fewer rules about how block grants may be spent.

In recent years Congress has given more block grants but fewer categorical and project grants. This has pleased state and local officials, who think they know best how to help their communities.

Federal Grants to West Virginia. Like other states, West Virginia receives many federal grants-in-aid. These grants make up about 27 percent of the money spent by our state government. In 1988 that was more than $850,000,000. Our state and local governments could not provide many of their services if they did not receive so much federal money.

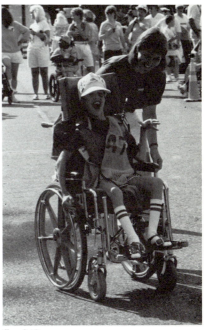

fig. 340
High costs are incurred in helping the handicapped live a good life. The government can help when personal income is not enough.

fig. 341

The chart in the text shows how federal funds are used in West Virginia. Look at the pictures in this section of the chapter, too. They show some of the many ways West Virginians have been helped by federal grants.

fig. 342

FEDERAL FUNDS RECEIVED BY WEST VIRGINIA AND HOW THEY WERE USED, 1987		
USE	Amount	Percentage (%) of Total Federal Funds Received by WV
Highways	$194,098,976	22.1
Agriculture	1,462,206	.2
Benefits for the Unemployed	18,623,010	2.1
Environmental Projects	31,463,507	3.6
Libraries	1,063,187	.1
Health Programs	125,306,555	14.2
Vocational Training	24,812,725	2.8
Welfare Benefits	356,255,443	40.6
Education	80,477,447	9.2
Other Programs	44,193,144	5.0
Total Received and Spent	$877,756,200	100.00

Source: *Analysis of Receipts and Expenditures* - State Auditor's Office.

REVIEW OF SECTION THREE:

1. What types of aid do state and local governments receive from the federal government?
2. Why do state and local officials prefer block grants to categorical or project grants?
3. Describe three ways in which federal funds have been spent in our state.

SECTION FOUR: FEDERAL AGENCIES IN WEST VIRGINIA   fig. 343

Bringing the Federal Government Closer to West Virginians. As we have seen, the federal government grants millions of dollars to our state every year. The federal government also helps us in another important way. Many federal agencies have offices in our state. Most people in our state do not want to travel to Washington, D.C., to get services from the federal government. The offices in West Virginia make it much easier for state residents to benefit from federal programs.

The chart in this section lists many of the federal agencies that have offices in West Virginia. All of them are part of the executive branch. The list leaves out federal courts and government corporations such as the postal service. Some of these agencies may have an office near your home. Some of the federal agencies in West Virginia are described below.

The Department of Veterans Affairs. Many West Virginians have served in the armed forces. The federal government provides services to veterans. It helps them pay for training or a college education and it offers them low-interest loans to buy homes. Some veterans or their families receive pensions, while veterans' hospitals provide medical services.

The Department of Veterans Affairs provides these and other services to veterans. The department has offices in Beckley, Clarksburg, Huntington, and Martinsburg. There are also hospitals for veterans in each of those cities.

The Social Security Administration. Most Americans who work must contribute part of their income to the federal social security fund. The fund has several purposes. The major purpose of the fund is to provide pensions for people when they retire. The fund also helps unemployed workers, people who are disabled, and the families of workers who die.

The Social Security Administration is part of the Department of Health and Human Services. It has sixteen offices in West Virginia to help people receive social security benefits.

The U.S. Army Corps of Engineers. The major rivers of West Virginia are vital to our state's economy. They are a means of shipping goods cheaply. Our largest cities and many of our industries are located on the Ohio, Kanawha, and Monongahela rivers. However, goods could not be shipped on these rivers year-round if

AGENCIES OF THE EXECUTIVE BRANCH OF THE FEDERAL GOVERNMENT WITH OFFICES LOCATED IN WEST VIRGINIA

★ Department of Agriculture

★ U.S. Army Corps of Engineers

★ Environmental Protection Agency

★ General Services Administration

★ Federal Highway Administration

★ Department of Housing and Urban Development

★ Geological Survey/Water Resources Division

★ Office of Surface Mining

★ Internal Revenue Service

★ International Trade Administration

★ Department of Labor

★ U.S. Office of Personal Management

★ Bureau of the Public Debt

★ Small Business Administration

★ Social Security Administration

★ Bureau of Alcohol, Tobacco and Firearms

★ Department of Veterans Affairs

★ National Weather Service

★ Federal Bureau of Investigation

★ Federal Aviation Administration

fig. 344
Locks and dams built by the Army Corps of Engineers largely prevent flooding and disasters such as this one at the turn of the century on the Monongahela River.

the water level was not controlled. High water and low water are dangerous to barge traffic. One duty of the U.S. Army Corps of Engineers is to keep barges moving on the rivers. It has built locks and dams on the rivers to control the water level.

The Corps of Engineers is a part of the Department of Defense. It has a large office in Huntington. A colonel in the United States Army is in charge of the office, but most of the employees are civilians who work for the army. Many are engineers who plan and direct the large projects of the corps.

The Corps of Engineers also builds dams to help prevent flooding in West Virginia. The lakes that are formed by the dams store water that can be released during droughts. You may have visited some of our lakes: Bluestone, Sutton, Tygart, Summersville, East Lynn, R.D. Bailey, Burnsville, Beech Fork, Bloomington, and Stonewall Jackson. All of these lakes and their recreational areas were provided by federal money and the Corps of Engineers.

The National Weather Service. The National Weather Service is part of the Department of Commerce. It records weather conditions and forecasts the weather. The National Weather Service has offices in Beckley, Charleston, Elkins, Huntington, and Parkersburg. It also has nine weather radio transmitters and sixty-five climate stations in

West Virginia. The transmitters broadcast weather reports to the public on special channels. Climate stations record the temperature and the amount of rain or snow that has fallen.

The National Weather Service provides a great deal of useful data. Weather information is very important to farmers, airline pilots, and construction companies.

REVIEW OF SECTION FOUR:
1. Why do federal agencies locate offices in West Virginia?
2. Name two federal agencies that have offices in West Virginia. How do they help the people of our state?

REFERENCES:

1. Gitelson, Alan R., Robert L. Dudley, and Melvin Dubnik. *American Government.* Boston: Houghton Mifflin Co., 1988, pp. 43–67.
2. McClenaghan, William A. *Magruder's American Government.* Boston: Allyn and Bacon, Inc., 1983, pp. 64–85.
3. Wit, Daniel, P. Allen Dionisopoulis, and Robert Gennette. *Our American Government and Political System.* River Forest, IL: Laidlaw Brothers, 1983, pp. 103–21.

fig. 345
May 12, 1985, was a day when West Virginians joined the rest of the nation in literally joining Hands across America to express their determination to help the homeless in America.

fig. 346
Dr. William E. Coffey

fig. 347
Dr. Frank S. Riddel

About the Authors

William E. Coffey is a native of Charleston, West Virginia. He received his undergraduate, master's, and doctoral degrees in history from West Virginia University.

Dr. Coffey's academic experience includes teaching at Potomac State College, the American University in Cairo, Egypt, and Marshall University. He served on the faculty of Marshall University in the Department of Social Studies from 1969 to 1985. During that time he taught World Civilizations, the American Capitalism Seminar, and West Virginia History, Geography and Government. He also developed and taught a course on the American coal industry. Dr. Coffey is the author of several articles relating to West Virginia history and the coal industry. He coauthored *West Virginia Government* with Carolyn M. Karr and Frank S. Riddel.

In 1985 Dr. Coffey became an assistant to the president of Marshall University and in 1986 was appointed assistant vice president for academic affairs. He remained in that position until 1989. Dr. Coffey is currently associate dean for faculty affairs at the Office of the Chancellor of the California State University.

Frank S. Riddel is a native of St. Marys, West Virginia. He earned undergraduate and master's degrees from Marshall University and a doctoral degree from Ohio State University.

Dr. Riddel's professional experience includes teaching at Gallia Academy High School in Gallipolis, Ohio, and Barboursville High School in West Virginia before joining the Marshall University faculty in 1968. He has also taught at the Ironton Branch of Ohio University and has conducted numerous workshops for social studies teachers throughout West Virginia. He is professor of social studies at Marshall University and has served as social studies program coordinator since 1985. He teaches West Virginia History, Geography and Government and World Civilizations at Marshall University.

Dr. Riddel is the author of several articles on the history and politics of Spain during the Franco era, coauthor of *Modules in Political Inquiry* and the editor of an anthology entitled *Appalachia: Its People, Heritage and Problems.* He also coauthored *West Virginia Government,* which was published by the West Virginia Historical Education Foundation in 1983.

About the Foundation

The Foundation was organized in 1950 as a nonprofit West Virginia corporation. Its principal objective is to publish books about West Virginia and by West Virginians. Some Foundation books include *West Virginia History* by Phil Conley and William Thomas Doherty, *West Virginia Studies: Our Heritage* by William Thomas Doherty, *West Virginia Reader* by Phil Conley, *West Virginia in the Civil War* by Boyd B. Stutler, and *Captain Matthew Arbuckle* by Joseph C. Jefferds, Jr.

Editor

Marshall Buckalew, M.A., J.D., LL.D., former president of Morris Harvey College/The University of Charleston. Author of *The Life of Morris Purdy Shawkey.* Editor of *West Virginia Studies: Our Heritage* and *West Virginia Government.* Graduate of Morris Harvey College, West Virginia University, and Harvard Law School.

Associate Editor

Eugenia G. Thoenen, B.A., former copy editor for *Cosmopolitan* magazine and assistant editor for the University of New Mexico Press. Graduate of the University of New Mexico. Associate Editor of *West Virginia Studies: Our Heritage* and *West Virginia Government.*

Assistant Editor

Nicholas Winowich, B.A., M.L.S., former Library Director, Kanawha County Public Library, Charleston, West Virginia. Graduate of Bethany College and Carnegie Mellon University.

Assistant to the Editor

Eileen Cain Stanley, a native of Ritchie County, has read all manuscript material. Her suggestions to the Editor for improving the quality of this publication have been invaluable.

Consultant

Frank J. Krebs, B.A., M.A., Ph.D., former teacher, principal, superintendent of schools, professor of history and sociology, and vice-president of Morris Harvey College. Coauthor of *The History of the West Virginia State Federation of Labor,* and author of *Hayes and the South* and other books and magazine articles. Graduate of Mount Union College and Ohio State University.

fig. 348
Designers Eve Faulkes and Clifford A. Harvey, who are also professors of graphic design at West Virginia University

fig. 349
Lynn Pagendarm, Neil Hawkins, and Kevin Harrington are among the WVU design students who helped develop some of the charts and graphs shown in this book on the Macintosh computer.

Credits

Figures listed alphabetically by source

Arthur, Terry, the White House, 196; Barna, Mark, 301; Office of Robert Byrd, U.S. Senator, 145; Charleston Newspapers, 227; Cremer, Kate, 161; Commission on the Bicentennial of the U.S. Constitution, 4, 65; Dallas, Robin, 317; "Dominion Post," Morgantown, 125, 254, 277; Erlander, Daniel, 80; Evans, Michael, the White House, 100; Ferrell, Dale, 236, 248; Fitzpatrick, Bill, the White House, 171; Gram Lee Collection, 15, 27, 34, 59, 62, 121; Goodwin, Mark, 331; Governor's Office, 242, 269, 271, 274, 291, 306; Haines, L. Victor, cover, 182, 222; Harrington, Kevin, 183, 266, 289, 343; Hawkins, Neil, 321; Hoffmeister, Margo, 210, 256; Horton, Michelle, 81, 198; Kammerdeiner, David, 302; Karlin, Millie Cooper, 239, 353; Library of Congress, 20, 21, 35, 41, 44, 45, 51, 52, 53, 66, 67, 87, 89, 107, 109, 110, 111, 114, 123, 128, 150, 173, 175, 189, 217, 279; McGrath, Rose, 348; Miller, Douglass, 169; Nagy, Dan, 78; National Archives, 33, 36, 38, 40, 43, 46, 76, 98, 166, 168, 176, 190, 200, 201; National Computer Center, 207; National Portrait Gallery, 37, 39, 50, 68, 88, 90, 91, 96, 106, 152, 170, 178, 179, 197, 219; Ockerse, Thomas, 16; Pacich, George, 315;

Pagendarm, Lynn, 70, 211, 307; Penn, Timothy, 79, 82; Purcell, Steven, the White House, 143; Ratliff, Gerald, 185, 268 top; Sanders, Scott, 9, 94; Schumacher, Karl, the White House, 100; Scott, Tracy, 48, 49, 160, 212, 304; Second Story Design: Eve Faulkes and Clifford Harvey, 1, 2, 3, 5, 6, 10, 11, 12, 14, 18, 19, 22, 23, 24, 25, 26, 28, 29, 30, 32, 42, 47, 55, 57, 58, 60, 61, 63, 64, 69, 71, 72, 74, 77, 83, 85, 86, 92, 93, 95, 97, 99, 100, 101, 102, 103, 104, 105, 107, 108, 112, 113, 115, 116, 117, 118, 120, 122, 124, 126, 127, 130, 131, 133, 134, 135, 136, 137, 138, 139, 141, 142, 144, 147, 148, 149, 151, 153, 154, 155, 157, 158, 159, 164, 165, 167, 181, 184, 186, 187, 188, 191, 192, 195, 202, 203, 204, 205, 206, 208, 209, 214, 215, 216, 220, 224, 226, 229, 234, 235, 237, 238, 240, 241, 242, 243, 244, 245, 246, 247, 249, 250, 251, 252, 253, 255, 257, 258, 259, 260, 261, 263, 264, 265, 267, 273, 276, 278, 281, 282, 283, 284, 285, 286, 287, 288, 290, 293, 294, 295, 296, 297, 298, 300, 303, 305, 308, 309, 310, 311, 312, 313, 314, 316, 318, 319, 320, 322, 323, 324, 325, 326, 327, 328, 329, 330, 331, 332, 333, 334, 335, 336, 339, 340, 341, 342, 349, 350, 351, 352; Snow, Ron, 268 bottom, 272, 280, back cover; Souza, Pete, the White House, 199; Valdez, David, the White House, 17, 75, 172; West Virginia State Archives, 119, 180, 223, 225, 231, 232,

233, 338; West Virginia Department of Commerce, 140, 218, 262, 292, 299; West Virginia Division of Culture and History, 56; The West Virginia Historical Education Foundation, Inc., 132, 227, 346, 347; West Virginia and Regional History Collection, 221, 228, 230, 338, 344; White House Photo Archives, 8, 73, 129, 177, 193, 345; Whitmore, Robert, 156, 163, 213; U.S. Postal Service, 84, 146, 194.

Glossary

Act: (see Law).

Adjourn: to end a meeting or a session of a legislative body or a court.

Ambassador: the highest-ranking representative of a government in a foreign country.

Amend: to change a bill, law, or constitution.

Amendment: a change made in a bill, law, or constitution.

Anarchy: the absence of any form of government.

Antifederalists: those who opposed the ratification of the U.S. Constitution in 1787.

Appeal: a request by a convicted person for a review of his or her case by a higher court.

Appeals Court: a federal or state court that has the authority to hear appeals from a lower court.

Appellate Jurisdiction: the power of some federal and state courts to review the decisions of lower courts.

Articles: the seven major divisions of the Constitution of the United States that describe how the federal government is to be organized and how it is to function.

Articles of Confederation: the plan of government used by the United States from 1781 until the ratification of the Constitution in 1789.

Assessor: the county official responsible for determining the value of property so it can be taxed.

Attorney General: the chief law officer of the United States or the state of West Virginia. The Attorney General of the United States is appointed by the president to head the Department of Justice. The attorney general of West Virginia is an elected official.

Auditor: the West Virginia official who must approve any payments made from the state treasury.

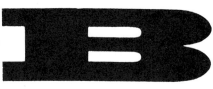

Bail: Money, bonds, or property deposited with a court as a guarantee that an accused person will show up for his or her trial.

Balanced Budget: a budget in which revenues (income) equal expenditures (expenses).

Ballot: a piece of paper on which voters indicate their choices during an election.

Bicameral Legislature: a legislative body that is divided into two houses. Both the U.S. Congress and the West Virginia Legislature are bicameral.

Bill: a proposed law. At the federal level a bill must be approved by both Congress and the president before becoming a law. In West Virginia both the legislature and the governor must approve a bill before it becomes a law.

Bill of Attainder: a law that permits a person to be punished without receiving a fair trial.

Bill of Rights: the first ten amendments to the Constitution of the United States, which guarantee all Americans certain basic rights. The West Virginia Constitution also contains a Bill of Rights.

Board of Education: the West Virginia Board of Education is responsible for establishing rules and regulations for all elementary and secondary schools in the state. Each county also has an elected Board of Education that manages the public schools within the county.

Board of Public Works: The West Virginia Board of Public Works is made up of the governor, secretary of state, auditor, treasurer, attorney general, commissioner of agriculture, and superintendent of schools. Its only responsibility today is to decide how much public utilities will be taxed.

Bonds: a written guarantee issued by governments to those from whom they have borrowed money promising to repay the money plus interest after a certain period of time.

Brief: a written statement presented to a court by a lawyer that explains the arguments of one side in a case.

Budget: a yearly spending plan showing the amount of revenue (income) expected, the sources of that revenue, and proposed expenditures (expenses). The federal budget is prepared by the president but must be approved by Congress. West Virginia's budget is prepared by the governor but must be approved by the legislature.

Cabinet: the group of people who head the executive departments of the federal government and who also serve as advisers to the president.

Campaign: the activities of political candidates and their supporters that are aimed at winning an election.

Candidate: a person who is running for a political office.

Caucus: a meeting of the members of a political party. Caucuses are held for such purposes as nominating candidates for office, selecting the party's legislative leaders, and deciding the party's position on proposed laws.

Census: the official count of all the people in the United States, which is taken every ten years.

Checks and Balances: the method provided for in the U.S. Constitution to balance the powers of the three branches of government by providing each branch with ways to check, or limit, the other two branches.

Chief Executive: the president is the nation's chief executive because he heads the executive branch of government. At the state level, the governor is the chief executive.

Chief of State: the president's role as the living symbol of the United States and the ceremonial head of the nation.

Circuit Courts: the West Virginia courts that hear both civil and criminal cases as well as appeals from the magistrate courts. There are thirty-one circuits courts in the state.

City: a municipality that has met the requirements established by the state legislature for incorporation. In West Virginia, a city must have a population of at least two thousand.

City Council: the lawmaking body of a city government.

City Manager: an appointed official who carries out city ordinances and supervises city affairs under the direction of the city council.

Civil Laws: laws concerned with disputes between individuals or between citizens and the government.

Civil Rights: the rights guaranteed to all Americans by the Constitution and certain laws passed by Congress.

Civilization: a complex culture that has cities and a system of writing.

Civil War: the war (1861–1865) between the eleven Southern states that attempted to withdraw from the U.S. and the states that remained loyal to the Union. As a result of this war, West Virginia became a separate state.

Claims Court: a federal court that hears cases involving financial claims against the federal government.

Clan: a group of families united under one chieftain. Members of a clan generally believe they are descended from one ancestor.

Closed Primary: a primary election in which voters may vote only for their political party's candidates.

Cloture: a method of limiting debate or ending a filibuster in the U.S. Senate. A three-fifths majority of the full Senate must approve a motion for cloture for it to pass.

Colonist: a person living in a colony.

Colony: a settlement in one land that is ruled by a government in another land.

Commander in Chief: the president's role as commander of all the armed forces of the U.S. At the state level, the governor is the commander in chief of the state militia or national guard.

Commerce: trade, or the exchange of goods, within nations or between nations.

Commerce and Slave Trade Compromise: the agreement reached by the Constitutional Convention in 1787 that Congress would have the power to regulate commerce but would not be allowed to tax exports. Neither could Congress interfere with the slave trade for twenty years.

Commission Form of Government: a form of municipal government in which the voters elect commissioners who are in charge of city departments. As a group, the commissioners pass municipal ordinances and determine city policies.

Commissioner of Agriculture: the elected executive official in West Virginia who heads the Department of Agriculture.

Committee: A group in either house of a legislature that is responsible for studying bills, conducting investigations, or working with members of the other house to solve problems. Much of the work of Congress and the West Virginia Legislature is done by committees.

Committee Chair: the person who heads a committee in the U.S. Congress or the West Virginia Legislature.

Committee on Committees: A committee made up of several members of Congress from the same party that assigns party members to the various standing committees. Both political parties have a committee on committees in each house.

Community: a group of people who live in the same area, are governed by the same laws, and who have common interests.

Commute: to shorten the sentence of a convicted person. The president and governors have the power to commute certain sentences.

Compromise: an agreement between individuals or groups in which each side gives up some of its demands.

Concurrent Powers: powers shared by the federal and state governments.

Concurring Opinion: a statement about a case written by a Supreme Court justice who agrees with the court's decision on the case but for reasons that differ from those of other justices.

Confederate States of America: the alliance of eleven Southern states that attemped to withdraw from the United States and become an independent nation between 1861 and 1865. Their defeat during the Civil War brought the Confederacy to an end.

Confederation: a loose alliance of independent states that decide what powers the central government will have. The United States was a confederation from 1781 until the ratification of the Constitution in 1789.

Conference Committee: a committee made up of members of both houses of Congress or both houses of the West Virginia Legislature. Conference committees are responsible for eliminating differences in bills passed by the two houses.

Congress: the legislative branch of the United States government, which is made up of the Senate and the House of Representatives.

Congressional District: the section of a state in which the voters elect one member of the House of Representatives.

Congressional Record: a written account of the proceedings of both houses of Congress, which is published daily when Congress is in session.

Conservative: a person who is opposed to most political, social, and economic change.

Constituents: the people who are represented by members of the West Virginia Legislature.

Constitution: a written plan of government such as the Constitution of the United States, which describes how the government is to be organized and how it is to function.

Constitution of 1863: the first constitution of West Virginia, which was in effect from 1863 until it was replaced by a new constitution in 1872.

Constitution of 1872: the second constitution of West Virginia. It was adopted in 1872 and is still in effect.

Constitutional Convention: the meeting in Philadelphia in 1787 at which the Constitution of the United States was written.

Constitution of the United States: the plan of government adopted by the United States in 1789.

Consumer Sales Tax: a tax paid by those who purchase certain goods and services in West Virginia.

Continental Congress: the governing body of the American colonies during the Revolutionary War.

Copyright: the legal right given to an author or artist to publish or sell his or her work for a certain time and to prevent others from copying the work without permission.

Corporation Income Tax: a tax on the profits of corporations. Both the federal government and the government of West Virginia tax corporate profits.

Council-Manager Form of Government: a form of municipal government in which the voters elect a city council that passes ordinances and hires a city manager to

act as the city's chief executive.

County: a political subdivision of a state. In West Virginia there are fifty-five counties. Each county has an elected government.

County Commission: the elected officials who serve as the legislative and executive body of West Virginia's county governments.

County Seat: the town or city in which the county government is located.

Courts of Appeals: the twelve federal courts, below the level of the Supreme Court, to which convicted persons may appeal their cases. The West Virginia Supreme Court of Appeals reviews the appeals of people convicted of breaking state laws.

Criminal Laws: laws that define crimes such as robbery or murder and provide for the punishment of those who commit crimes.

Currency: coins or paper money.

Custom: old practices that a group of people commonly follow.

Customs Court: the federal court that hears cases involving taxes on imported goods.

Customs Duty: (see Tariff)

Declaration of Independence: the document adopted by the Second Continental Congress on July 4, 1776, which declared the independence of the American colonies from England.

Deficit Spending: spending more money than is being taken in.

Delegates: representatives who attended the Constitutional Convention; representatives who attend political party conventions; members of the West Virginia House of Delegates.

Delegate District: a section of West Virginia in which the voters elect at least one member of the House of Delegates.

Delegated Powers: (see Enumerated Powers).

Democracy: a system of government in which political power is held by the people who elect public officials to represent them.

Democratic Party: one of the two major political parties in the United States.

Dictator: a powerful political leader over whom the people have no control.

Dissenting Opinion: a statement about a case written by a Supreme Court justice explaining why he or she disagrees with the decision of the majority of justices.

District Courts: the federal trial courts having original jurisdiction in most cases involving federal laws.

Drafting a Bill: putting a bill in written form so it can be introduced to a legislative body.

Due Process of Law: the right to a fair trial.

Economy: the way in which a nation produces, distributes, and consumes goods and services.

Elastic Clause: Article I, Section 8 of the Constitution, which states that Congress may pass laws that are "necessary and proper" to carry out its enumerated powers.

Election: the process through which voters select people for public office or decide what should be done about some public issue.

Electoral College: the group of electors from each of the states and the District of Columbia who officially elect the president and vice president.

Electoral Votes: the votes cast by members of the Electoral College for president and vice president.

Electors: representatives from each state and the District of Columbia who are elected by the voters to choose the president and vice president.

Embassy: the residence and office of an ambassador in a foreign nation.

Eminent Domain: the power of the government to purchase private property for public use.

Enumerated Powers: the powers granted to the federal government by the Constitution.

Estate Tax: a tax placed on the property of a person when he or she dies.

Excise Tax: a tax placed on certain goods such as gasoline and tobacco products that must be paid by the consumer.

Executive Branch: the branch of government (federal, state, or local) which carries out the laws.

Executive Departments: the major departments of the executive branch of either the federal or state governments.

Executive Office of the President: the agencies and advisers who work closely with the president to help him carry out his duties.

Expenditures: money spent to meet the expenses of a government.

Exports: goods sold to other countries.

Ex Post Facto Law: a law passed after an act is committed that makes the act illegal.

Extended Session: a session of the West Virginia Legislature that extends beyond the regular sixty-day session to give legislators time to complete the state budget.

Extradition: the return of an escaped prisoner or accused person from one state to the state where the crime was committed.

Federal Bureau of Investigation (FBI): the agency of the Department of Justice that investigates most federal crimes.

Federal Government: the national government of the United States.

Federalists: those who supported the ratification of the U.S. Constitution in 1787.

Federal System: a system of government in which political power is divided between the national and state governments.

Fees: payments charged by governments for licenses and various types of services.

Felonies: serious crimes such as murder or kidnapping.

Filibuster: a method used in the U.S. Senate to delay or stop the passage of a bill by making extremely long speeches.

General Election: an election in which the voters elect public officials. Voters may cast their ballots for candidates of any party.

Gift Tax: a tax that must be paid by anyone giving a valuable gift to another person. This does not apply to husbands and wives.

Government Corporation: businesses, such as the Postal Service, that are owned and operated by the federal government.

Governor: the chief executive of state government.

Governors Succession Amendment: the amendment to the West Virginia Constitution permitting a governor to succeed himself in office.

Grand Jury: a group of people that decides whether or not there is enough evidence to hold an accused person for trial.

Grants-in-Aid: grants of federal funds to state and local governments to help those governments pay for various types of programs and services.

Great Compromise: the agreement reached by the Constitutional Convention in 1787, which gave all states equal representation in the Senate and representation based on the size of their populations in the House of Representatives.

Great Depression: the period from 1929 to 1940 during which the United States suffered from very serious economic problems.

House of Delegates: one of the two houses of the West Virginia Legislature. It has one hundred members who serve two-year terms.

House of Representatives: one of the two houses of Congress. It has 435 members who serve two-year terms. The number of members from each state is determined by the size of its population.

Impeachment: the process of bringing charges against a government official. The House of Representatives has the power to impeach federal officials. At the state level, the House of Delegates may impeach state officials.

Implied Powers: powers not specifically given to Congress by the Constitution but suggested by the elastic clause that permits Congress to pass laws that are "necessary and proper" to carry out its enumerated powers.

Imports: goods purchased from foreign nations.

Independent: a voter or candidate for office who does not belong to a political party.

Independent Agencies: federal executive agencies created by Congress to carry out special tasks and enforce rules and regulations in areas that are not the responsibility of the executive departments.

Independent Regulatory Commissions: twelve independent commissions created by Congress to regulate several economic and scientific activities. They are part of the executive branch.

Indict: to charge a person with a crime. It is the responsibility of grand juries to determine whether there is sufficient evidence to indict people accused of crimes.

Initiative: a procedure by which the citizens of some states can propose a law or an amendment to the state constitution by obtaining a certain number of signatures on a petition.

Interest: money that must be paid for the use of borrowed money.

Interest Groups: organized groups who try to influence government officials.

Internal Revenue Service (IRS): the agency of the Treasury Department responsible for collecting income taxes.

Interstate: between and among states. Interstate commerce refers to trade among states.

Invest: to put money into a business, stocks, bonds, or other articles of value in the hope of making a profit.

Joint Committee: a committee made up of members of both houses of Congress. Joint committees are formed to conduct investigations and to deal with matters of interest to both houses.

Judicial Branch: the branch of government (federal, state, or local) that interprets and applies the laws. One of the major duties of the courts, which make up this branch, is to decide if laws have been broken and to punish lawbreakers.

Judicial Reform Amendment: an amendment to the West Virginia Constitution adopted in 1974. It created a unified court system for the state.

Judicial Review: the power of certain courts to determine whether or not acts of the legislative and executive branches are constitutional.

Jurisdiction: the authority of a court to hear and decide a case (see Appellate jurisdiction and Original jurisdiction).

Jury: a group of people who are chosen to hear evidence and make a decision in a court case (see Grand jury and Petit jury).

Justice: a member of the United States Supreme Court or the West Virginia Supreme Court of Appeals.

Law: a written rule that explains how people are expected to behave. Laws are passed and enforced by governments.

Legislative Branch: the branch of government (federal, state, or local) that makes the laws.

Legislature: the lawmaking body of a government. Congress is the national legislature. Each state also has a legislature.

Limited Government: a government whose powers are limited by a constitution that describes what the govern-

ment may and may not do.

Literacy Test: a test once used in certain states to determine if a person could read and write. Those who failed the test were not permitted to vote. Such tests are now illegal as a qualification for voting.

Lobbyist: a paid representative of an interest group who tries to influence government officials, particularly legislators.

Magistrate: a judge of a magistrate court. In West Virginia, magistrates are elected to a term of four years.

Magistrate Court: a court presided over by a magistrate. In West Virginia, magistrate courts hear both civil and criminal cases of a minor nature.

Majority Leaders: the leaders of the majority party in both houses of Congress and both houses of the West Virginia Legislature. It is their responsibility to do all that they can to gain support for bills favored by their party.

Majority Opinion: a statement about a case written by a Supreme Court justice explaining why a majority of the justices voted as they did.

Majority Party: the party with the most members in a house of Congress or a house of the West Virginia Legislature.

Marshal: an official of each federal district court who makes arrests, locates witnesses, and keeps accused persons in custody.

Mass Media: methods of communicating, such as newspapers, magazines, radio and television, by which masses of people are reached.

Mayor: the chief executive of a municipal government.

Mayor-Council Form of Government: a form of municipal government in which the voters select a city council that passes ordinances and a mayor who carries out those ordinances.

Militia: a force of volunteer soldiers. State militias are now called the National Guard.

Minority Leaders: the leaders of the minority party in both houses of Congress and both houses of the West Virginia Legislature. It is their responsibility to do all they can to gain support for bills favored by their party.

Minority Party: the party that has fewer members than the majority party in a house of Congress or a house of the West Virginia Legislature.

Misdemeanors: less serious crimes such as reckless driving and trespassing.

Modern Budget Amendment: an amendment to the West Virginia Constitution that makes the governor responsible for preparing the state budget and submitting it to the legislature.

Monarchy: a form of government headed by a king or queen who has inherited his or her position.

Multiparty System: a political system that has several major political parties rather than one or two.

Municipal Charter: a plan of government for a municipality.

Municipal Corporation: a city, town or village that has a municipal government.

Municipal Court: a court that hears cases involving violations of municipal ordinances.

Municipal Government: the government of a city, town, or village.

Municipal Ordinances: laws passed by municipal governments.

Municipality: (see Municipal corporation).

National Convention: a meeting of representatives of each of the major political parties held every four years to choose candidates for president and vice president and to draw up the party platform.

National Debt: the amount of money owed by the United States government.

Naturalization: the process by which citizens of foreign nations become American citizens.

Nominate: to select a party's candidates for public office.

Nominee: a person selected by a political party to run for public office.

Nonpartisan Election: an election in which the candidates are listed on the ballot without a party label.

Office of Management and Budget (OMB): the executive agency that helps the president prepare his budget proposal and supervises the spending of government funds.

Oligarchy: a government controlled by only a few people.

Open Primary: a primary election in which the voters may vote for the candidates of any party.

Original Jurisdiction: the authority of a court to be the first to hear certain types of cases.

Pardon: an official act by the president or a governor that frees a person who has been convicted or accused of a crime.

Parliament: the legislative body of a nation that has a parliamentary system of government, such as Canada or Great Britain.

Party Platform: a written statement adopted by a political party's national convention describing the party's position on important issues and the program it proposes to deal with those issues.

Party Whips: the assistants to the majority and minority leaders in Congress and the West Virginia Legislature. Party whips are responsible for persuading party members to support or oppose, certain bills. They also see that party members are present for important votes.

Patent: the legal right given to an inventor to make and sell his invention for a certain time and to prevent others from copying the invention.

Personal Income Tax: a tax paid to the federal and state governments on the income earned by an individual.

Petit Jury: a group of people who decide whether a person accused of a crime is guilty or innocent.

Petitions: written requests sent to government officials that are usually signed by many citizens.

Pocket Veto: the power of the president to veto a bill by refusing to sign it before Congress adjourns.

Political Action Committee: (PAC): a committee representing a corporation or an interest group that raises campaign contributions and provides those funds to political candidates favored by the organization represented by the committee.

Political Party: an organized group that attempts to elect its members to public office.

Polls: places where people vote during an election.

Poll Tax: a special tax that some states once charged people before they were permitted to vote. Poll taxes are now illegal.

Popular Sovereignty: a principle of American government that means that political power rests with the people.

Preamble: the introduction to the Constitution of the United States, which describes the goals of the Constitution. The West Virginia Constitution is also introduced by a preamble.

Precinct: an election district in a county or city. Each precinct has a polling place where residents of the precinct vote on election day.

President: the chief executive of the United States who heads the executive branch of the federal government.

President Pro Tempore: a member of the U.S. Senate who presides over the Senate when the vice president is absent.

President of the Senate: the presiding officer of the West Virginia Senate.

Primary Election: an election in which voters choose candidates to run for office in the general election (see Closed primary and Open primary).

Property Tax: a state tax paid by people on the property they own.

Prosecuting Attorney: the chief legal officer of a county who prosecutes people accused of crimes.

Ratification: the approval of a constitution or an amendment to a constitution.

Real Property: land, minerals, and buildings on which property taxes are collected.

Recall: the power of the voters of some states to remove an elected official from office in a special election.

Referendum: a procedure in which the voters may approve or reject amendments to the state constitution and/or other acts of the legislature.

Register: to place one's name on the list of eligible voters in the office of the clerk

of the county commission in order to be able to vote.

Regulatory Agencies: (see Independent regulatory commissions).

Reorganized Government of Virginia: the state government of Virginia created in Wheeling in 1861 by opponents of Virginia's secession from the Union. The Reorganized Government remained loyal to the Union during the Civil War and gave permission for West Virginia to become a separate state.

Representative Government: a system of government in which the people elect representatives to make political decisions.

Representatives: members of the United States House of Representatives.

Reprieve: an order from the president or a governor postponing the carrying out of a sentence handed down by a court.

Republican Party: one of the two major political parties in the United States.

Reserved Powers: powers reserved for the states or the people by the Constitution of the United States.

Revenue: income collected by a government.

Revenue Estimate: the governor's determination of the amount of revenue that will be collected during the next year. The West Virginia Legislature cannot approve expenditures that are higher than the governor's revenue estimate.

Search Warrant: a document issued by a judge that permits the police to search in specific places for evidence of a crime.

Secession: the withdrawal of a state from the Union.

Secretary: the official who heads an executive department of the federal

government, such as the secretary of defense.

Segregation: separating people by race. Before the Supreme Court began to make such practices illegal, black Americans in many states were forced to make use of separate public facilities such as schools.

Select Committees: a temporary committee of Congress or the West Virginia Legislature that is appointed to deal with a special problem.

Senate: one of the two houses of Congress or the West Virginia Legislature. Two U.S. senators are chosen by each state for six-year terms. The West Virginia Senate has thirty-four members who serve four-year terms.

Senatorial District: a section of West Virginia in which the voters elect two members of the West Virginia Senate.

Senators: members of the U.S. Senate or the West Virginia Senate.

Seniority System: the practice of giving the position of committee chairperson to the member of the majority party who had served the longest time on the committee. Party caucuses now determine who will chair Congressional committees.

Separations of Powers: the division of political power among the three branches of government.

Severance Tax: a tax in West Virginia that must be paid by companies that mine coal, cut timber, pump oil and gas, or quarry limestone and sandstone.

Sheriff: the chief law enforcement official and treasurer of a county.

Social Security: the federal program that provides financial assistance to the unemployed, retired workers, the disabled, and the families of workers who have died. The program is supported by a tax paid by workers and their employers.

Speaker of the House: the presiding officer of the U.S. House of Representatives and the West Virginia House of Delegates.

Special Courts: federal courts established by Congress to deal with special types of cases, such as the United States Tax Court.

Special Session: a session of Congress or the West Virginia Legislature that is held to consider special issues or problems after the regular session has adjourned.

Standing Committee: a permanent committee of Congress or the West Virginia Legislature.

State of the State Address: the message delivered each year by the governor to the West Virginia Legislature in which he describes the condition of the state and recommends new programs and laws.

State of the Union Message: the message delivered each year by the president to Congress in which he describes the condition of the nation and recommends new programs and laws.

Strong-mayor Form of Government: a form of municipal government in which the voters elect a city council that has limited powers and a mayor who has a great deal of power.

Suffrage: the right to vote.

Supreme Court: the highest court in the United States. Its decisions are final.

Supreme Court of Appeals: the highest court in West Virginia.

Tariffs: rate of a duty (tax) to be paid for the importation for articles of merchandise.

Tax: a payment businesses and people are required to make to a government.

Tax Court: the special court created by Congress to hear cases involving disputes between taxpayers and the federal government.

Tax Limitation Amendment: an amendment to the West Virginia Constitution limiting the size of property taxes.

Term: the length of time for which a public official is elected to office.

Territory: an area such as Puerto Rico that is owned and governed by the United States but is not a state.

Third Parties: political parties other than the Democratic and Republican parties.

Three-fifths Compromise: the agreement reached by the Constitutional Convention in 1787 that each slave would be counted as three-fifths of a person in determining the population of a state.

Townships: a unit of local government in some states. Under the Constitution of 1863, West Virginia's counties were divided into townships. However, they were eliminated by the Constitution of 1872.

Treason: the betrayal of one's country by helping its enemies.

Treasurer: the West Virginia official who is the custodian of all state funds and who pays the state's bills.

Treaty: a written agreement between two or more nations.

Trial Jury: (see petit jury).

Tribes: a group of several clans led by one chief.

Two-party System: a political system in which there are two major political parties.

Unconstitutional: not in agreement with the Constitution of the United States or the West Virginia Constitution.

United States Attorney: an official of each federal district court who prosecutes those accused of breaking a federal law and defends the federal government in civil cases.

Veto: the refusal of the president or a governor to approve a bill passed by Congress or the state legislature.

Vice President: the federal official who is to become president if the president dies, resigns, or is removed from office. The vice president also presides over the United States Senate.

Weak-mayor Form of Government: (see Mayor-council form of government).

Wheeling Convention: the meetings held in Wheeling in 1861 at which the reorganized Government of Virginia was created and the decision was made to establish the state of West Virginia.

White House Office: the president's closest advisers and aides. The White House Office is part of the Executive Office of the President.

Writ of Habeas Corpus: a court order requiring that an accused person be brought before a judge so it can be determined if there is sufficient evidence to hold the person for trial.

Index

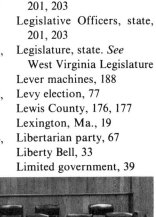

fig. 350, *The jury box*

fig. 352, *A constituent*

fig. 353, A disgruntled Uncle Sam